THE ACTOR'S CHECKLIST

CREATING THE COMPLETE CHARACTER

Third Edition

THE ACTOR'S CHECKLIST

CREATING THE COMPLETE CHARACTER

Third Edition

Rosary Hartel O'Neill
Loyola University

WADSWORTH
CENGAGE Learning™

Australia • Brazil • Japan • Korea • Mexico • Singapore • Spain • United Kingdom • United States

WADSWORTH
CENGAGE Learning

The Actor's Checklist: Creating the Complete Character, Third Edition
Rosary Hartel O'Neill

Publisher: Holly J. Allen

Assistant Editor: Darlene Amidon-Brent

Editorial Assistant: Meghan Bass

Senior Technology Project Manager: Jeanette Wiseman

Senior Marketing Manager: Mark Orr

Marketing Assistant: Alexandra Tran

Marketing Communications Manager: Shemika Britt

Project Manager, Editorial Production: Megan E. Hansen

Creative Director: Rob Hugel

Executive Art Director: Maria Epes

Print Buyer: Judy Inouye

Permissions Editor: Bob Kauser

Production Service: Azadeh Poursepanj, G&S Book Services

Copy Editor: Mike Nichols

Cover Designer: Brittney Singletary

Compositor: Newgen

For product information and technology assistance, contact us at
Cengage Learning Customer & Sales Support, 1-800-354-9706

For permission to use material from this text or product, submit all requests online at
www.cengage.com/permissions
Further permissions questions can be emailed to
permissionrequest@cengage.com

Library of Congress Control Number: 2005931609

ISBN-13: 978-0-495-05047-6

ISBN-10: 0-495-05047-4

Wadsworth
10 Davis Drive
Belmont, CA 94002-3098
USA

Cengage Learning is a leading provider of customized learning solutions with office locations around the globe, including Singapore, the United Kingdom, Australia, Mexico, Brazil, and Japan. Locate your local office at: **www.cengage.com/global**

Cengage Learning products are represented in Canada by Nelson Education, Ltd.

To learn more about Wadsworth, visit
www.cengage.com/wadsworth

Purchase any of our products at your local college store or at our preferred online store **www.ichapters.com**

Printed in Canada
3 4 5 6 7 09

This book is dedicated to
the bravest people I know:
my children—Rachelle, Barret,
Rory, and Dale—who shared me;
my husband Bob, who loved me;
and my enthusiastic editor, Holly Allen,
who believed in me. Bravo!

BRIEF CONTENTS

DETAILED CONTENTS

PREFACE

Acting is a time-honored art. Its oral tradition has been handed down for years, and its written tradition has flourished since the twentieth century. The Russian master Constantin Stanislavski revolutionized the teaching of acting when he formalized the "hands-on" process. This book examines eight principles he clarified and presents them for your understanding today. It is designed to teach the serious beginning actor the art of acting.

The Actor's Checklist provides techniques for use in both classroom and production situations. Primarily intended for an initial acting course, the book will serve as a guide to your expressiveness when you begin to operate completely on your own.

The Actor's Checklist will help you if you are a theater or film student by grounding you in principles of believability. The film actor's authenticity is challenged by magnification on a giant screen, the stage actor's by duration in a two-hour uninterrupted performance. Because of the flexibility of chapters you can use the text when in improvisation and scene study classes or when in production. Rooted in principles of truthful behavior, this handbook supplements other texts by giving you a central roadmap. A timeline constrains the building of a role. This book will hasten you along your path to excellence.

My understanding of these principles has been enhanced by interaction with more than two hundred artists across America and Europe. Much study was conducted while rehearsals and performances were in progress. I have implemented ideas with my students in France, Germany, and New York, with members of the professional theater company I founded and ran at Southern Rep, a state theater of Louisiana, and with the Times Square Playwrights professional theater company in New York City. This book has been classroom tested for more than twenty years. The eight topics can be taught in a sixteen-week semester, allowing two weeks for the implementation of chapters and audition techniques.

In New York City, I want to thank Allen Hubby at Drama Books; Larry Harbison at Samuel French; Aldon James at the National Arts Club, and Tom Thorton, director of the Times Square Playwrights.

I would also like to thank the many helpful actors for their comments during the writing process. Individuals who deserve praise include Vincent Capone; Collette Knight, my able assistant; and Jillian Chrisman.

Thanks go to my acquisitions editor, Holly Allen, for her determined support. She believed in the worth of this book and saw the third edition through to completion. I am grateful always for my true friend and husband, Bob Harzinski.

Rosary Hartel O'Neill, Ph.D.
New York, 2005

INTRODUCTION

Acting is a daring art. An actor walks out nightly before an audience of strangers and expresses himself fully in public. His knees may be weak, but the audience sees only what the trained actor wishes it to see.

As you study acting you will gain more poise; you will learn how to appear comfortable in the most stressful of situations. Notice how your personality expands because of your increased creativity. Acting frees you to open yourself up, to try new things, to relate to all sorts of situations and people.

One recent study of corporate America claims that a person's rise to success is in direct proportion to his or her sense of audience. By studying acting you will learn to trust your impulses; you will know how to read between the lines; you will acquire the ability to relate to people with whom you have nothing in common. The skills you learn as an actor will help you complete your first job interview, present a new product line to a group of conservative investors, get the person of your dreams to date you.

Although based on the teachings of the great acting teacher Constantin Stanislavski, this book includes insights by other famous acting teachers, such as Uta Hagen, Sanford Meisner, Lee Strasberg, Michael Chekhov, and Stella Adler, integrated with Carl Jung's theories for tapping the unconscious. Of course, it is also based on what I have learned in my twenty years of experience as an actress, acting teacher, director, playwright, and founding artistic director of Southern Rep Theater.

You must practice to be successful at anything you do in life. This book provides you with a checklist of eight techniques used to inspire strong performances. Practice them, commit them to memory; with them you will build a solid foundation so that someday, either onstage or off, you will rivet your audience!

THE ACTOR'S CHECKLIST

CREATING THE COMPLETE CHARACTER

Third Edition

1

OBJECTIVE
What do I want?

This chapter deals with objective: what your character wants.

*You will become as small as your controlling desire, as great as
your dominant aspiration.*

James Allen

■ WHAT IS DRAMA?

This book outlines the essential checklist for an actor to create
a phenomenal performance. Aristotle in fifth-century Athens
said drama is the imitation of action. Action holds the key to any
role. Acting means doing. We understand a story by what the actors do onstage. To act is to do. Remember a pivotal moment in
your life: a wedding, a funeral, a graduation. Don't you see yourself parading down the aisle, throwing a rose onto the casket,
accepting the diploma? Yes, you may say, but what you were
feeling was more important than the action. The observer understands that feeling through action.

We can never disconnect our physical actions from our inner
motivations. As long as we are alive, we'll think, feel, move. Our
emotional, intellectual, and physical selves are interconnected.
Death ends action. When we rehearse what we are doing onstage, we are always assessing what we are thinking or feeling.
But we capture thought and feeling through physical action.
Thought and emotion are volatile, butterfly-like, hard to grasp
and re-create. Physical action can be specified and repeated.

What we do stirs up and is stirred up by thoughts and feelings. The key principle of acting is *to play action* in each beat of the script.

What is a beat?

Some say the term *beat* comes from the Russian pronunciation of *bit*, because disciples of Stanislavski spent countless hours exploring each bit of a scene. A **beat** is a slice of a scene with the same ingredients. It is the smallest unit of conflict. Sequences of beats create the pyramid of dramatic action. Each character confronts conflict in a series of beats that creates the scenes, and the play.

You must break down the material in each scene into interesting beats. Your interpretation results from how you shape these units. The script is your blueprint. You base your choices for the beats on information discovered in the text. "Working moment to moment" is a phrase actors use to describe a method for discovering each beat of the text.

What things make up a beat?

In a beat, you are looking for four elements: an objective (something to want), an action (something to do), an obstacle (something to overcome), and an inner image (something to motivate). These elements stimulate the tension in each beat. You probably already call upon some of them instinctually, because they are based on your normal reactions as a human being. In the next several chapters, we'll study these elements.

■ WHAT IS AN OBJECTIVE?

An objective is what your character wants. In each beat or bit of stage life, you're wanting something (objective). In life, your desires are often unconscious; onstage, you must experience the longings, conscious and unconscious, of your character.

Also called an "intention," "purpose," or "need," an objective motivates your action.

For example, onstage you don't just eat your dinner. You do so in a way that tells another character something about what you want—for example, a date, some money.

After getting what you want, you might try another objective. Continue to pursue your objective until you succeed or another objective replaces it.

How do I name objectives?

To name objectives, ask yourself, "What do I want now, and from whom?" In the following example, an actress has jotted down objectives she discovered when improvising a scene.

STRUCTURED EXERCISE: BLANCHE'S ENTRANCE

A Streetcar Named Desire by Tennessee Williams, Scene 1

Observe how the actor changes objectives by breaking her sequence into a beginning, middle, and end.

OBJECTIVE	ACTIONS
	Beginning
to alert any vagrants inside	to enter
	to close the door
	to listen for sounds
	to drop the suitcase
	to scan the living/dining room
	to look for messages
	Middle
to reassure myself I am welcome here	to explore the apartment
	to scan the papers on the table
	to tiptoe into the bedroom
	to reexplore the living room
	to worry when Stella will be back

OBJECTIVE	ACTIONS
	End
to overcome my shock	to find some liquor
	to scan the living room
	to rummage through a cabinet
	to search in the drawers
	to peer under a couch
	to slip into the kitchen
	to spot liquor
	to hurry into the living room
	to perch on the couch
	to gulp the liquor
	to relax
	to lean back on the couch
	to calm self

Why should I use active verbs?

When naming objectives, use the infinitive form of an active verb. "To excite Stella" is more dynamic than "wanting to make Stella enthusiastic about my coming to her house." Word your objective so it inspires you to pursue the action.

to arouse Stella

to annihilate Stanley

to slug Mitch

Try violent, provocative, or even sexual verbs. No one but you knows the words you're using!

EXERCISES

1. *My Secret.* Talk truthfully about yourself. Who are you? Where do you come from? What do you hope to gain from the class (objective)? Then share one secret desire.

2. *My Dream.* What is the biggest desire you have right now? To get into a great school? To marry someone? To save your

parents' marriage? To become a famous actor? Share this dream with the class. Identify someone in a play or film who is playing the same objective. Optional: Stage a scene from this play or film.

What are strong objectives?

Lord, grant that I may always desire more than I can accomplish.

Michelangelo

Strong objectives compel you to risk daring action. Observe which need arouses a physical sensation, making you breathe heavily, break out in a cold sweat, clear your throat.

WEAK OBJECTIVE	POWERFUL OBJECTIVE
1. to have you hear this story	1. to mesmerize you
2. to transcend your superiority	2. to crush you
3. to give you some comical information	3. to convulse you with laughter

A well-written scene may work with thin objectives, but fiery ones will make it astonishing.

The forcefulness of your objective may come from the fact that it is hidden. Objectives delude you into believing that if only they would materialize, satisfaction would ensue. Although you anticipate winning, whatever you are craving moment to moment you usually don't get.

How do objectives counteract anticipation?

Strong objectives impel you to change another character's outlook and thus overcome anticipation. For example, if your character anticipates a marriage proposal, getting a rejection is more painful. You might keep imagining moment to moment his slipping that ring onto your finger.

If a character's intelligence assures correct anticipation of what is to come, she might misjudge how she will feel when specific needs are thwarted. Where possible, drift in the direction of false hope for a strong objective so as to startle yourself when different information is delivered.

■ OPPOSING OBJECTIVES

How do you find strong major objectives?

A major objective is your overall need in a scene. Warring objectives create electricity onstage. When your need is blocked, suspense mounts.

Analyzing the closing of the scene to determine what your character has or hasn't obtained will often reveal your major objective.

Strong objectives require opposition. In most scenes, the objectives of the major characters collide. For example, one character wishes "to bewitch," and the other wishes "to distance" the other. When alone, a character may play opposites within herself.

When you are onstage with someone else, even when not apparent in the dialogue, that other character's objective differs from yours. Warring objectives even ground the love scene. In *Romeo and Juliet*, Romeo wants to seduce Juliet, and Juliet, fearing for Romeo's life, wants him to leave.

How can another person block my objective?

Onstage, you are continually trying to get your desire fulfilled through someone: another person, the audience, a wiser self. A more interesting scene develops if you choose not to like what you get.

You are agitated by the other character's manner of presentation. You feel the other character could have been sweeter, smarter, more considerate in the going. Or you immediately want something else. Your obsessions penetrate below the dialogue.

You are trying to get through to someone, to change her, to make him feel a certain way. In moving that person, you move the audience.

Between two passionate people, one person's desire provokes another. In Eugene O'Neill's *Beyond the Horizon*, (act 1, scene 2) Andrew wants to break free from his family. Pay attention to the opposing objectives.

Andrew: (*facing his father*) I agree with you, Pa, and I tell you again, once and for all, that I've made up my mind to go [and leave the farm].

Mayo: (*dumbfounded—unable to doubt the determination in Andrew's voice—helplessly*) But why, Son? Why?

Andrew: (*evasively*) I've always wanted to go.

Robert: Andy!

Andrew: (*half angrily*) You shut up, Rob! (*Turning to his father again*) I didn't ever mention it because as long as Rob was going I knew it was no use; but now Rob's staying on here, there isn't any reason for me not to go.

Mayo: (*breathing hard*) No reason? Can you stand there and say that to me, Andrew?

Mrs. Mayo: (*hastily—seeing the gathering storm*) He doesn't mean a word of it, James.

Mayo: (*making a gesture to her to keep silence*) Let me talk, Katey. (*In a more kindly tone*) What's come over you so sudden, Andy? You know's well as I do that it wouldn't be fair o' you to run off at a moment's notice right now when we're up to our necks in hard work.

Andrew: (*avoiding his eyes*) Rob'll hold his end up as soon as he learns.

At their peak, such clashing objectives strip you and your opponent bare. Note Robert's and Ruth's speeches later, in act 2, scene 1, where husband and wife play the objective "to destroy each other."

Ruth: What do you think—living with a man like you—having to suffer all the time because you've never been man enough to work and do things like other people. But no! You never own up to that. You think you're so much better than other folks, with your college education, where you never learned a thing, and always reading your stupid books instead of working. I s'pose you think I ought to be *proud to* be your wife—a poor, ignorant thing like me! (*Fiercely*) But I'm not. I hate it! I hate the sight of you. Oh, if I'd only known! If I hadn't been such a fool to listen to your cheap, silly, poetry talk that you learned out of books! If I could have seen how you were in your true self—like you are now—I'd have killed myself before I'd have married you! I was sorry for it before we'd been together a month. I knew what you were really like— when it was too late.

Robert: (*his voice raised loudly*) And now—I'm finding out what you're really like—what a—a creature I've been living with. (*With a harsh laugh*) God! It wasn't that I haven't guessed how mean and small you are—but I've kept on telling myself that I must be wrong—like a fool!—like a damned fool!

Fantasize you are Ruth or Robert. Imagine what's going on inside you. How do your eyes feel? What are you putting on the line in this confrontation?

How can the audience assist with my objective?

Some characters' most intimate encounters occur in a monologue. You must figure out why your character can't reveal herself to the other characters but bares her soul to the audience.

Troubled characters often reach out to the audience to solve a burning problem. A character contemplating suicide could urge the audience (as a wiser presence) to tell him what to do. Imagine Hamlet playing the following lines as begging the answer from the audience:

Hamlet: To be, or not to be, that is the question:
Whether 'tis nobler in the mind to suffer
The slings and arrows of outrageous fortune,
Or to take arms against a sea of troubles
And by opposing end them. To die, to sleep—
No more; and by a sleep to say we end

The heart-ache and the thousand natural shocks
That flesh is heir to: 'tis a consummation
Devoutly to be wish'd.

How do you confront yourself?

Besides addressing the audience, you often talk to—even
battle with—yourself. Imagine the conversation you had with
yourself when you were in a dilemma, and you expected a wiser
part of yourself to respond. You could talk to yourself to keep
from cracking up, to gain control over your circumstances, or
to test your sanity. The simple fact that you talk to yourself
means one part of you seeks to control another.

How can I confront someone offstage?

When alone onstage, you may want something from someone
who has departed or who is arriving. When somebody exits,
your character may continue confronting him, or you may begin daydreaming about your next interaction.

Maybe you nuzzle a shirt in hopes of picking up a lover's scent.
Perhaps you smash your heel into the glass of a photograph.

■ OBJECTIVES IN EACH RELATIONSHIP

A relationship is a link between characters. Your character's
way of talking, touching, listening may differ drastically depending on whom he wants something from.

Relationships give rise to specific objectives. I want my sister to support me because she is my sister, and I expect support
from my family. I want to protect my lover, and I expect him to
act responsibly.

How are my relationships personalized?

Personalize the other character. Does s(he) have a temper like
your mother's, scolding eyes like your dad's, humor like your
best friend's?

Ask yourself, "If she was actually my sister, wife, or best friend, what would I want? How would I behave?" If the analogy doesn't work, choose any real person like the other character. Associate the two, such as by relating both are dark-eyed, German, or stubborn. Then play to that real person within the actor playing the character.

After the personalization is wedded in your heart, drop this adjustment. You will experience needing something from that other character. Make sure the relationship has a strong hook into you, much like a hook in a fish's mouth. Not only do you respond to these tugs, but each tug wounds you.

How do physical relationships drive my objectives?

The day is gone, and all its sweets are gone! Sweet voice, sweet lips, soft hand, and softer breast. O for a life of Sensations rather than of Thoughts!

John Keats, letter to Benjamin Bailey, November 22, 1817

Your emotions make themselves known through physical sensations. Cliché phrases like "This person sets my heart racing," "makes my stomach churn," or "leaves me cold" indicate sensual responses. Ask yourself, "How does the other character affect me physically?"

Notice what you do when you're excited by a suitor, when you're hungry for a hug from Mother, when you're thwarted by a boss. How does your body adjust? What thoughts and sensations are provoked by this bodily reaction? What do you do?

How do psychological relationships stimulate my desires?

Do you allude to me, Miss Cardew, as an entanglement?

Gwendolen, *The Importance of Being Earnest* by Oscar Wilde, act 2

Putting certain mental conditions on a relationship can sharpen your impulses. For example, let's specify the psychological condition "in love." If a couple has been dating for six months and are getting married, they may crave closeness. He may hold her hand. They may read the paper together. Conversely, if the couple has been dating for six years, they may be a bit blasé; they might need some space. Different mental relationships affect responsiveness onstage.

Why is responsiveness important?

Responsiveness, or the electricity between characters, is present when actors refer to a scene as "cooking!"

Dreams awaken you to the ambiguity of your needs and expand responsiveness. Imagine yourself, as in a dream, to be overtaken by the encounter. Open yourself to the unpredictable. Relinquish your inhibitions so that you can begin experiencing the fantastic needs of each relationship.

CLASS GAMES

1. *Crawling Babies.* Blindfolded, imagine yourselves as crawling babies. Explore another actor through touch. Describe his or her physical characteristics. Then identify the names of neighbors you bump into.

2. *Building a Machine.* Heighten physical chemistry by building a group machine. Create instances in which you touch in different places and react with different sounds.

3. *Watching a Lineup.* Have the class break up into groups of five or six and go onstage. Other class members guess the background of actors (single, only child, athletic) from the way each is dressed.

■ REHEARSING OBJECTIVES

What should I focus on in rehearsals?

When you go onstage, the question is, "Am I persuading you to give me what I want?" You must experience another character *right now*, relating to—and usually resisting—you. Keep your objective with another actor alive, as something you must fulfill *now*. Focus on the present.

Onstage, your character is tied to the other character, like a water skier to a speedboat. Fantasize how dramatically you respond when it races ahead, turns, stalls, stops. You are responding continually; reactions occur not only on the line, but also before and after you say a line.

Play a scene as if the character opposite you is the most astonishing creature you've ever met. Concentrate on that actor so fully you don't have time to think about yourself.

Repetitious exercises help to tie your objectives to the other character. Needing to repeat the other's gesture exactly encourages you to keep focused on him. If you are looking for some slight change in another's behavior, you have to listen with your whole being to see whether she's meeting that objective. Being sensitive to what that individual is doing, you respond truthfully to her every move.

CLASS GAMES

1. *Farewell.* In groups of two to six, improvise a farewell situation. Stage the sequence first realistically, then in an exaggerated way, as if in a nightmare. Have other class members guess the circumstances.

2. *Repetitious Exercise.* In pairs, repeat what you hear your partner saying five or six times, then ask for something. Continue this pattern for several minutes, back and forth. Focus on staying with your partner's every move. Some subjects that the partner could talk about include your outlook, your looks, your health. For example: "You're looking very ill," "I'm looking very ill," repeated six or seven times. Then: "You're feeling better," "I'm feeling better," and so forth.

3. *Your Style.* Stand opposite a partner. Reciting your name and vital statistics, walk toward the partner and then have him or her do the same. What did each of you notice about how the other person moved and spoke? Now imitate that.

EXERCISES

1. *Silent Task.* Pair off. Decide on a relationship such as parent-child or sister-brother. Use an activity, such as making a salad, packing a suitcase, straightening the room, during which your silent response communicates what the relationship is.

2. *Improvising Relationships.* List ten qualities that suggest a couple who has been married five years, as opposed to fifteen years. Stage two silent improvisations, with a physical task done differently; for example, the way you set the table may telegraph a comfortable marriage.

Should I get to know other actors?

The more comfortable you are with other actors, the better you can play your objectives. Trust encourages you to react intuitively as the character. Use rehearsal to get to know other actors, so you can manipulate, bargain with, hypnotize, and bewitch them onstage.

Sometimes you may have to show affection toward an actor whom you dislike. Find a way to neutralize your negativity. For example, if she is playing your wife, imagine that she inherited an annoying trait from her mother, whom you don't like anyway. So you dislike her mother's fault, but your wife is perfect.

If possible, spend time offstage with anybody your character relates to onstage. If not, observe his picture, find out about him, watch his behavior offstage. You want an opinion about that actor, a physical response to him. Try to discover what you admire or resent about him. It may be something unspoken, but if you notice that the actor playing your boss has a nervous habit of chewing on the edge of his nail, it could strengthen your resistance if it makes you cringe. Offstage, an actor you dine with may continually freshen her makeup. You could use this information onstage, in a scene where you compliment the character, a rival, on her looks.

How do I work off another actor?

To work off another actor, you must experience what you want is residing in her. You need to do something to her to get what you want. In rehearsals, practice stirring up the actor playing opposite you so that she is in a different state by the end of the scene. For example, make her concerned rather than complacent, enthusiastic rather than bored, compassionate rather than angry. Remember, when you move that other person, you move the audience.

You transform a concept such as "to seduce" into a real experience by relating to the other actor. What do you like about him? How does he make you feel? What about him (the texture of his hair, warmth of his fingers, his radiant humor) do you find irresistible? Find something compelling about the other actor. Allow yourself to be drawn to this quality. The intoxication of acting in a love scene opposite a great actor is that he convinces you that he is madly in love with you—so much so that you must resist pursuing his affections offstage.

What should I look for in the other actor onstage?

To keep your objective alive, observe what the other actor is doing. See whether you are getting your need met. Initially you may need to practice the scene slowly, to let the other actor "move in on you"—a professional term meaning to experience you onstage. Mark places in your script where you check to see whether you're getting what you want. Is the other actor as happy or sad as you wanted? Measure whether you are succeeding in meeting your objective by the reactions you provoke.

What should I listen for?

Listen to determine whether you're getting your objective. In real life, we can sometimes allow our minds to wander. But actors must listen. Listen with specific focus on what you want from a relationship. Interpret the meaning of each message to the relationship. For instance, you are uncovering your groom's motivations, your brother's disdain. When listening closely, you are intent on experiencing the thoughts, feelings, sensations of another. Try to perceive what the other actor is giving you in this relationship. Sensitize yourself to nuances of his behavior. You are listening for his objective so that you can immediately respond in character.

■ CHECKLIST

1. Am I playing strong objectives?

2. Who or what is blocking them?

3. Are my relationships personalized?

4. Am I listening to get my objective?

■ FINAL PROJECTS

1. *Progressive Exercise.* Throughout the next several chapters, you will pursue a series of related exercises. Each chapter adds an element to strengthen your acting. Rehearse several times with your partner and use many objects.

   EXERCISE 1: Pick a partner. You are strangers with opposing objectives who meet at an empty campus or park.
   Begin the scene in silence with each of you engaged in a physical activity. Then one of you should begin the verbal conflict in which your main objective is in total opposition to your partner's. Hand in any homework on the exercise. The scene should last five minutes and stop when one of you wins or someone calls a halt.

2. *Total Conflict.* Create a sequence with a partner in which a conflict erupts because the two of you have totally different objectives. For example, your roommate wants to marry you, and you decide to move overseas. Spend time discussing your relationship and setting up a specific place. Use the environment and the facts you make up to pursue your objective. Use real props to help you believe in the space and pick opposing objectives that truly provoke you. Start the improvisation with two minutes of silence in which you each do an activity that leads to the conflict. Then one of you should begin the verbal conflict.

3. *Open Scene.* Choose a specific relationship and place for the following scene. Make sure your and your partner's objectives conflict. Each of you should pick one overall objective to play, for example, "to make Adrian laugh," or "to wound Pat." Do the first two minutes of the scene in silence. Each of you should perform a physical task that leads to the conflict. Focus on winning your objective. (Note that the scene is called an "open scene" because it allows for a great range of interpretation. Have fun!)

Adrian:	I'm just not ready.
Pat:	You don't want me to move in?
Adrian:	It's not that.
Pat:	You do want me to move in?
Adrian:	I don't know.
Pat:	Look, Adrian, this is ridiculous.
Adrian:	I know it's ridiculous.
Pat:	Then for God's sake make a decision. That's all I want.
Adrian:	I'm too tired.
Pat:	Adrian.
Adrian:	Can you wait one more day?
Pat:	No.
Adrian:	Well, I can't make the decision right now.
Pat:	Every time it ends this way.

Adrian:	Tomorrow, I promise. Really, really.
Pat:	I can't force you to make a decision. I'm warning you, though, it's getting to the point where I don't care.
Adrian:	(*pausing*) Eight o'clock?
Pat:	I guess.
Adrian:	I love you.
Pat:	Tomorrow.

4. *Monologue to an Individual.* Study the following monologue that the poetic young Eugene addresses to Laura, his mother's beautiful new boarder, in act 1, scene 2 of Ketti Fring's dramatization of Thomas Wolfe's novel *Look Homeward, Angel* and identify a possible overall objective. Ask yourself what specifically you want the other person to experience. What major objective will you use to change that individual's emotional state? Find your major objective by practicing the monologue with another actor from class. Use active infinitives. Other possible monologue selections are cited in Appendix F.

OVERALL OBJECTIVE: <u>"TO + VERB"</u>

Eugene:	Have you ever touched one? [. . .] A locomotive. [. . .] Have you ever put your hand on one? You have to feel things to fully understand them. Even a cold one, standing in a station yard. You know what you feel? You feel the shining steel rails under it—and the rails send a message right into your hand—a message of all the mountains that engine ever passed—all the flowing rivers, the forests, the towns, all the houses, the people, the washlines flapping in the fresh cool breeze—the beauty of the people in the way they live and the way they work—a farmer waving from his field, a kid from the school yard—the faraway places it roars through at night, places you don't even know, can hardly imagine. Do you believe it? You feel the rhythm of a whole life, a whole country clicking through your hand.

5. *Monologue to the Audience.* In small groups, practice the following monologue addressed to the audience from act 2

of *A View from the Bridge* by Arthur Miller. Focus on your objective, on what you want the other group members to feel. Identify the objective needed to move individuals from one frame of mind to the next. Make notes next to the text. Note: A forceful objective should change the audience's state of being.

OBJECTIVE (WHAT DO I WANT MY PARTNER [THE AUDIENCE] TO FEEL?):

Alfieri: On December twenty-seventh I saw him next. I normally go home well before six, but that day I sat around looking out my window at the bay, and when I saw him walking through my doorway, I knew why I had waited. And if I seem to tell this like a dream, it was that way. Several moments arrived in the course of the two talks we had when it occurred to me how—almost transfixed I had come to feel. I had lost my strength somewhere. (EDSDIE *enters, removing his cap, sits in the chair, looks thoughtfully out*) I looked in his eyes more than I listened—in fact, I can hardly remember the conversation. But I will never forget how dark the room became when he looked at me; his eyes were like tunnels. I kept wanting to call the police, but nothing had happened. Nothing at all had really happened.

2

ACTION
What am I doing?

This chapter deals with what you do physically.
Each beat is composed of a unit of similar actions.

As I grow older, I pay less attention to what men say. I just watch what they do.

Andrew Carnegie

■ WHAT IS AN ACTION?

Action = "to Do"

Action means "to do." Onstage, you are always engaged in action for an objective. A beat or small piece of a scene is a sequence of similar actions. Your life is also composed of sequences of action. Some days the sequences are vivid. Imagine some of the highlights from your life: receiving a graduation diploma, reciting your wedding vows, embracing a dying friend. You have experienced more moving episodes or beats than you'll ever play onstage.

How do I name actions?

Onstage, after knowing what you want, you must identify your action to get it. Because acting is doing, you are looking for verbs that capture inner and outer movements, verbs that stimulate thought and activity. You name action in an attempt to clarify (and thus repeat) the instinctual choices you make in rehearsal. By choosing clear verbs, you pinpoint the distinctions in choices. "To badger" differs from "to irritate." The range of colors in your performance depends on your ability to identify and re-create many shades of action. In one sequence, you might use all these actions when flirting: "to coo, to toy, to expose, to tease, to humor, to entice, to tempt, to giggle."

To name actions, use the infinitive form of an active verb. For example, for the action "to wait," use the active verb "to amuse myself." It forces you to discover what you're doing, whereas "to wait" encourages passivity. When rehearsing actions, jot down verbs you are playing: "to punish, to ignore, to attack, to distract," and so forth. At home, find other verbs to experiment with in rehearsals. Succinct terms like "to dump him" work better than lengthy descriptions like "to get this person out of my life."

You follow impulses to discover actions in rehearsal. The more you understand what you're doing, the more actions may come to mind. By naming action, you clarify what you did so that you can do it again. Precision and detail are encouraged through such experimentation.

A thesaurus can help you clarify what you're doing. Use verbs like "to con" or "to punch his eyes out" that evoke an emotional response in you. Study books on human behavior. Psychology books like Eric Berne's *Games People Play* can reveal the manipulating action of a scene. Your character may be engineering a game "to get revenge," as in "Now I've got you, you son of a bitch!" or to "show off," as in "Look, Ma, no hands!" or "to blame," as in "See what you made me do!"

Remember, action that can be put into words and repeated is yours. Homework that reviews and strengthens what you do in rehearsal can help your subconscious store it. In performance, when you know what you're doing, you play free. You simply react to what is given to you moment to moment.

What is psycho-physical action?

Onstage, you'll be looking for physical and psychological action to reach your objective. Your physical action is what you do with your body. Your psychological action is what you think.

But all action is psycho-physical. You can't separate your thoughts from your body. Although some actions are more physical than others, all have a psychological component. For example, the physical action "to slug the robber" will have some psychological factors affecting it. Oftentimes action is misinterpreted as purely movement around the stage, but really action has more to do with inner movement like "to get revenge" as it is expressed in your stage choices. So when choosing action, imagine what your character is thinking, experiencing. How does her body feel? What is she sensing? What images are stirring up her thoughts?

Nearly all stage actions are psychological, that is, they express your character's thoughts. Your character is constantly performing mental activities such as judging, envying, resenting, evaluating, repenting, worrying. Human beings are thinking machines. You spend much of your time assessing things. You can stop walking, but you can't stop thinking. Try right now, for one minute, to stop assessing things. It's impossible.

How do I physicalize an action?

To *physicalize* means to find the outward, physical expression of the internal, psychological action. Often a psychological action will have a completely physical expression. If your psychological action is "to punish someone," you might attempt to slap him. If your action is "to flirt," you might adjust your friend's collar. Look for different ways to relate psychological action to the body. In the balcony scene of Shakespeare's *Romeo and Juliet*, Romeo woos Juliet with his words. The actor might perform several physical activities while speaking, such as leaping the wall, throwing a rose to Juliet, staring at her, or caressing her cheek. For instance, Romeo could rush toward Juliet when saying "For stony limits cannot hold love out," because the line's action demonstrates the power of love (act 2, scene 2, line 67).

Active choices urge you to do something physical with the line. Imagine a scene in which you have to apologize to someone so he'll forgive you. If the text says, "I'm terribly sorry," you could just speak the words, but then you're not acting. In acting, you actively engage in behavior that communicates the remorse. For instance, you could drop to your knees or sob when you say the line.

Remember, you can concentrate on only one action at a time. If you play two actions, you must choose which is predominant. The lesser action becomes an activity. An activity is a task you do while engaged in the primary action. For example, think of the difference between an eating scene in which the main action is "to gobble down your food" and one in which the action is "to seduce."

Why is using a physical task important?

Because the audience can't tell what you're thinking, an activity or task helps you express your thoughts. For instance, you can suggest erotic thoughts by the way you handle your food. Find timely tasks that stir your emotions. If your action is "to withdraw," and it is appropriate, you could be packing. Imagine the thoughts, feelings, sensations tied to the way you deal with certain objects: a new résumé, a wedding ring, a plane ticket, a passport. If you're packing, are you worried about making the flight, about meeting someone, about leaving home? Later on, in scripted work, certain tasks, clothes, and objects may be specified by the playwright.

Clothing and objects can help you physicalize your actions. If your action is "to interview for a job," your attire will influence your action. If you are dressed in a dirty jacket and sweaty gloves, your actions will be different from those you perform when in a pristine pinstripe suit.

How can I use an unrelated physical activity?

Do a complex task—fixing a radio, making a soufflé, manicuring your nails. Re-create precisely all the steps in the activity. Next, find a monologue totally unrelated to the activity. Identify the main action in the monologue and practice it separately.

Next, do the monologue while performing the task. (Note: Just put the monologue to the activity and see how a physical task empowers action.)

Why are physical actions important?

Stanislavski discovered that through physical actions, actors tap into psychological actions. By grounding you in the reality of the scene, physical actions help you focus your thoughts.

Climactic scenes, such as that of Oedipus pulling out his eyes, revolve around physical action. In the latter part of his life, Stanislavski concentrated on physical actions as the road to emotional involvement. Whenever possible, he encouraged playing them in order to galvanize the actor's sense of moment-to-moment reality.

Stanislavski stressed physical actions because they communicate immediately with an audience and simultaneously create the actor's sense of reality. They encourage both actor and audience to believe what is occurring onstage. For example, if you want to get across the idea that you want desperately to recover from an illness, you may succeed with a physical action like meticulously taking your temperature every five minutes.

Why do I need stamina?

Stamina will help you sustain a range of actions so you can behave imaginatively in whatever role you play. A change of voice, a tilt of the head, a shift in the gait—all require physical dexterity. Stamina encourages you to act in quick rhythm and tempo and to respond sharply to the other actors.

For any interpretation, you play hundreds of actions. Learn to recognize the demands being placed on your body and voice. Some actions require training in combat techniques, whereas others require vocal adjustments. Even when portraying a wounded character, you must project the incapacitation to the audience through your trained body and voice. A full year before he tackled Shakespeare's military hero Othello, Laurence

Olivier went into daily training, running track and vocalizing his lower voice. Of all of the qualities necessary for actors—talent, training, stamina—Olivier placed stamina first. Even in his eighties, he swam sixty laps a day. Actors know that being in shape gives you an edge in performing action. Great actors are often fanatics about the human body.

CLASS GAMES

1. *Total War.* The object of this improvisation is never to stop making verbal sounds or talking. Two people go onstage and verbally attack each other. First option: two roommates. One condemns the other for wrecking the car; one for destroying a best outfit. Second option: a newly married couple. She attacks him for losing interest; he attacks her for flirting with his best friend.

2. *Objects on a Tray.* Collect in class twenty-five diverse objects and place in a pile. Actors have two minutes to observe, then two minutes to jot down all the objects remembered. Action: to remember more objects than anyone else. Objective: to impress the group.

3. *Grocery Store.* Sit in a circle. One actor begins, "I packed my bag for Grandmother's house, and in it I put an *a* (apple)." The next actor repeats all that went before and adds a *b* item. The next actor adds a *c* item and so forth. An actor who forgets or mistakes an item is eliminated from the circle. Action: to list the most objects. Objective: to stay in the circle.

EXERCISES

1. *The Stranger.* Observe a stranger doing some activity such as eating or shopping. Record only the physical actions and re-create them in class. Afterward tell the class the thoughts you suspect may have prompted these physical actions.

Imitate the stranger exactly. Try to experience how different gestures and rhythms feel.

2. *Professional Procedures.* Observe one of the following groups of people. Write down and re-create the actions of a person in one group. Stage the sequence.

   a. three waiters or waitresses serving
   b. three freshmen studying
   c. three beauticians combing hair
   d. three teachers lecturing
   e. three janitors cleaning

3. *Emergency Room.* Do an improvisation in which one of you plays an admitting clerk at a hospital emergency room and another a patient seeking help: a prostitute, long-lost friend, foreigner, doctor, your mother, your brother, a rival in love, your therapist.

■ FINDING ACTION IN SCRIPTS

How do I develop a range of actions?

You develop a range of actions by breaking down the scene. Begin by choosing your character's objective, then your actions in each beat. Actions should be clear, creating something the audience can see. Naming what you're doing helps you distinguish and sustain interesting choices. Note how one actor has named the actions in the following beat.

BEAT 1: SLIPPING ONTO THE BUS

Scene: a bus in New Orleans

Objective: to win sympathy from the driver

Major action: to slip by the bus driver

ACTIONS

1. to hurry onto the bus

2. to slug change into the fare box

3. to look for twenty more cents

4. to scramble inside my bag

5. to dump out my wallet

6. to moan

7. to rub my back

8. to check my pockets

9. to wave my eviction notice

10. to droop my shoulders

11. to ransack my bag for change

12. to slam more change into the box

13. to knife the driver with a dirty look

14. to stride down the aisle

In this beat, all the actions are related but *varied*. To keep audience interest, never repeat actions unless that repetition makes an important dramatic point. Your goal is to reveal your character through actions that are both exciting and fresh. Note in the "Bus Observation" that follows how objectives motivate action.

BUS OBSERVATION

Scene: a bus in New Orleans

Objective: to win sympathy from the driver

OBJECTIVE	ACTION
1. to win approval from the driver	1. to hurry onto the bus
2. to win approval from the driver	2. to slug change into the fare box
3. to win approval from the driver	3. to look for twenty more cents
4. to stall the driver	4. to scramble inside my bag
5. to stall	5. to dump out my wallet
6. to soften the driver	6. to moan
7. to soften	7. to rub my back

8. to soften	8. to check my pockets
9. to overcome the driver	9. to wave my eviction notice
10. to overcome	10. to droop my shoulders
11. to overcome	11. to ransack my bag for change
12. to punish the driver	12. to slam more change into box
13. to punish	13. to knife the driver with a dirty look
14. to pulverize the driver	14. to stride down the aisle

How do I extend my range in a beat?

You extend range by how you view your character. When in doubt, lean your interpretation toward the strong action coming from the strong trait: acting madly in love rather than sort of attracted, brokenhearted rather than hurt, furious rather than upset. These extremes of character inspire the peaks of your action and allow for moderate choices in between because it's easier to tone down a choice than to bolster it up.

When a script emphasizes one character action, you can extend your range by implementing an opposing one. For example, if you are playing an icy spinster, look for the moments when she is warm. Play her passionate when she says, "I'm perfectly calm, Mrs. Falk." Give your choice the benefit of complexity. Look for your character's opposing emotional traits. In *My Life in Art*, Stanislavski said: "Understand, I said to one of them, you are playing a hypochondriac. You are nagging all the time, and seemingly take care only that your part might, God forbid, not be that of a hypochondriac. But why worry about it when the author himself has taken care of it already? When you play a good man, look for the places where he is evil, and in an evil man look for the places where he is good."

Discover opposing actions by studying the play. Some roles, such as a messenger, for instance, may be vaguely written. Add your own imaginative characterization. Small roles sometimes present an opportunity for testing outrageous actions, like those of a "playboy," "rock singer," or "astronaut." Because you may resist negative actions, phrase actions in an enticing way. In life, you excuse distasteful actions. You see yourself as determined, not bullheaded; as carefree, not sloppy; as fun-loving, not foolish; as harried, not negligent. Onstage, play the positive. Interpret the character so positively that even repulsive actions seem natural.

■ REHEARSALS

How do I discover my actions in rehearsals?

In rehearsals, you pinpoint your objective, then test, discard, and set actions. Some choices may fit naturally the first time. Others may have to be rejected before you discover an interpretation that works. I come from the practical school of acting, where you test action. You do it, fix it, change it, adjust it, rather than thinking about action, analyzing it, researching it, and discussing it. Both schools are important, but because you must *play* a scene, the sooner you can get on your feet and test actions, the better.

Begin by establishing the physical framework of the sequence. Find out what your character is wearing. Then experiment with what task your character could be doing. If you choose a task like "to study," you might investigate your character's particular routine. What might your character do when studying? Would you paint your fingernails, sip hot tea, flick on the radio, sharpen pencils? Start by imagining items you could use on your desk. Possible objects might include index cards, papers, prayer beads, liquor, or a snack. Rehearse with different objects. Keep those that provoke the most interesting thoughts and reactions.

What is a main action?

Besides a physical task, look for your character's main action. In any scene, usually one person is doing something, and another is resisting it. Commit yourself to your main action, so you will buffer any opposition to it. Notice which major action works best with your lines. When possible, work closely with the other actors. The opposing actions you choose will set up the structure of the scene. In fact, the tension of a scene is caused by this collision of actions.

To get yourself into the action, experiment with playing it in the moments before a scene begins. Let's say, for example, that your character is a famous writer who has been hounded by critics. The play opens with the unexpected arrival of the critics. Your action upon entering is "to kick the critics out." You might imagine, offstage, that you have been battling for a week with *New York Times* reporters. When you recognize them, you play your action with venom. You hurl abuse.

Examples of main actions that propel characters in scenes are "to advance and to retreat," "to trap and to escape," "to confront and to ignore," "to collect and to hide the money," "to brag and to ignore," "to seduce and to withdraw." With strong main actions, the tension in a scene mounts. The lines gain weight and meaning. The phrase "I'm playing opposite so-and-so" really means that you are playing action *against* someone else's. Your main actions collide. (In monologues, you could be playing against another side of yourself.)

How do minor actions support my main action?

Besides choosing your main action, you must experiment with how you play the actions in different beats. If, for example, you are insulting the critics, you must listen for how they receive that action before proceeding to the next one. All action grows out of reaction. When you connect with a living, breathing actor, you will adapt your actions to affecting her. These minor actions or strategies keep you in the moment. Remember, variety provokes interest, so you're searching for contrast in your approach to different beats.

For example, if your main action is "to hurl abuse," test the smaller actions you are playing to get this across. Imagine yourself in similar circumstances. For instance, you might remember a time you tried to force someone out. What did you do? Yell, threaten, curse, toss things? How did the sequences change based on the responses you provoked?

In the following scene from *Death of a Salesman,* one actor tests the action "to retreat" when he wants to get his wife's sympathy. He has jotted down some possible line-by-line actions such as complaining, moaning, blaming, next to the text. Note: Write down your actions in pencil so you can adjust them as rehearsals proceed.

DEATH OF A SALESMAN: NOTES ON WILLY'S OPENING BEAT

Objective: to get my wife's sympathy

Possible action: to retreat

ACTIONS

	Linda:	(*hearing WILLY outside the bedroom, calls with some trepidation*) Willy!
To moan	Willy:	It's all right. I came back.
	Linda:	Why? What happened? (*Slight pause.*) Did something happen, Willy?
To avoid	Willy:	No, nothing happened.
	Linda:	You didn't smash the car, did you?
To needle	Willy:	(*with casual irritation*) I said nothing happened. Didn't you hear me?
	Linda:	Don't you feel well?
To complain	Willy:	I'm tired to death. (*The flute has faded away. He sits on the bed beside her, a little numb.*) I couldn't make it. I just couldn't make it, Linda.
	Linda:	(*very carefully, delicately*) Where were you all day? You look terrible.
To collapse; to blame	Willy:	I got as far as a little above Yonkers. I stopped for a cup of coffee. Maybe it was the coffee.

But the breathtaking part of it all was not so much the planning as the fantastic skill with which the planning was concealed.

Eva Le Gallienne, *The Mystic in the Theatre: Eleonora Duse*

How should I rehearse actions line by line?

Line-by-line actions are the tiny doings you play on or between your different lines. Sometimes line-by-line actions oppose what you say. But normally what you are doing supports the words. For example, the action "to startle" might underlie the line "Gotcha!"

Find an action for each line and moment. In art, we judge greatness by the virtuosity of the sequence of actions—the way a ballerina spins a pirouette, a violinist builds to a high note. You, too, can develop an exciting moment-to-moment plan for a role. Remember: genius is 1 percent inspiration and 99 percent perspiration!

You can discover actions in various ways. Work out the approach that's best for you. Acting involves making choices. There is this group of actions that is going to say this, and this group of other actions that is going to say that. Which way is best? Try out different approaches and see. Look for choices that affect you emotionally.

Be as spontaneous as possible during the rehearsal process. In French, the word for "rehearsal," *essay*, means "an attempt."

During rehearsals, you try on actions for expressiveness. Gradually you piece small units into bigger and bigger sequences. Work as much as you can in detail, and keep in mind the overall action of the scene. You will be discovering ideas for small sections and intermittently reviewing larger sections of the play to build the sweep of the scenes.

Find time to practice daily, unit by unit, so you can string together an interesting progression of actions. It is far better to rehearse twenty minutes daily than two hours once a week. Daily rehearsals develop your memory and imagination. Stopping rehearsal with partial work done stimulates you to do homework, ruminate, and return invigorated with fresh insights.

How should I rehearse the build of a scene?

As you grow comfortable with line-by-line actions and beats, focus rehearsals on discovering the momentum of the scene. In her autobiography, the actress Tallulah Bankhead gave this advice: "I'm the foe of moderation, the champion of excess. If I may lift a line from a die-hard whose identity is lost in the shuffle, I'd rather be strongly wrong than weakly right."

A compelling series of actions ripens your emotions. But keep a lid on them. Your actions must build to the climax of the scene. The audience feels more for you if you are trying to hold yourself together than if you're falling apart. Never play all you are experiencing.

Some artists defy others with their actions, especially during climactic scenes. One actress playing a grieving mother chose bold physical actions to communicate her grief. When her dead little girl's rag doll was tossed onto the floor, she broke free of those consoling her, dashed across the stage, and flung herself down on the doll. Another actress simulated possession by the devil. Audiences of young and old stood up and blocked others' view to see how the actress was hissing to attract the devil, writhing with pleasure, her tongue out, her eyes rolled back. Both actresses' extreme choices for action arose from insightful observation and rehearsal. They pushed the boundaries of self-expression with the range of truthful actions building inside their performances.

How do I prepare for a scene?

Besides preparing with physical warm-ups for the body, you must prepare for the scene's action emotionally. You do this by getting in touch with your character's action before your first entrance. Some actors come to the theater early and use the time while getting into costume and makeup to start thinking the thoughts (psychological actions) of the character before the entrance.

Others improvise the offstage life of the character and actually practice different improvisations during final rehearsals. At some point before your entrance you'll need to isolate yourself from backstage reality and focus on the character's offstage action. Allow yourself at least ten minutes. Often, choosing a physical action your character might do right before entering helps concentration. For example, if you're fixing yourself up for a date in your first stage action, you could start combing your hair offstage.

■ IMPROVISATION

What is improvisation?

Improvisation is the act of composing a sequence without previous study or preparation, spontaneously reacting to your fellow actors on stage in a relaxed and truthful way. Extemporizing develops impulses as a primary tool; you must rely on them.

How does improvisation help rehearsal?

Improvisation is a method for testing action in rehearsal. Until you set your interpretation for a scene, you are improvising to some extent. You are reacting with lines and movements in new ways to express your impulses. You are trying out choices to see which ones bring the strongest results from other characters. Experimenting with different approaches helps you discover nuances of meaning. You will find the appropriate impulses for a scene and the actions they lead to.

Improvisation can teach you about your character. In rehearsal, set up specific improvisations to help you relate truthfully as the character. Establish a given framework of opposing objectives, then invent the scene spontaneously, using your own words. If you are playing a farewell scene, try saying goodbye in different ways. Or do the opposite: Improvise the time you first met. Memory of the real encounter will thicken your relationship in the departure scene.

What are structured improvisations?

The progressive exercises at the end of each chapter of this book can be viewed as structured improvisations. They are structured in that they are rehearsed and have a framework supporting them. They are improvisations in that, though rehearsed, the verbal exchange is somewhat fluid. Progressive exercises excite your feelings by filtering more and more background into each encounter. Information leads to detail in your choices and to specific actions.

After you restage an improvisation, it becomes a "structured" improvisation because you have chosen elements to keep. Most acting in plays begins in a free format and develops a tighter and tighter structure. Your challenge is to stay in touch with your impulses and the spontaneity originally felt in rehearsal. You are making the frozen format as exciting as the free. You are acting as if it's the first time.

■ CHECKLIST

1. Have you broken your scene down into beats?

2. What is your major action?

3. Have you physicalized your actions?

4. Do you have line-by-line actions?

■ FINAL PROJECTS

1. *Progressive Exercise.* This exercise is related to the one in chapter 1, so you have the same partner. Rehearse this sequence several times.

   EXERCISE 2: An empty apartment. Two years have passed since Progressive Exercise 1. You and your partner are intensely related. Each of you plays opposing objectives with a strong action.

   Many minor objectives and actions may also influence you in the scene.

Begin the scene in silence with each of you engaged in a physical activity. Then one of you should begin the verbal conflict. Hand in your written backgrounds.

2. *Sequencing Actions.* Choose a major action and a series of actions for one of the following descriptive sequences from a play. (One example has been partially completed.) Test various possibilities, then stage the most interesting one in class.

Buried Child by Sam Shepard, Act 1

ACTIONS: **OVERALL ACTION: <u>TO RELAX SELF</u>**

1. to stare   (*Gradually the form of* DODGE *is made out, sitting on the couch,* [1] *facing the TV. . . .* DODGE *slowly tilts his head back* [2] *and stares at the ceiling for a while, listening to the rain.* [3] *He lowers his head again and stares at the TV. He turns his head slowly to the left and stares at the sofa next to the one he's sitting on. He pulls his left arm out from under the blanket, slides his hand under the cushion, and pulls out a bottle of whiskey. He looks down left toward the staircase, listens, then uncaps the bottle, takes a long swig and caps it again. He puts the bottle back under the cushion and stares at the TV. He starts to cough slowly and softly. The coughing gradually builds. He holds one hand to his mouth and tries to stifle it. The coughing gets louder, then suddenly stops when he hears the sound of his wife's voice coming from the top of the staircase.*)

2. to check distraction

3. to follow program

_____

_____

_____

_____

_____

'Night, Mother by Marsha Norman

ACTIONS: **OVERALL ACTION:** _____

_____   (MAMA *stretches to reach the cupcakes in a cabinet in the kitchen. She can't see them, but she can feel around for them, and she's eager to have one, so*

_____

ACTIONS:
_____

_____

_____

_____

_____

she's working pretty hard at it. This may be the most serious exercise MAMA ever gets. She finds a cupcake, the coconut-covered, raspberry-and-marshmallow-filled kind known as a snowball, but sees that there's one missing from the package. She calls to JESSIE, who is apparently somewhere else in the house.)

Serenading Louie by Lanford Wilson (Hill & Wang, 1985), Act 1, Scene 1

ACTIONS: **OVERALL ACTION:** _____

_____

_____

_____

_____

_____

_____

_____

(*Nearly evening. The only light is on the desk*)
Carl: (*Coming from the kitchen as he closes the outside door, he calls from offstage*) Sweetheart?
(*he enters*) Honey? . . . Mary?
(*he yells up the stairs*) Hey, baby? (*He goes to the patio door, yells out*) Mary?
(*He shuts the door, turns, and sees the light; he goes to the desk, picks up a note, and sits as he reads it. He lets the note float from his hand back to the desk, shuts his eyes a moment, reaches to the desk lamp, and turns it off.*) (*Blackout*)

The Ghost Sonata by August Strindberg, Scene 1

ACTIONS: **OVERALL ACTION:** _____

to walk

to carry

to remove

to place

to wipe

to drink   to wash   to style hair

(*The milkmaid comes in from around the corner, carrying a wire basket filled with bottles. She is wearing a summer dress, with brown shoes, black stockings and a white cap. She takes off her cap and hangs it on the drinking fountain; wipes the sweat from her brow; takes a drink from the cup; washes her hands; arranges her hair, using the water in the fountain as a mirror.*)

3. *Sibling Rivalry.* Stage a scene between two siblings, such as the greeting scene between Blanche and Stella in *A Streetcar*

Named Desire or the bedroom scene between Biff and Happy in *Death of a Salesman*. Choose psychological and physical traits that reflect the character's and your own uniqueness. Make sure the actions of the two siblings totally clash.

4. *Framing the Action.* Do a physical task for two minutes while you focus on an action. Then let the task evolve into a monologue. Look for ways to physicalize your actions. The following monologue is partially analyzed to demonstrate the process. Additional monologues are in Appendix F.

Ludlow Fair by Lanford Wilson

ACTIONS:	TASK: <u>TO SET MY HAIR</u>
1. to destroy	Agnes: [1][*Throw down old rollers*] [2]I'm going to be
2. to complain	a mess tomorrow. [3]I probably won't make it to work, let alone lunch. [4]A casual lunch, [5][*Toss a bobby pin*
3. to predict	*in trash*] [6]my God. I wonder what he'd think—stupid
4. to qualify	Charles—if he knew I was putting up my hair for him; catching pneumonia. No lie, I can't wait till
5. to mock	summer to see what kind of sunglasses he's going
6. to curse	to pop into the office with. Probably those World's Fair charmers. A double unisphere. (*Turns*) Are
	you going to sleep? (*Pause. No reply*) Well, crap.

3

OBSTACLES
What's in my way?

This chapter deals with the elements that impede the action
and thus create suspense. Your obstacle intensifies action by
thwarting it.

Life is either a daring adventure or nothing.

Helen Keller

■ WHAT IS AN OBSTACLE?

An obstacle is something that stands in the way of your action
and stops you from getting what you want. In every beat, you
are doing something, wanting something, and something is
stopping you. By blocking what you're pursuing, the obstacle
creates unpredictability, which excites the audience to partici-
pate mentally. Think about how alert football players are when
the score is tied with two minutes to go. Deadlines occur in
both comedy and drama.

Why are obstacles important?

Actions require obstacles to sustain attention. Obstacles challenge you to intensify what you do to get what you want. You
have to pursue a full range of actions to overcome obstacles.

Note in the "Bus Observation" that follows how obstacles intensify action.

BUS OBSERVATION

Scene: a bus in New Orleans

Main obstacle: driver's indifference

ACTION	OBJECTIVE	OBSTACLES
1. to hurry onto the bus	to win approval from the driver	slippery floor
2. to slug change into the fare box	to win approval	narrow coin slot
3. to look for twenty more cents	to win approval	empty wallet
4. to scramble inside my bag	to stall the driver	messy papers in bag
5. to moan	to soften the driver	no time
6. to rub my back	to soften	heavy topcoat
7. to check my pockets	to soften	pockets full of objects
8. to wave my eviction notice	to overcome the driver	other passengers' impatience
9. to droop my shoulders	to overcome	driver's indifference
10. to slam more change into the box	to punish the driver	broken fare box
11. to knife the driver with a dirty look	to punish	driver's indifference
12. to stride down the aisle	to pulverize the driver	unsteadiness on feet

Obstacles create the suspense in a scene. A carefully rehearsed plan of action, focused on overcoming the opposition, encourages the gradual growth of emotion and lends depth to your acting. To quote Stanislavski (*My Life in Art*): "What was good was that we saw how you controlled yourself more and more, until at last something tore into you, and you could control yourself no longer." Never play the obstacle—that is, don't telegraph how much it bothers you. Instead, focus on the action. You sustain audience interest by showing how much you can bear.

What is a major obstacle?

In every scene, your character struggles against a major obstacle, which blocks your main action. The other character usually creates this obstacle. Your opposing needs lead you to actions that clash in some way. To find the obstacle, ask, "What person is stopping me in each scene?"

The major obstacle to one character's persecuting his mother is her comforting him. An actor playing Hamlet once made the choice of the extreme action of throwing a corpse into his mother's lap and pushing the corpse's face into hers. This assault would block his mother's action of calming him down.

Major obstacles need not be negative. Young lovers might differ about whether to consummate their affection. Because of the suspense, the audience wants to know what will ensue.

Notice how the opposing objectives "to protect" and "to seduce" create the colliding actions of the young lovers in this excerpt from act 2, scene 2 of *Romeo and Juliet.*

Juliet: How came you hither, tell me, and wherefore?
          The orchard walls are high and hard to climb,
          And the place death, considering who you are,
          If any of my kinsmen find you here.

Romeo: With love's light wings did I o'erperch these walls;
          For stony limits cannot hold love out,
          And what love can do, that dares love attempt;
          Therefore your kinsmen are no stop to me.

Juliet: If they do see you they will murder you.

When actions clash, one of two outcomes can result: The actions of both of you are evenly blocked, or one of you overcomes the other.

EXERCISES

1. *Opposing Action.* List actions that oppose the following ones:

Objective: to abandon you	Opposing objective: to pick you up
ACTION	OPPOSING ACTION
1. to pack my suitcase	1. _____
2. to distance you	2. _____
3. to change clothes	3. _____
4. to leave	4. _____
5. to write a paper	5. _____
6. to practice my exercises	6. _____
7. to straighten the room	7. _____
8. to pay remaining bills	8. _____

Consider the following opposing actions. How do they differ from the ones you wrote?

ACTION	OPPOSING ACTION
1. to pack my suitcase	1. to unpack your suitcase
2. to distance you	2. to embrace
3. to change clothes	3. to undress you
4. to leave	4. to corner you
5. to write a paper	5. to party
6. to practice my exercises	6. to dance with you
7. to straighten the room	7. to ransack the room
8. to pay remaining bills	8. to massage your feet

2. *Overcoming My Distance.* In pairs, practice throwing a ball back and forth. Keep widening the distance between the two of you.

3. *Getting Attention.* Rehearse a sequence in which you play the objective "to seize another's attention" while he focuses on ignoring you. This can represent a major obstacle.

4. *Touching and Tension.* Rehearse a sequence using two or three different distance ranges between the characters. Study the power of touch versus distance onstage in establishing the necessary tension in a scene.

What are minor obstacles?

Minor obstacles are smaller ones that fortify the major obstacle. They create variety by erupting unpredictably throughout a scene. In the following scene, which opens act 3 of Arthur Miller's *All My Sons*, Jim's major obstacle is Mother's silence about her missing son, Chris.

One actor playing Jim discovered minor obstacles by observing the conditions and thoughts that made playing the action more difficult. He noted his major need in a scene (to calm Mother) and the minor obstacles that blocked him (poor visibility, lateness, tiredness). Minor obstacles can extend for a period of time (like Mother's ceaseless rocking) or for just a few moments (like someone at the bedroom window).

ALL MY SONS: JIM'S OBSTACLES

Major obstacle: Mother's silence	Action: to make conversation
Possible minor obstacles:	Objective: to calm Mother
lateness	*Two o'clock* the *following morning.* MOTHER *is*
tiredness	*discovered on the rise, rocking ceaselessly in a*
rocking unnerves me	*chair, staring at her thoughts. It is an intense,*
spooky moon	*slight sort of rocking. A light shows from the*
my previous search for him	*upstairs bedroom, lower floor windows being* *dark. The moon is strong and casts its bluish* *light. Presently,* JIM, *dressed in jacket and hat,* *appears from the Left, and seeing her, goes up* *beside her.*
poor visibility	Jim: Any news?

someone watching at bedroom window, when she doesn't sleep she cracks up	Mother:	No news.
	Jim:	(*gently*) You can't sit up all night, dear, why don't you go to bed?
ceaseless rocking	Mother:	I'm waiting for Chris. Don't worry about me, Jim, I'm perfectly all right.
seven hours of waiting	Jim:	But it's almost two o'clock.
	Mother:	I can't sleep. (*Slight pause*) You had an emergency?
her incessant prying the Muhlers	Jim:	(*tiredly*) Somebody had a headache and thought he was dying. (*Slight pause*) Half of my patients are quite mad. Nobody realizes how many people are walking around loose, and they're cracked as coconuts.
my new Ford her withdrawal she belittles me		Money. Money-money-money-money. You say it long enough. It doesn't mean anything. (*She smiles, makes a silent laugh*) Oh, how I'd love to be around when that happens.
her irritability	Mother:	(*shakes her head*) You're so childish, Jim. Sometimes you are.

Many minor obstacles strengthen action in this interpretation.

■ DISCOVERING OBSTACLES

What are physical obstacles?

Physical obstacles are natural barriers that block action externally. A blaring alarm that scares a thief when looting a building is a physical obstacle; so is a person like a tall guard who blocks a player when throwing a ball. Just as you look for physical actions to play, you should find physical obstacles. A physical obstacle communicates immediately with the audience and provides a tangible force that you can work against in a scene. Wherever possible, you should layer your work with physical obstacles because they are the easiest to control. It's much simpler to work against a tangible force than against a thought.

Physical obstacles trigger emotions because you don't have to *imagine* the obstacles. You simply play your action "to throw the ball," and a physical obstacle such as an opponent, distance, or a faulty glove creates the problem. A physical obstacle immediately agitates you. For example, if your action is "to get dressed," the obstacle of too-tight pants will frustrate you more than just thinking about being thin. Notice which items around you could stifle your action "to read" right now. Endless physical obstacles exist.

How can the place work as an obstacle?

The place can threaten your character's action. Think of how you've felt when walking to your car in a deserted parking lot or trying to sleep in a freezing apartment. Many locales automatically deter action. Some playwrights construct the environment as a major obstacle. Romeo wants to be in Juliet's bedroom rather than below the balcony. In another play, a character longs to roam outdoors rather than hide in the attic. In yet another, a character struggles to escape the ghetto.

A particular occasion in a particular place can inhibit action even further. Think of how you might act in church at the marriage of your fiancé to someone else, in the labor room at the birth of triplets, in the graveyard at the burial of your father. Whatever you choose to do on these occasions often has consequences. After a choice is made, you can't turn back. Key events—marriages, births, deaths, departures—in special places pressure the action of many characters: the auction of an estate, a secret forgery in a conventional community, a birthday at a Mississippi mansion, a hanging in Salem, an only brother's wedding in a small southern town, the purchase of a first house in postwar Chicago, the death of a child in Texas.

How can the place create real problems?

The place can create real problems by physically hindering you. We move more onstage than in real life. A floor plan that creates obstacles for the characters heightens interest in the action. Allow physical conditions of your environment (such as noise, dirt, light) to agitate you. For example, if noise is stopping you from studying, you might move across the room, retreat under the covers, pound on the wall, or stuff cotton into your ears. When you are setting up the space, consider not putting everything within arm's reach. Cross to get your makeup or shaving kit as opposed to having it right next to you. Let the chair at a table be pushed in, so you must pull it out to sit down, just as you would in real life. If you are playing a love scene, start out across the room from your partner, rather than side by side, with little distance to overcome. Find a real problem in each place.

How can time work as an obstacle?

Whereas many characters face difficult places and events, others face the problem of time running out. They must face a jury, find a job, overcome an illness, get married. Some characters face the last days before their death.

If you are playing a scene in which time is an obstacle, use a timepiece whenever possible. Relate to a watch or some form of physical measurement of time at specific moments throughout the scene. Time is an obstacle only if it presents a real problem in a particular place. You've got to get to the church for the wedding, to the airport for that flight, and so on.

How do objects and tasks serve as obstacles?

Objects can easily block your character's action. Imagine the vexation of having to work at an office with a disconnected telephone or to dance at your senior prom in tight shoes. Objects such as a broken window shade, ringing alarm clock, or glaring light increase the adversity of your immediate environment.

Think about trying to open a stuck door to escape when an enemy is chasing you. Remember the frustration of having your computer crash as you're trying to type a critical exam paper.

In *Dream Girl* (1945), Elmer Rice has written into Georgina's opening monologue a series of frustrating objects.

DREAM GIRL: OBJECTS AS OBSTACLES

Possible action: to postpone getting up

Possible obstacles/objects: alarm clock, sunlight

Georgina: (*yawning heavily*) Ohhhh! (*Then, angrily, to the alarm clock*) For heaven's sake, will you please shut up? (*She shuts off the alarm clock, then leans over and pulls up an imaginary window shade. The bed is flooded with morning sunlight.* GEORGINA *moans, shakes her head, and stretches her arms*) Oh, dear! Another day! How awful! Who was it that said: "Must we have another day?" Dorothy Parker, I suppose. I wonder if she really says all those things. (*With a sigh*) Well, time to get up, I guess. (*She plumps herself down again and snuggles her head in the pillow*)

A physical task can also create a real problem for your character. A character may need to take deep breaths to calm her nerves without being observed by another, and this presents a real problem.

How can my clothing work as an obstacle?

Your character's clothing can hinder action. Have you ever tried to move gracefully in work boots or climb to your seat at a football stadium in high heels? Your costume influences all your physical actions.

Put yourself at risk in rehearsal. For example, if you are playing a homely teacher, wear some of your own tacky clothes, ugly accessories, and no makeup ("Oh, no!" you say). Find clothing that truly dictates what you do.

Clothing specific to an ailment can drastically restrict movement. Have you ever tried to clean house with your leg in a cast? Can you remember how embarrassed you felt when you clumped down an aisle with a cast on your leg? Most physical obstacles have some psychological component and vice versa.

Physical handicaps create great obstacles. Think of a blind man finding his way with a stick, an athlete hobbling on crutches, a veteran limping with a wooden leg. Many lead roles revolve around impairments: blindness, deafness, muteness, paralysis.

What are psychological obstacles?

At the root of our fullest involvement . . . is a deliberate disjunction of impressions, often what we see working against what we hear, or vice versa; often what we feel working against what we think.

J. L. Styan, *Drama, Stage and Audience*

Psychological obstacles are internal barriers within your character or other characters. Psychological obstacles are mental forces, disturbing thoughts and thwarting actions. A psychological obstacle can be an idea in your character's mind that hinders what you do. Often it means experiencing another's outlook blocking your actions. You find yourself unable to reach him because of his slanted point of view. You adjust your responses and try to move past resistance. You feel that if this person could only experience your predicament, he would help. For example, you warn a friend that he must sell his house. But he is easily distracted. Distraction stops you from getting your scene partner to focus on the crisis.

Onstage, you often try to influence the point of view of another character. In *Romeo and Juliet*, Romeo must overcome not just the physical obstacle of the balcony but also the psychological one of Juliet's outlook: her fears about her parents' disapproval. His obstacle is her attachment to her parents.

To overcome the psychological obstacle in this scene, Romeo should begin experiencing Juliet's point of view. He would ask himself, "What is she thinking as she looks at me? What is she imagining her parents will say if they walk in right now? Is she picturing her parents locking her up forever?"

Why are psychological obstacles important?

The most vexing obstacles onstage and in life are psychological ones. For example, you can't get another character to understand you, to love you, to support you. You can't pull yourself out of a depression. You can see and accept a locked door, but it's hard to deal with a locked-up personality. Onstage, you try different ways to break through internal barriers.

Often, you are dealing with an obstacle in another actor. You must try to overcome the way that character thinks. Mental barriers incite you to corner the other character to get what you want.

Sometimes a psychological obstacle is actually a second side of yourself. You are fighting against your own disturbing thoughts and feelings. When this happens, be sure to use many details of circumstances to make your thoughts gnaw away at you. Background material strengthens inner obstacles. Using your imagination, fill in the character's present and past with details from your own life and fiction. In the following exercise, mental obstacles of preoccupation pressure the action.

BACKGROUND FOR THREE-MINUTE SEQUENCE

I am an unemployed actress wanting to do something significant in my field, married to a neat, caring husband who has just lost his job.

What time is it?

4:45 P.M. Saturday, May 15, 1991, spring, light breeze outside. I'm wearing summer clothes. Cost of living is skyrocketing (esp. at grocery store) and may inflate with the president's energy plan pending Congress. My in-laws are due shortly for a first visit to our new house.

Where am I?

I am in the children's section of the living room, by the fireplace, in our house in the country town of Lambertville, New Jersey. Tom, my husband, is mowing the lawn, which he has not cut for two weeks. Lambertville is an expensive New York suburb. There are over fifty theaters in a seventy-five-mile radius of Lambertville. We have a mortgage of $820 a month.

My show is ending at Bucks County Playhouse. Everyone gleefully assumes I'll come back and reapply for a company position again. I just opened two rejection letters from theaters because of cutbacks. I cannot act at Bucks County next year. My in-laws loaned us money for buying this house and want us to settle happily here.

What do I want?

Main objective: to impress Tom's relatives

Immediate (mental) objective: to alleviate unemployment problem

ACTION: to clean

Subactions (physical)

1. to put on cleaning gloves, scarf
2. to clean fireplace
3. to dust mantel
4. to dust end table, phone
5. to dust end table, lamp
6. to dust coffee table
7. to clean bookcase
8. to clean chair

Psychological actions

1. to define what's wrong with my auditioning

What's in my way?

Major obstacle: time running out

Other obstacles: worry about unemployment problem

anger at presumptuous visit
desire to go to the movies

desire to read and rest before kids come home
damp, muggy afternoon
dislike for physical activity
Tom's neat streak
Tom needs to mow, then clean up
my stomach and nerves
headache
dinner unmade

State of mind

Events

I am discouraged and uneasy; I have constipation, piercing stomach cramps; I hate myself for failures on interviews; I had expected employment at another theater. I am angry about not being able to go to the movies and our surprise in-law visit tonight.

People (in thoughts)

Tom—want to keep his spirits up for tonight and for his job hunt.
Director Richards—want to tell him off for his rude interview.
Producer O—want to play up to him for a small role.
Actor B—want to tell him off for his hypocrisy.

Objects (surrounding me)

Phone—want it to ring and resolve problem.
Rug—want it to return my stock money.
Lamp—want it to take me back to Japan where I was on a fellowship.
Chair (*by phone*)—want money from parents, not gifts.
Sofa and table—want to forget how I had to scrape when married in acting school.
Coffee table—want to forget how Tom searched to find $8 table.
Bookcase—want to forget all work I did to excel; stop being acting student.
TV—want to forget my failure to make money as an actress and dust; want Tom to make more money.

Note: The actress may not think of these thought/obstacles in the same order or use all of them for each performance. She is loading her work with mental obstacles because they are capricious and may vary each performance. All these obstacles distract her from the action of cleaning.

Also, during performance, she will not force herself to concentrate on them. The work of recalling and specifying obstacles comes in rehearsal. And the battle is to keep cleaning.

How do psychological obstacles encourage vulnerability?

Stanislavski considered psychological obstacles the most useful and powerful because they are intricately tied to your feelings. Vulnerability, the ability to be wounded easily, is a major trait of good actors. It means you allow your ideas about the other characters and yourself to hurt you. You are continually deepening your interpretation of the problem while trying to overcome it. Good actors transform themselves into vulnerable, unpredictable characters. They intrigue the audience by the range of their adjustments to inner obstacles.

CLASS GAMES

1. *Mirror Exercise.* Stand opposite each other in pairs. (Send a classmate out of the room.) Choose a leader to perform a physical movement and a follower to simultaneously mirror the action. Objective: to prevent your classmate from identifying the leaders. Obstacle: difficulty in synchronizing with your partner.

2. *Handicap Walk.* Divide class in half. Members of one half walk across the floor as fast as they can, pretending they have broken ankles. Where is the pain avoided when walking? The other half chooses the most authentic walk. Discuss.

3. *Physical Obstacle List.* Make a list of the physical obstacles (places, events, people) that could have impeded you today from reaching class. Actor with the longest list reads it to the class.

4. *Rope Pull.* Split the class in half. Have class members tug back and forth on the obstacle of an imaginary rope.

5. *Number Shoot.* Sit in a circle. Count off around the circle, with each actor taking a number. Then Actor Number One calls out, "One says to Three." Actor Number Three might respond, "Three says to Eight." Then Eight responds with something like, "Eight says to Four." An actor is put out of the circle if she does not respond immediately to her number or calls upon an incorrect number (the number that was just called or the number of an actor already eliminated). Action: to call the correct number. Objective: to stay in the circle. Obstacle: distraction.

EXERCISES

1. *Physical Obstacle Sequence.* Re-create one of the following: (a) someone writing a paper with a broken pen; (b) someone cooking a meal with the wrong utensils; (c) someone reading without glasses; (d) someone escaping while blindfolded. Concentrate totally on performing the action several times until it becomes organic.

2. *Problem Computer.* Think of several possible problems with a computer: a stuck key, broken space bar, uncooperative mouse. Type a particular term paper pretending you're working against one particular problem. Repeat the exercise in class.

3. *Blindfolded Breakfast.* Get up and make breakfast while blindfolded. Repeat the exercise in class.

4. Observe and re-create a person working against a physical obstacle, for example, someone climbing the stairs with a sprained ankle, typing a paper with a broken typewriter, or cooking a meal with the wrong utensils. Then do this assignment with:
   a. one objective, one action, one obstacle
   b. one objective, one action, two obstacles
   c. one objective, two actions, one obstacle

d. one objective, two actions, two obstacles

e. two objectives, two actions, one obstacle

f. two objectives, two actions, two obstacles

■ REHEARSING OBSTACLES

How can difficult obstacles help me?

Difficult obstacles focus you totally on the action. The harder it is for you to do something—climb a mountain, make a phone call, unlock a door—the more carefully you'll commit yourself to each choice. Tough obstacles are the best gifts you can give yourself in a scene.

Onstage, your character must make urgent decisions, think quickly, react to some extremely painful pressure. That's one of the reasons why when I coach a scene, I'll say, "Put more pressure on her, make her respond to you. React to what she just said; did you hear that? Yes, repeat it for me, respond to that." Onstage, someone is always forcing another to do something. In my early years of teaching acting, I used to sit back and analyze for about twenty-five minutes what the obstacle was for the actors, and then I'd say, "Come back next class and do that scene," and I would see the same results I saw earlier. But now I referee the scene in class, and when I know the actors are physically experiencing the obstacles, I then step out. Sometimes I'm a devil's advocate, setting up an argument, egging it on, and after it gets ignited, stepping out of it.

How can I strengthen each obstacle?

Strengthen each obstacle by eliminating the phrase "My character is not concerned about this problem" from your vocabulary. Hook yourself into only one option: Your character is more determined to overcome the obstacles than you are!

Imagine yourself playing the Commuter in the following opening scene. Ask yourself, "When has someone confronted me like this?" Experience the Man's opposing point of view. Try to recall when you felt suspicious of someone.

Man: Well, I've been meaning to talk to you. I hope you won't mind. I suppose you're an easygoing type and—you missed your train?

Commuter: By not more than a minute. I rush into the station, and it pulls out before my very eyes.

Man: You could have run after it.

Commuter: Of course, it's silly, I know. If I hadn't been loaded down with all those damned packages, bundles, boxes, God knows what else! Like a jackass! But you know women—errands, errands—it never stops! It took me three minutes, believe me, just to get out of the taxi and get my fingers through all those strings, two packages to a finger.

Man: You must have been quite a sight. You know what I'd have done? I'd have left them in the cab.

Commuter: And my wife? Oh, yes! And my daughters? And all their friends?

Man: Let them scream. I'd enjoy it enormously.

Commuter: That's because you probably have no idea what women are like when they get to the country in the summer!

Man: But of course I know. Precisely because I do know. (*a pause*) They all begin by saying they won't really need anything.

(from Luigi Pirandello's *The Man with the Flower in His Mouth,* 1926; translated by William Murray, 1970)

Ask yourself, "What stranger from my life would I have difficulty overcoming? What could I personally risk losing to this man?" For example, a missed train could unnerve you if you are unarmed, carrying your paycheck, and confronting a drug addict. What's at stake? Possibly your life.

Study the play! Better to have too many obstacles than too few. The more your character has to lose, the more suspenseful the obstacle. For example, in a tragedy, his life is what a character has to lose. In a comedy, you might risk something vital to you like all your money, if you're greedy, or your looks, if you're vain. Remember in rehearsals to give yourself the right to experiment, to play, and to fail. Often you must go past the mark to find the limits imposed by the obstacles.

■ CHECKLIST

1. What is my major obstacle? Who is doing this to me?
2. What little obstacles are stopping me moment to moment?
3. How are the place, time, and events stopping me?
4. How are the other characters hindering me?

■ FINAL PROJECTS

1. *Progressive Exercise.* This exercise is related to the ones in chapters 1 and 2, so you have the same partner. Rehearse this sequence several times.

   EXERCISE 3:   A stalled train. Two more years have passed. You and your partner are intensely related. You each play an opposing objective and action, and each has one main obstacle in the sequence. One of you has a physical handicap, and one has a professional handicap.
   Many minor obstacles may also affect you in the scene. Begin the scene in silence, with each of you engaged in a physical activity. Then one of you should begin the verbal conflict. Hand in your written background for the exercise.

2. *Lost Object.* Re-create a sequence with objects in which you have one major objective (to find something), one action (to hunt), and one physical obstacle (something hidden). Make up background information that puts you at great risk because of the lost object. Rehearse in a familiar place with

someone actually hiding the object from you. Then re-create the sequence in class. Hand in your background and plan for the scene's objectives, actions, and mental and physical obstacles.

3. *Opposing Dreams.* Pick a partner and set up a scene in which your needs and your partner's are in total conflict because of your personal convictions. A conflict might be that I need to move to New York, and you want me to stay in the Midwest. Between rehearsals, get to know your partner by doing something together—going to lunch, to the park—unrelated to the scene. Use this real memory of friendship to make you want to overcome your estrangement. Stage the scene. Hand in your homework on the exercise.

4. *Time Running Out.* Choose a simple task in a familiar place, using objects related to your need and the obstacle of too little time.

4

INNER IMAGES
What motivates my action?

This chapter evaluates the use of sources from your own life that stimulate the character's action.

As an actor, you enter the field out of this intense desire to make a contribution, to do something very fine in the art world, to use your pain, anguish, and life experience to lighten the load or make someone else's perceptions keener. You want the human race to advance out of your sacrifice of yourself because at least 50 percent of what you relive onstage is very painful. *Even in comedy it's somewhat painful to intensely remember things that are already gone.*

Joe Warfield, actor

■ WHAT IS AN INNER IMAGE?

An inner image is a picture flashing before your mind's eye that fires your needs. Inner images running through your head color how you think and react to each situation. Some images influence you momentarily. A ring may remind you of a friend's engagement, graduation, or death. Haunting images may have an intense and/or constant effect on your psyche and thus on your actions.

Both actors and characters experience inner images. Onstage, you try to find images from your life that are similar to ones the character might have. Many inner images can create a charged mental state. For example, a character might literally shrink from thoughts of her mother's boyfriends.

Actors describe inner images as substitutions, personal sources, or inner objects. *Substitutions* means images from your life that replace each thought of the character. When putting words on paper, the playwright envisioned a complete character with an active mind. Fabricating personal images for things mentioned onstage helps you develop the mind-set to react as the character.

The inner image alters your state of being, what you're actually experiencing.

Why are inner images important?

Inner images root you in the character's experience while at the same time connecting you with your own impulses. Like an electric current, they spark your actions. In *Romeo and Juliet*, for example, if Juliet contacts her image of some unattainable lover (possibly the actor playing Romeo) right before she says the line "O Romeo, Romeo! wherefore art thou Romeo?" that connection will inspire the action "to lament." Similarly, the memory of a velvet-textured rose might stimulate the action of another line, "That which we call a rose by any other name would smell as sweet."

Your images charge your performance, especially your dialogue. In physical action scenes, actors may give inner images less focus, but in highly verbal scenes, actors must intensify inner images. The voice beams from a source of inner images, and no matter how perfect the outer instrument, it will not be effective if the power is disconnected. If you are physically wrestling with another onstage, you rehearse a pattern of physical moves. If you are wrestling with your thoughts, you fight a pattern of images. Onstage, you may evoke, then fight, something as intangible as a series of memories and sensations. The more inner images motivating a role, the less you will feel the need to always be "acting."

In the "Bus Observation" chart that follows, the actor has noted inner images that will intensify her actions. The images are idiosyncratic and cryptic, but filled with personal meaning for the actor. You, too, have certain memories and mental pictures that stir your actions.

BUS OBSERVATION

Scene: a bus in New Orleans

Main obstacle: driver's indifference

ACTION	OBJECTIVE	OBSTACLE	INNER IMAGE
1. to hurry onto the bus	to win approval from the driver	slippery floor	Hertz airport van
2. to slug change into the fare box	to win approval	narrow coin slot	clogged streetcar slot
3. to look for twenty more cents	to win approval	empty wallet	dirty Indian nickels
4. to scramble inside my bag	to stall the driver	papers in bag	secret pouch in black bag
5. to dump out my wallet	to stall	many wallet photos	high school photos
6. to moan	to soften the driver	no time	spinal chart
7. to rub my back	to soften	heavy topcoat	Dr. Lewis's pills
8. to check my pockets	to soften	pockets full	stitched pockets
9. to wave my eviction notice	to overcome the driver	other passengers' impatience	Magazine Street rental note
10. to droop my shoulders	to overcome	driver's indifference	Daddy's sad shoulders
11. to ransack my bag	to overcome	messy bag	pencils, pens, writing supplies

ACTION	OBJECTIVE	OBSTACLE	INNER IMAGE
12. to slam more change into box	to punish the driver	broken fare box	Grandma Nix's noisy money box
13. to knife the driver with a dirty look	to punish	driver's indifference	Mother Johnson's expression
14. to stride down the aisle	to pulverize the driver	unsteadiness	Blue Ribbon award

Why should I keep inner images secret?

Although you should write your substitutions down, do not tell the other actors and artists what sources you are using. Concealing your substitutions enhances their mystery, heightens others' concentration, and will ultimately fortify yours. Remember, you and the other actors need to believe in what you're doing onstage. Secrecy encourages your sense of truth.

Some directors impose secrecy. In one play in which an argument about fixing a flat tire took place, the director took two actors out into the parking lot and made them actually change a tire, then swore them to secrecy. Whenever they got to that spot in the play, that real secret bonded them together, creating an extraordinary spark.

How do I contact useful images?

Contacting useful inner images is easy. It requires just the openness to connect with your past experiences. Your procedures need make sense only to you. Nobody has to know what is going on inside your head! Imagine yourself talking to a fortune-teller who calls up fantasies from your life. Sometimes you'll have to embrace troubling images, and even mental discomfort. Creating inner images for a role for the first time can be as challenging as lifting weights. Keep contacting different sources, and powerful ones will eventually take hold.

Why is relaxation the first step?

Relaxation helps you develop the concentration needed to focus on an imaginary world. It readies your mind and body for suggestion. Start with vocal and physical warm-ups, or practice controlling your breathing. Find a quiet place, sit in a comfortable position, and pay attention to your breath flowing in and out for at least twenty minutes. Focus within yourself. Some people find peace in the moment between the inhale and exhale; they feel in perfect harmony with themselves. Through quiet meditation, you can relax and gradually reawaken your inner self. When you find that center of being, you will know that you already possess all the resources needed for any moment onstage.

How should I rehearse?

In rehearsals, allow images associated with the words of your dialogue to surface and to stir your emotions. Develop points of reference from your own life for every person, place, or thing related to, talked about, or listened to onstage.

Let your body experience the lines; observe what feelings come up; discover what images stimulate your feelings. Although most actors contact images through the sense of sight, in some scenes other senses predominate, such as when hearing a mournful tune, smelling an enticing scent, feeling the texture of a loved one's skin. External stimuli such as lighting effects, sound effects, costumes, and furniture can also heighten substitutions and enrich your inner life.

How can inner images help me make an entrance?

Calling upon inner images can help you make a strong entrance. Determine your character's state of mind before you enter. What inner images lead you to the initial action? If after entering, your character must reprimand a friend, you would do it differently depending on what thoughts are going through your head. To contact inner images for your entrance, ask your-self, "How am I feeling right now?" In *Building a Character* Stanislavski wrote: "At any moment, you could contact many different emotional states, such as you're concerned, cold, hungry, distracted, sad, tired, lonely. Allow one of them to lure you into what the character is experiencing. This stream of images, fed by all sorts of fictitious inventions, given circumstances, puts life into a role."

Knowing that you have to perform intensifies your inner life. All of a sudden, you start to vibrate with more energy, focus, and attention. For some actors, it's as if someone is holding a gun to them saying they're going to die any second. It heightens their awareness.

What is an inner monologue?

An inner monologue is a silent conversation with yourself as the character. It helps you activate your character's stream of consciousness. Some actors use an inner monologue to keep inner images flowing. They verbalize responses going on in the mind while the action is occurring. For example, if another character reveals your secret, you might say to yourself: "Oh, my God, I didn't know he knew that!"

In an inner monologue you are evaluating what the other character does—every facial gesture, sound, pause, breathing pattern—before responding. Notice how you talk to yourself, how angry you are, because of what you are seeing. Listen to yourself in rehearsal. Test different associations that stir your thoughts.

For example, one character's inner monologue upon arriving at her married sister's tiny apartment after a long, tiring journey might be: "I sure could use some bourbon to calm my nerves. Gosh, the place is a dump and so small. Where's the booze? What's that smell? Cigarettes. Oh, I was afraid he smoked! Disgusting. Well, I'd better keep quiet. I'm broke, and I don't want him to throw me out! God, what a tiny little place. I hope they don't make love every night—loudly. The walls are paper thin."

What is an inner problem?

In your inner monologue you may address your character's inner problem, the concern that agitates you in a sequence. Even if your character is worried about something pleasant, such as which dress to wear to a party, you operate from a dissatisfaction onstage. Sometimes a character may search out loud for a resolution to the problem. At other times, the character may not verbalize the problem. For example, even though the topic of betrayal is never mentioned, a character may leave someone at the close of the scene. But because betrayal is what leads to the departure, the actor needs to work against this inner problem all along.

Channel your images toward the inner problem of the character. For example, my character's inner problem might be insecurity. I begin with the thought "I am (picture my new car outside) indifferent about this workshop because I am (hand trembling) afraid I will do poorly and don't want to (stained white dress) embarrass myself." Notice how contacting images helped me move from indifference to insecurity.

What are sense memory and emotional memory?

Sensory work re-creates the context of the emotion. Build a
house, and the emotion will return to live there again.

Dale Moffit, actor training specialist, Southern Methodist University

An inner image is often a relived memory. Sense memory is a technique for reliving physical sensations; certain inner images can trigger them: a sweaty forehead, labored breathing, a raspy throat, a pounding heart. Notice which image triggers which sensation.

For instance, the memory of hot tennis shoes on the pavement brings back the oppressive heat of summer; the image of a sandy beach evokes the prickly sensation to your feet; recalling the sound of dry wind screaming over the water makes you experience that wind in your face. Reliving a detail of a past event can stimulate memory and help you relive a particular sensation. Onstage, you may have to experience such things as a sudden chill or high fever throughout a scene. To do so, you will contact and respond to one or more images through sense memory.

Emotional memory is a technique for reliving a detail of a past event to evoke a feeling, such as sadness. Try recalling an experience similar to one in the script, as it happened, with all the physical details. When an event in a scene arouses feelings, note the specific item that stirs them. That trigger lets you make an instantaneous connection with the moment. For example, to grieve over a friend's death, you might try to remember moments when you enjoyed him. Remember the time, the weather, the colors. Hear the sounds, see what you saw, feel the temperature. Find the precise images that evoke an emotion.

In the following description, one actor recalls a time when she cried at a hospital in order to evoke a feeling of sadness. "I am in a hospital waiting room with my mother, and images of my father's heart surgery are making me cry. For example, I see my father's lifeless hand on the operating table, feel the pressure of the doctor's fingers, hear the lilt of the nurse's voice, then smell the cold antiseptic aroma. As these images of my father on the operating table flash to mind, my throat dries up, I feel a lump in my chest."

Let me emphasize, first, that not everyone can use the technique of emotional memory, and it sometimes requires strict supervision. Second, it is largely a rehearsal technique. In performance, an actor should not abandon the circumstances of the play and substitute specific emotional scenes from his own life because this destroys any hope of a through line of action. You infuse the character's present with your experience, but you must stay with your action onstage!

■ SENDING INNER IMAGES

How do I send inner images?

After you know how to reexperience powerful images, you must learn how to send them to someone else. Sending inner images means provoking another person to experience them.

Send your images to another character by concentrating on getting them across through the words. Before speaking, you visualize mental pictures, which your words then reflect.

For example, another character could interpret the following sentence many ways, depending on the inner images you used: "That farmer should not be allowed behind the garage near the chicken coop." Some examples of subtext, the hidden images you use to give the words meaning, for the line include:

1. A pervert doing strange sensual things behind an empty shed

2. A robust planter approaching a minefield of bombs in a village shack

3. A chicken thief disguised as a farmer slipping into a forbidden area

Make sure that when you send your words to another character, she not only understands the meaning of your lines, but also sees what you see in your mind's eye while you are speaking. If you focus on communicating your images, you will contact not only the other character but also the audience.

Remember, you cannot simultaneously be in your own world and look into someone else's eyes—you can't focus within and without at the same time. Inner images stop when you direct your attention to outer things.

CLASS GAMES

1. *The Bouncing Ball.* All members of the class bounce a ball in five different ways—like a sad, ecstatic, sluggish, withdrawn, and irritable person—by using different inner images. Notice how easy it is to move from one trait to the next by changing mental pictures.

2. *Recitation.* In pairs, recite to a partner the details of your daily behavior. Note that you cannot simultaneously recall events and retain active eye contact with your partner. You

need to look inward at specific images, if just for a second, before speaking directly to the partner.

3. *Recalling Events.* Right now, make a list of ten things you did last night. Notice how you have to look inward before writing down each thought.

1. _____

2. _____

3. _____

4. _____

5. _____

6. _____

7. _____

8. _____

9. _____

10. _____

4. *Collage.* Pick a character in a famous play. Create a human collage that could graphically illustrate a character's inner life. One by one class members join in the group painting.

EXERCISES

1. *The Entrance.* Practice entering and answering the telephone by just saying "Hello." Visualize five inner images as you go to pick up the receiver. Notice the series of images that influences you the most. Stage three ways to say "Hello" based on different inner images for class.

2. *Inner Problem.* Choose a strong inner problem based on dire circumstances to relate to while doing a physical task that is now a habit to you.

3. *Psychological Endowment.* Bring into class an important object from your life to talk about. Don't prepare in advance what you are going to say. When you start talking you should

experience a real stream of consciousness inspired by the object.

Why should I check my partner?

Check your partner to assess how your inner images are being received. She should be responding *while* you are speaking and vice versa. Don't make the mistake of letting the end of the preceding speech stimulate your lines; find the loaded words *inside* the speech that excite your responses. In many sequences, especially fight scenes, you may actually need to overlap the ending of another's line to keep the momentum going.

Experiment with pauses. Use them sparingly and make "X" marks in your script where you stop to evaluate whether the other character is listening. Generally, pauses work best inside a series of lines. Notice how in the following exchange, a pause before Brack's line "No!" would slow down the momentum of the conflict, but a pause in the middle of the line could create suspense.

Hedda: —so they found him there?

Brack: Yes. With a fired gun in his pocket. Mortally wounded.

Hedda: Yes—in the chest.

Brack: (*no pause*) No! (*Pause*)—in the guts.

Especially important at the beginning of a scene, pauses provide the listener space to understand your thoughts. Make a conscious effort to set up a few psychological pauses so that the other character receives the images you are sending. But don't overdo them. Long pauses are not necessarily significant. You've got to earn pauses by speaking fast most of the time.

How do I rehearse for inner images?

Rehearse a two-person scene and concentrate on letting inner images flow freely before your mind's eye. After saying each line, describe under your breath what you are experiencing.

What is your mood as you observe your thoughts, feelings, and sensations? Test different associations that might connect to your lines to uncover meaningful inner images. Practice the scene again and observe what the other character does during the scene—every facial gesture, sound, pause, and breathing pattern—before responding. Describe everything in an inner monologue. Actually write out the inner monologue as spoken.

Fill in explosive inner images for the scene. Notice which areas have the greatest lack of images, then rerun the scene, focusing on those sections.

Try the experiment of having one actor keep to the text while the other actor speaks not only the text but also all the thoughts that come to mind during the scene. The second "text," made up of the actor's thoughts, may sometimes coincide with the words, but the actors should not let this confuse them. Rather, they should discover that two conversations are going on in the scene—the text and the thoughts of the characters.

■ CHECKLIST

1. Am I contacting exciting inner images?

2. Am I relaxed enough to induce vivid thoughts?

3. What inner monologue is controlling my thoughts?

4. Am I using inner images to make my entrance and exit? To move the other characters?

■ FINAL PROJECTS

1. *Progressive Exercise.* This exercise is related to the one in chapters 1–3, so you have the same partner. Rehearse this sequence several times.

   EXERCISE 4:   A hospital waiting room. Two more years have passed. You and your partner are intensely related. You each play a strong action with an objective and obstacle. One of you has a professional handicap and one a physical handicap.

Each of you should tap your past to find a vivid series of inner images. Each of you has an inner problem that never comes up in the scene.

Begin the scene in silence engaged in a physical activity. Then one of you should begin the verbal conflict. Hand in your written work on the exercise.

2. *Sense Memory.* Make up an inner image chart, divided into positives and negatives, for sight, hearing, smell, touch, and taste. For each of the senses, list five things that you really love (such as a fifty-foot spruce Christmas tree) and five that you hate (such as your dog's vomit). Notice how contacting each image makes you feel.

FIVE SENSES CHART

SENSE	POSITIVE EXAMPLES	NEGATIVE EXAMPLES
Sight	1. ———————	1. ———————
	2. ———————	2. ———————
	3. ———————	3. ———————
	4. ———————	4. ———————
	5. ———————	5. ———————
Hearing	1. ———————	1. ———————
	2. ———————	2. ———————
	3. ———————	3. ———————
	4. ———————	4. ———————
	5. ———————	5. ———————
Smell	1. ———————	1. ———————
	2. ———————	2. ———————
	3. ———————	3. ———————

	4. _____	4. _____
	5. _____	5. _____
Taste	1. _____	1. _____
	2. _____	2. _____
	3. _____	3. _____
	4. _____	4. _____
	5. _____	5. _____
Touch	1. _____	1. _____
	2. _____	2. _____
	3. _____	3. _____
	4. _____	4. _____
	5. _____	5. _____

3. *Emotional Memory.* Review every month of the past two years for an important inner image and make a list. Initially you may remember just certain surroundings—the wallpaper in your room or a picture on the wall—but by contacting them, your memories will grow. Allow this experience to encourage you to keep a daily record of your impressions. When appropriate, hand in your list.

4. *Singing Shakespeare.* Stage a one-page Shakespearean sequence or a sonnet. Then perform it with you and a classmate singing the lines back and forth. Contact vivid images to support you in singing out Shakespeare. This technique helps you focus inward, then fire information powerfully on the phrase, as in song.

5

THE SCORE
How do I chart what I'm doing?

This chapter describes a written record that helps to reinforce your actions by clarifying your choices each moment onstage.

There is still that mystery of an actor who can repeat every detail because of his work and his life. The best actors try the most things in rehearsal. They are never satisfied, always looking for more adjustments and retaining them, and therefore, in performance they achieve the greatest heights.

Gilles Gleizes, French director

■ WHAT IS A SCORE?

A score is a written account you keep of how to play a role. It assists you in layering complexity into your acting. Like a musician's sheet music, your score charts the combinations you play. It solidifies the rehearsal process. At home, you study the play, fantasize about the role, and note choices already determined in rehearsal. At the next rehearsal, you re-create choices and open yourself to more inspiration. A strong score provides clarity and precision. It involves testing certain possibilities and choosing to play fully a particular course. A good score helps you store details in your unconscious, so when performing you can react spontaneously. It provides you with the specifics to re-create any moment you've originally found.

How do I write a score?

To write an exciting score, you need the ability to transcribe accurately what you do. Although scores may vary from actor to actor, an effective score usually captures the elements of conflict for each act, scene, beat, and line of the role. It isolates the action (What am I doing?), the objective (What do I want?), the obstacle (What's in my way?), and the inner image (What's my personal source?). Some actors record actions, objectives, obstacles, inner images in the margins. Some note objectives in big print and actions in small print. Most abbreviate inner images to conceal personal substitutions. Many actors make a chart of all the elements of conflict and use it as a checklist opposite each page of text.

How does the score keep my acting in shape?

The score provides the structure for a physical and mental workout for you as the character. That's why this book was written: to guide you effortlessly through a routine for developing your finest performance.

A score—like your background homework—will increase your self-confidence and your ability to get work earlier in your career. You may skirt much of the frustration of rejection. You may be paid to act rather than to do other work that would distract you from your art!

Who first used the term *score*?

Stanislavski first used the term *score*. He said we should call this long catalogue of minor and major objectives, units, scenes, and acts the *score of a role*.

> . . . One can call them natural objectives. There can be no doubt that such a score, based on such objectives, will draw the actor—physically speaking—closer to the real action of his part. (It) . . . stirs the action actor to physical action.
> The first requirement is that the score have the power to attract . . . excite the actor not only by its external physical truth

but above all by its inner beauty. . . . Let us now add depth to the score. . . . The difference will lie in the inner life . . . inner impulses, psychological intimations . . . that constitute the inner tone. . . . We can experience varying emotions when playing a score with the same objectives but in different keys . . . quiet or joyful . . . sad or . . . disturbed or in an excited key. . . . One's score which is to portray human passions, must be rich, colorful, and varied. . . . An actor must know the nature of a passion . . . how to cull (from the text) the component units, objectives, moments, which in their sum total add up to a human passion. . . . The score saturates every particle of an actor's inner being. . . . In this innermost . . . core . . . all the remaining objectives converge as it were, into super objective . . . the concentration of the entire score. . . . For the actor the through action is the *active attainment of the super objective.* (*An Actor's Handbook* by Constantin Stanislavski, edited and translated by Elizabeth Reynolds Hapgood, Theatre Arts Books, New York, 1963, pp. 124–125)

■ FINDING THE ELEMENTS

The important thing is not to stop questioning.

Albert Einstein

How do I find my super objective?

The most important element in the score is the super objective of your role. A super objective is an overall aim. Writing a score begins with finding the purpose, or super objective, of the play. It's the playwright's vision that drove him to write the play. Ask yourself, "Why did the playwright write this story? What aim motivated her creation of these events?" The super objective of the play contains its meaning. Read the play many times to discover its super objective. Better still, try to fall in love with the play, so you feel it in your bones. Read the play as if you are living through it.

Certain super objectives, especially those about love and money, drive many plays. Some popular super objectives include "to save someone," "to kill someone," "to marry someone," "to punish someone," "to get rich off someone," "to protect someone."

Understanding the super objective of the play will help you relate to the super objective of your character. This burning passion motivates each action and propels you through the play. As you reread the script, you will begin to sense your character's fundamental need. Like a magnet, your super objective draws you toward major objectives from scene to scene.

How do I score major objectives?

To score major objectives, write down the specific goal you want to achieve at the top of each sequence. This major objective is always blocked—usually by the major objective of another character.

Tennessee Williams's *Suddenly Last Summer* is about a young woman, Catharine, who is about to have a lobotomy. The play runs on the super objective "to save Catharine." In scene 1, Mrs. Venable wants to get the doctor to quiet her niece with a lobotomy. Dr. Cukrowicz tries to persuade her to support nonsurgical treatment. By the end of the scene, the collision of their major objectives has created the play's first crisis. Notice the doctor's major objective running beneath the following lines.

SUDDENLY LAST SUMMER

Doctor's major objective: to get her to forbid surgery

Doctor: (*quietly*) My God. (*Pause*)—Mrs. Venable, suppose after meeting the girl and observing the girl and hearing this story she babbles—I still shouldn't feel that her condition's—intractable enough! to justify the risks of—suppose I shouldn't feel that nonsurgical treatment such as insulin shock and electric shock and—.

Mrs. Venable: SHE'S HAD ALL THAT AT SAINT MARY'S! Nothing else is left for her.

How do I score immediate or line-by-line objectives?

A major objective provokes a series of immediate needs from beat to beat. If your major objective is "to make someone love you," the first goal is "to get a date," the second is "to get a kiss." Immediate objectives are these specific, even line-by-line aims that emotionally charge the score. By naming them, you start to store them in your unconscious.

Because of their momentary nature, you are more likely to forget immediate objectives. Write them down in pencil so you can make adjustments as rehearsals progress and new discoveries are made. Let me emphasize, there is nothing wrong with a repeated objective when varied actions are tried to accomplish it. Repeated actions, however, run the risk of boring the audience. Avoid them unless the repetition makes an important dramatic point.

In the following scene (act 4, scene 2) from O'Neill's *Ah, Wilderness!* Muriel "wants to enrapture Richard." Notice how the actress has jotted down immediate objectives for certain lines. She might enter wanting "to attract Richard," but after she gets that, she might play "to wound him for ignoring her." Then, perhaps, she tries "to arouse him."

AH, WILDERNESS!: MURIEL'S SCORE

Notes: role of Muriel	Super objective: to win Richard
Major action: to flirt	Major objective: to enrapture
Scene tag: flirting on the beach	Spine: to seduce

ACTIONS	*(Just now she is in a great thrilled state of timid adventurousness. She hesitates in the shadow at the foot of the path, waiting for* RICHARD *to see her; but he resolutely goes on whistling with back turned, and she has to call him)*	IMMEDIATE OBJECTIVES
1. to warn	Muriel: [1] Oh, Dick. Richard: *(turns around with an elaborate simulation of being disturbed*	1. to attract

*in the midst of profound medita-
tion*) Oh, hello. Is it nine already?
Gosh, times passes—when you're
thinking.

Muriel: (*coming toward him as far
as the edge of the shadow—*

2. to admonish
3. to blame

disappointedly)[2] I thought you'd be
waiting right here at the end of the
path.[3] I'll bet you'd forgotten I was
even coming.

2. to wound
3. to wound

Richard: (*strolling a little toward
her but not too far—carelessly*) No,
I hadn't forgotten, honest. But I got
to thinking about life.

4. to goad

Muriel: [4]You might think of me for a
change, after all the risks I've run to
see you! (*Hesitating timidly on the

4. to arouse

5. to coo
6. to tease
7. to whisper

edge of the shadow)[5] Dick! [6]You
come here to me.[7] I'm afraid to go
out in that bright moonlight where
anyone might see me.

5. to arouse
6. to arouse
7. to arouse

Richard: (*coming to her—
scornfully*) Aw, there you go again—
always scared of life!

8. to criticize

Muriel: (*indignantly*) [8]Dick Miller,
I do think you've got an awful nerve
to say that after all the risks I've run

8. to disarm

9. to demonstrate
10. to remind

[9]making this date and then sneak-
ing out![10] You didn't take the trouble
to sneak any letter to me, I notice!

9. to disarm
10. to disarm

Note in this score the occasional contradiction between immediate objectives and major objectives. For example, "to wound"
(immediate objective) appears incongruent with "to enrapture"
(major objective). Such inconsistencies linking the thread of
the through line ultimately strengthen the impact of the major
objective.

What is a through line or spine?

Just as your character is driven by a super objective, your performance is driven by a through line of action, the main thing you do to achieve the objective. The through line is often referred to as the "spine" of the role because it supports your performance, running from the beginning to the end of the play.

The spine is the track your character pursues to reach his destination. It is composed of the many small actions you perform scene by scene, all oriented in the direction of your super objective. If the play is well written, the spine of your actions will become apparent early on in scoring them.

In *A Streetcar Named Desire*, Stanley Kowalski's spine is brute force. He has run the streets most of his life. This rough quality permeates his every action—how he behaves with his wife, with his friends, with his pretentious sister-in-law, Blanche. His bestiality intimidates Blanche. Because she has been raised in a mansion, never cooked a meal, made a bed, or traveled alone, she recoils when shaking Stanley's dirty hand. The following chart shows how a director has determined that the spine of Stanley is "to bully" and that of Blanche "to enchant."

NOTES FROM *ROGET'S THESAURUS*: THE SPINE

Stanley/strength:	powerful, forceful, physical, brutal, lustful, stamina, nerve, virile, muscular; spine = to *bully?*
Blanche/fragility:	sensitive, tact, frail, nice, dainty, exact, delicate, discriminating, fastidious; spine = to *enchant?*

How does scoring clarify my major action?

The scoring process helps you relate to your major action in a scene as part of your spine. Notice in the example from *Ah, Wilderness!* how the actress playing Muriel has identified her major action "to flirt" and her spine "to seduce Richard." A certain number of major actions recur in scripts. Giving each scene a tag such as "flirting on the beach" reminds you of your major action.

Why do I need to note line-by-line actions?

Each major action is composed of smaller line-by-line actions. Scoring, for the most part, is jotting down line-by-line actions. Changing action holds interest. For example, in the *Ah, Wilderness!* beach scene, to achieve her major action, "to flirt," Muriel could use several tactics. First, she might warn her boyfriend, next she might admonish him for a past decision, then she might blame him. Muriel might also play actions such as "to wail," "to groan," and "to complain," actions resulting in non-verbal sounds—grunts, moans, sighs, intakes of air.

Along with the actions beneath lines and sounds, observe gestures, your blocking, and stage directions for possible line-by-line actions. Some playwrights offer no stage directions; others, such as O'Neill, specify them as vital clues to the character. Keep yourself open to all possible options for actions.

How do I discover line-by-line actions for characters from different periods?

Discovering actions for characters in different historical periods may require outside reading. Begin by trying to clarify what you are doing. Many things that are described or said may be unclear to you.

Obstacles must be noted in any score because they stimulate variety. When you say an actor is boring, you mean she repeats the same wooden choices. Obstacles provide an easy way to offset predictability. They make you yearn to play different actions by impeding what you are currently doing.

Use the score to strengthen obstacles' possibilities. Which ones are the most effective? Which excite the greatest interest? After discovering your main obstacle, note how you break down minor ones. Obstacles encourage transitions—you disregard a specific line of action and substitute another. In rehearsal, test a range of obstacles because you can always eliminate choices.

How do I find obstacles with my score?

To find obstacles, strengthen the opposition in each scene. Discover the elements stopping you from reaching someone. Work to move that other character and jot down what you are overcoming. Search for obstacles that frustrate your action. For example, should your character throw a pebble to get another's attention? Practice the option of standing far away from him and see whether the obstacle of distance strengthens your action. Strong obstacles will agitate your thoughts and provoke a series of powerful inner images.

Should I score my inner images?

Absolutely! Sufficient inner images will keep your actions motivated. Sometimes you'll forget your inner images in a performance. One night you'll be so excited, and everything will be going perfectly. Then the next night, you'll dry up completely and wonder: "What is it I thought about that made it so interesting before?" So you must jot down the mental pictures that create the sparks. Remember, even when a character commits the most hideous crimes, you can find inner images that unite you. Keep sensitizing yourself to whatever makes you believe in your actions and write them down.

Should I score every line?

Sometimes a student will ask: "I don't have to score each line, do I? Four different lines in my scene are the same." No, scoring doesn't have to change for every line. But in any interpretation, you should explore every possible nuance.

The more you break down the action, the more expressive you become because of the variety you are generating. Have you ever heard a pianist trill a note? You could play it "bong bong," but "brrrremmm" is more interesting! So I encourage actors to score not only lines, but also pauses, gestures, and sounds.

The most important part of a score is your actions because a range of actions makes you compelling to watch. You express meaning through the little things you are doing with your hands, with your feet, with your body, and with your face. Obstacles, inner images, and objectives affect the little doings, and the score records them, on paper and in your unconscious. In performance, you react spontaneously, like a master pianist gliding through a concerto without sheet music.

■ SCORING AND REHEARSING

Every composer knows the anguish and despair occasioned by forgetting ideas which one has not had the time to write down.

Victor Hugo, nineteenth-century playwright

How can rehearsals help me score?

A score is easiest to record while you are in rehearsal, in the discovery mode. As you test adjustments, simply jot down the strongest ones. You are clarifying choices—something most actors do automatically. Begin on the simplest level, to accumulate your action, objective, obstacle, and inner image. Then further break down each sequence after you determine more detail.

Slow down and absorb what is going on around you! Experience the choices one by one in the progress of your role. Test vivid choices (actions, objectives, obstacles, inner images). Notice moments when the other character responds the way you want. Update and delete items from your score as your interpretation develops. Practice the script in tiny chunks and in bold run-throughs to experience the vitality behind your score.

CLASS GAMES

1. *Blindman's Bluff.* Play blindman's bluff (also called "Marco Polo"). Blindfold and spin one member of the class. Classmates hide around the room as he counts to fifteen. The

blind person must touch and identify someone to win. Sit down afterward and quickly score the scene.

2. *Physical Condition.* All actors in class pantomime the action of "to apply makeup" or "to shave" with the physical condition of being drunk, sleepy, or nauseated. Sit down afterward and score the scene. Discuss.

How can a thesaurus help me add range to the score?

Using a thesaurus when you are foggy about a moment can help you clarify choices. Note the synonyms for the following elements. Each presents a slightly different variation of the moment. Which of the words affects you the most? Which do you fear playing? Why? Which could be the "hot" choice for you?

ACTION	OBJECTIVE	OBSTACLE	INNER IMAGE
1. to teach	1. to inspire you	1. deaf	1. Judy at dominoes
2. to instruct	2. to excite you	2. outside noise	2. Harry at Audubon Park
3. to guide	3. to arouse you	3. you completely lack power to hear	3. algebra II test
4. to counsel	4. to enliven you	4. your unwillingness to hear	4. Ms. Tate at cafeteria
5. to discipline	5. to invigorate you	5. your determination not to listen	5. Newton's car garage

Describe each action, objective, obstacle, and inner image with exciting terminology. As you work on meaning and experiment with detail, you will find yourself effortlessly memorizing your dialogue.

1. *An Interview.* Set up a radio or television interview conducted by one character with another in which the interviewee is asked biological questions. Score the scene.

2. *Character Action.* Rehearse actions you would undertake when finding yourself in a doctor's office, a graveyard, or an empty park. Then rehearse actions a celebrity might undertake. Stage the actions first performed your way, then the way of the celebrity. Hand in both scores.

3. *Character Improvisation.* Pick one of your favorite characters in a play. Try to get into the skin of the character by practicing one or more of the following improvisations as your character. Stage and score one of the improvisations for class.

getting dressed	coming home from work
eating breakfast	talking on the phone to a lover
reading the mail	going to bed
handling problems at work	

What is a prompt book?

To allow space for scoring, many actors keep a notebook or journal, which they refer to as a "prompt book." Use a three-ring or spring binder so you can keep loose paper for notes and the script itself in the same binder. Make two copies of the script, pasting each page in the center of an $8\frac{1}{2} \times 11$-inch sheet. Place a blank sheet after each page of script. On this scoring page, make columns for objective, action, obstacle, and inner images. In the script next to the first line, write the number 1, referring to number 1 on the opposite scoring page. For each particular line or moment, jot down the objective, action, obstacle, and inner image used. Choose direct infinitive phrases for the actions and objectives.

The following three tables are semiadvanced acting scores. They demonstrate your goal: capturing intuitive ingredients of conflict in print.

THE GLASS MENAGERIE, SCENE 7: LAURA'S SCORE

(JIM *knocks glass horse off table. Music fades.*)

Laura: [121]Oh, it doesn't matter—

Jim: (*picks horse up*) We knocked the little glass horse over.

Laura: [122]Yes.

Jim: (*hands unicorn to* LAURA) Is he broken?

Laura: [123]Now he's just like all the other horses.

Jim: You mean he lost his—?

Laura: [124]He's lost his horn. [125]It doesn't matter. [126]Maybe it's a blessing in disguise.

Jim: Gee, I bet you'll never forgive me. I bet that was your favorite piece of glass.

Laura: [127]Oh, I don't have favorites—(*Pause*) [128]much. [129]It's no tragedy. [130]Glass breaks so easily. [131]No matter how careful you are. [132]The traffic jars the shelves and things fall off them.

Jim: Still, I'm awfully sorry that I was the cause of it.

Laura: [133]I'll just imagine he had an operation. [134]The horn was removed to make him feel less—[135]freakish! (*Crosses L., sits on small table*) [136] Now he will feel more at home with the other horses, the ones who don't have horns. . . .

Super objective: to marry Jim

Spine: to please

Major obstacle: shyness

Main action: to befriend

Scene tag: befriending the unicorn

ACTION	OBJECTIVE	OBSTACLE	INNER IMAGE
121. to convince self	to hide feelings	broken favorite	broken swan
122. to acknowledge	to hide feelings	Jim did it	broken mouse

ACTION	OBJECTIVE	OBSTACLE	INNER IMAGE
123. to examine	to observe break	darkness	sharp edges
124. to appraise	to state damage	hurt feelings	sharp edges
125. to convince self	to comfort self	hurt feelings	dirty rag doll
126. to convince self	to ignore upset	truly upset	swallow hard
127. to lie	to comfort Jim	truly upset	porcelain angel
128. to qualify	to let truth escape	reserved feelings	porcelain angel
129. to excuse	to comfort	the tragedy	suicide
130. to excuse	to lessen importance	its importance	shards
131. to assume carefulness	to lessen importance	not being careful	splinters
132. to simplify	to comfort	both upset	bull in china shop
133. to fantasize	to comfort	both upset	castoff
134. to fantasize	to recover	the tragedy	castoff
135. to improve	to encourage	the tragedy	crippled unicorn
136. to praise	to delight	the tragedy	medieval tapestry

"VISITOR FROM HOLLYWOOD," *PLAZA SUITE* BY NEIL SIMON: MURIEL'S SCORE

(*When the door opens, the two of them greet each other with enormous smiles.* JESSE *throws out his arms*) Muriel!

BEAT 1

Muriel: [1](*smiles, cocks her head*) Jesse?

Jesse: It's not.

Muriel: [2]It is. [3](*Pause*)

Jesse: Muriel, I can't believe it. Is it really you?

Muriel: It's me, Muriel.

Jesse: Well, come on in, for Pete's sakes, come on in.

BEAT 2

Muriel: [4](*enters with a rush and crosses to the far side of the sofa*)[5] I can only stay for a few minutes.

Jesse: (*closes the door and follows her to below the near side of the sofa*) My God, it's good to see you. (*They stand and confront each other*)

Muriel: [6]I just dropped in to say hello. [7]I really can't stay.

Jesse: You sounded good on the phone, but you look even better.

Muriel: [8]Because I've got to get back to New Jersey. [9]I'm parked in a one hour zone. [10]Hello, Jesse. [11]I think I'm very nervous.

Jesse: Hey! Hello, Muriel.

Super objective: to win Jesse's adoration

Spine: to captivate

Major obstacle: sex (I'm married)

Main action: to flirt

Main objective: to win his affection

Scene tag: the initial flirtation

Inner images for Muriel's initial entrance: Jesse is a visiting celebrity. I am a suburban housewife. I have not seen him since our high school romance days. I have never been inside the Plaza Hotel before.

   Major substitution: John Kennedy for Jesse.

   Initially walk through lobby to elevator to seventh floor, down hall (if someone sees me?). I don't belong here. Going to "Kennedy's" private suite is dangerous reputation-wise. Newsmen are always on the heels of famous people—looking for a flash story. Ted—Chappaquiddick. They could unearth all kinds of stories about my past. I live 1½ hours from here. JFK is an international celebrity. My family and friends are vulnerable for they don't even know I'm here. JFK doesn't live in NYC—special visit = more newsmen. I must get inside his apartment, although I don't know if he's alone within. He's been in NYC many times since we were together.

I was in the kitchen at 5:30 yesterday when Jesse called from New York. Children Elizabeth and John were watching TV; Larry was working. I never know whether Larry's coming home for dinner or not.

ACTION	OBJECTIVE	OBSTACLE	INNER IMAGE
BEAT 1			
1. to question	elicit his reason for calling me	he turns me on (main obstacle)	USC, short hair, glasses
2. to confirm it's me	elicit his reason for calling me		away long time and return home
3. to reconfirm	convince how well preserved I am	I'm married! (time, hotel hall, bedroom)	hair a mess, no sleep, shoes unpolished, outfit wrinkled, see apartment
BEAT 2			
4. to flirt: "same old me"	convince how well preserved I am		
5. to warn	expose his reason for calling		protect self
6. to convince of quick social visit	expose his motive for ravishing me	time on meter	excuse exit, return to Daddy
7. to tease	expose his motive for ravishing me		my "dignity"
8. to disregard compliment	titillate to expose desire	gorgeous room	
9. to postpone affair	warn to act dignified	nerves	muscled = David, he's hot, demands of Jersey
10. to confront lover honestly	remind of past intimacy	his fame	meter by Bonwit's

| 11. to define | nurture sympathy | G.N. restaurant |
| fear | for erratic actions | |

AH, WILDERNESS!, ACT 4, SCENE 2: RICHARD'S SCORE

[1] (RICHARD *starts to stroll around with exaggerated carelessness, turning his back on the path, hands in pockets,* [2] *whistling with insouciance "Waiting at the Church."*)

[3] (MURIEL MCCOMBER *enters from down the path, left front. She is fifteen, going on sixteen. She is a pretty girl with a plump, graceful little figure, fluffy, light-brown hair, big naive wondering dark eyes, a round dimpled face, a melting drawly voice. Just now she is in a great thrilled state of timid adventurousness.* [4] *She hesitates in the shadow at the foot of the path, waiting for* RICHARD *to see her,* [5] *but he resolutely goes on whistling with back turned, and she has to call him.*)

Muriel: Oh, Dick.

Richard: [6] (*turns around with an elaborate simulation of being disturbed in the midst of profound meditation.*) [7] Oh, hello. [8] Is it nine already? [9] Gosh, time passes—[10] when you're thinking.

Muriel: (*coming toward him as far as the edge of the shadow—disappointedly*) I thought you'd be waiting right here at the end of the path. I'll bet you'd forgotten I was even coming.

Richard: [11] (*strolling a little toward her but not too far—carelessly*) [12] No, I hadn't forgotten, [13] honest. [14] But I got to thinking about life.

Muriel: You might think of me for a change, after all the risks I've run to see you! (*hesitating timidly on the edge of the shadow*) Dick! You come here to me. I'm afraid to go out in that bright moonlight where anyone might see me.

Richard: (*coming to her—scornfully*) [15] Aw, there you go again—always scared of life!

Super objective: to marry Muriel
Spine: to capture Muriel
Major obstacle: her resistance
Main action: to punish

Main objective: to torment with desire

Scene tag: the making-up scene

ACTION	OBJECTIVE	OBSTACLE	INNER IMAGE
1. to stalk	to hide rejection	broken heart	dear John letter
2. to whistle	to hide feelings	she's late	broken agreement
3. to sneak a look	to see if she loves me	darkness	softness of skin
4. to adore	to find a sign of her love	her treachery	Judy O
5. to peal music	to comfort self	her treachery	deep blue eyes
6. to condescend	to belittle	her cruelty	
7. to dismiss	to rub it in	feeling of tragedy	dear John kiss
8. to disbelieve	to ignore her	her abandonment	
9. to discount	to distance	her sore feet	suicide of M. S.
10. to proclaim	to lessen her importance	passionate feeling	her letter
11. to play hard to get	to lessen her importance	her full figure	sand
12. to hesitate	to seize comfort	her coldness	Q. R. at pit
13. to reassure	to seize comfort	shadows	castoff ice
14. to philosophize	to recover pride	her rejection	castoff letter
15. to scorn	to excite adventure	her love for Dad	her father's hat

How do I find and rehearse beats?

Rehearse a section in which your objective and your partner's totally conflict. Each partner should pick a passionate opposing point of view that you can personally relate to. Each of you should choose an activity. Start with two minutes of silence, then begin the verbal conflict of the scene.

How do I score a beat and sequences?

The line-by-line components of an actor's score may be grouped into beats. If a scene is long, similar beats may be grouped into sequence. A beat is a small section of a scene in which an actor has a single obstacle, adjustment, physicalization of action until achieving, or not achieving, a specific goal. The beat changes when the action changes. One actor may change an action without the other actor(s) changing, but that shift in action moves the scene in a new direction. Many differences in one action are possible in a beat. (Think of all the variations in behavior in a farewell action.) A typical beat pattern of an actor might be:

BEAT: objective → action → adjustment → physicalizations

Physicalizations—external expressions of the action—are not always there but usually grow out of the intensity of the need.

Break your scene into beats or sequences of beats (if the scene is long).

What if I have scored beats, but the acting remains uneven?

1. Look over and eliminate from your score whatever you aren't playing onstage. Don't include material that is never used. A score should record only what you are actually doing. Study what sections of your score have the largest gaps. Work in detail on various choices for these sections; discover missing elements by testing choices opposite from those being played.

2. A score is only as good as its first missing link, connecting moments in a chain of development. One or more transitions can stop one moment from evolving into the next. Too long a pause, an afterthought, or an inappropriate adjustment between lines can throw off the truth and momentum of an

entire scene. Work the scene for transitions between beats and then for its pauses.

3. Run the entire scene without words. Observe where the character's physical life feels weak or unclear and work on these gaps. After the physical life becomes solid in each beat, reintroduce the words.

4. Freely test different thoughts behind certain beats and do not worry about making mistakes. (The value of a score may be observed in its clarity, specificity, and aliveness—how it actively empowers the conflict.)

How do I set choices with my score?

Setting choices means finalizing the score for your performance. Your performance may still ripen emotionally, but essentially your plan for the role is solidified. Because a pause or an inappropriate movement can destroy momentum, eventually every actor needs to stick to what has been rehearsed and researched. In an improvisation, you're freely inventing as you go. But making your choices for a script spontaneous can result only from knowing what your form is—by keeping a score.

How does the score help me in performance?

Chance favors the prepared mind.

Louis Pasteur

The longer the run of the play, the more valuable an accurate score becomes. It protects you from losing your bearings onstage. Because of it, you will always be able to repeat your most brilliant performance. After opening night, you can continue to enrich your score. After they are in the run, many actors still work on their scores several hours a day—deepening choices, emotionally charging the body and voice.

To keep your score alive over a long period of time, keep working as your own coach. Most people will accept a certain level of quality from you. They don't really push you to the ultimate homework you can do. Are you training your body and voice? All that takes tremendous personal discipline. No one makes you write a score, create a background, do research, or experiment! It's not like being on an athletic team where the coach reprimands you if you don't train.

The score allows you to play free—to act with great expressiveness—because it supports you with an invisible framework. You contact your burning passion—the major objective in the scene—and then you play 100 percent to get it.

■ WHAT IS HOMEWORK ON CONFLICT?

Your feelings and actions can be augmented by homework on conflict. You must clearly understand the procedures involved for this homework, then identify when the conflict is or is not working. Two main types of homework are a score and a history (see chapter 8) of the role.

In the score, you record the components (objective, action, obstacle, inner image) of each scene. In the history, you research, imagine, and create the character's past and future life circumstances, fueling the conflict. You should score (analyze and record) each stage moment and write out character histories. Note the differences and similarities in the following two acting scores from *The Lady of Larkspur Lotion* by Tennessee Williams and *Company* by Stephen Sondheim. The major distinction is that the strength and length of the action in a musical must correspond to the structure of the musical phrase.

What is the function of a score and a history?

When you create a score and a history, you construct the conflict with a blueprint or map for reference. Experienced actors can re-create from memory, but if focus wanes, they must have some structure to consult or else the scene's conflict could collapse.

> Like a dull actor now;
> I have forgot my part, and I am out,
> Even to a full disgrace.
> (*Coriolanus*, act I, scene i)

A score provides you with a record of acting choices discovered in private and in rehearsal. Don't fail to do this work, spend extra rehearsal time discovering the life of the character and actions for each individual moment of a scene. Annotate the voices made during rehearsal. A score clarifies the path of development of the characters so distraction cannot sidetrack you from the path of truth.

Scoring solidifies what you play from moment to moment; unconscious performance choices become conscious. At any given time, you can review the score to discover elements missing in a performance. If you cannot put into language an acting choice, you may never see it again. Record on the score discoveries made in private and in rehearsal about what the character is wanting, doing, avoiding, and identifying with at each moment of the play.

THE LADY OF LARKSPUR LOTION BY TENNESSEE WILLIAMS

SCENE: a wretchedly furnished room in the French Quarter of New Orleans. There are no windows, the room being a cubicle portioned off from several others by imitation walls. A small slanting skylight admits late and un-encouraging day. There is a tall, black armoire, whose doors contain cracked mirrors, a swinging electric bulb, a black and graceless dresser, an awful picture of a Roman Saint and over the bed a coat-of-arms in a frame.

[1]Mrs. Hardwicke-Moore, a dyed-blonde woman of forty, is seated passively on the edge of the bed as though she could think of nothing better to do.

There is a rap at the door.

MRS. HARDWICKE-MOORE:	(*in a sharp, affected tone*) [2]Who is at the door, please!
MRS. WIRE:	(*from outside, bluntly*) Me! (*Her face expressing a momentary panic,* MRS. HARDWICKE-MOORE *rises stiffly.*)
MRS. HARDWICKE-MOORE:	[3]Oh [4]. . . [5]Mrs. Wire. [6]Come in. (*The landlady enters, a heavy, slovenly woman of fifty.*) [7]I was just going to drop in your room to speak to you about something.

MRS. WIRE:	Yeah? What about?
MRS. HARDWICKE-MOORE:	(*humorously, but rather painfully smiling*) [8]Mrs. Wire, [9]I'm sorry to say that I just don't consider these [10]cockroaches to be the most desirable kind of roommates—[11] do you?
MRS. WIRE:	Cockroaches, huh?
MRS. HARDWICKE-MOORE:	[12]Yes. [13]Precisely. [14]No I have had

THE LADY OF LARKSPUR LOTION BY TENNESSEE WILLIAMS

OBJECTIVE	ACTION	OBSTACLE	INNER IMAGE
1. to resuscitate self as proper *virgin*	to repress nightmare	fallen past, overdue rent, no credit, no money, lack of rentals, no friends, faded books	Don/NYC, "nothing negative," no beauty parlor, drink hidden in bath bottle
2. to appraise visitor	to inquire like a courtesan	street crime creditors	male callers? high hopes
3. to arrange self and room	to cover shock	street crime creditors	rent now, hates noise, smells apartment
4. to confirm it's hidden	to check liquor on breath	heat	curly black hair Anita
5. to sidetrack rent issue	to fawn welcome	her rage, greed, heartlessness	hard metal
6. to reassure her for waiting	to entreat entry	her rage, greed, heartlessness	
7. to convince of my devotion	to sneak in white lie	her rage, greed, heartlessness	
8. to warm her	to ingratiate		white/pink room, JB's office

OBJECTIVE	ACTION	OBSTACLE	INNER IMAGE
9. to tickle her fancies	to distract with bubbly conversation	landlord's inspection	Francesca, first floor
10. get a week's free rent	to point out villains	landlord's ruthlessness	grown their shells
11. get a week's free rent	to encourage agreement	landlord's ruthlessness	
12. get a week's free rent	to confirm	landlord's ruthlessness	
13. get a week's free rent	to pinpoint enemy	landlord's ruthlessness	manor bathtub
14. to seize sympathy	to confirm awkwardness	landlord's ruthlessness	Orkin-New Orleans

THE LADIES WHO LUNCH (LYRICS OF MUSICAL SCORE)

[1]I'd like to propose a toast

[2]Here's to the ladies who lunch,

[3]Ev'rybody laugh.

[4]Lounging in their caftans and planning a brunch

[5]on their own behalf.

[6]Off to the gym, then to a fitting,

[7]claiming they're fat,

[8]And looking grim 'cause they've been sitting,

THE LADIES WHO LUNCH

OBJECTIVE	ACTION	OBSTACLE	INNER IMAGE
1. to arouse the audience's indignation	to call for a toast	self-exposure	Sallie, G. N. "drunk," humiliation of my husband two-timing me, "the girls," $, noise/music

			in bar, Bobby's naiveté, other's disinterest
2. to expose hypocrisy of losers	to salute my comrades		Washington Roosevelt Hotel
3. to get the audience to squeal with laughter	to crack a joke	I'm the failure	Bruce/piano
4. to keep audience mocking them	to point out idleness		Sallie, long red robe, "writer," tennis
5. to keep audience mocking them	to expose their self-interest		Mary's birthday
6. to keep audience putting them down	to commend their preservation	avoid self-exposure	
7. to force audience to mock them	to expose	thick tongue	Spa G. N.
8. to force audience to mock them	to point out their emptiness		cocked hat, three spots

How can I use a checklist for the score?

After you have developed a certain ability to score, use this checklist to enrich your emotional life onstage. Follow this checklist loosely, using it as a reference more than as a bible, and adjust it to your needs because it will vary somewhat with each actor and with each character.

■ CHECKLIST

What am I urgently doing and why?

A. Line Analysis

   1. What am I doing on each line and why? What do I want from my partner, and what is stopping me? (What are the objective, the

action, and the obstacle? For example, "I want to make him laugh in order to win his confidence; but he ignores me.")

2. Who or what is my object of attention on what line? Where is my focus? (This can sometimes be the same throughout the play.) What inner image am I experiencing?

3. What activity, bit of business, or gesture can I find that will support my action, clarify it, strengthen it?

4. What adjustment must I take, if any, toward the line? (Consider to whom the line is being said, the place, the time, and circumstances surrounding it to determine how it should be said.)

B. Beat Analysis

1. Follow outline for line analysis.

2. A beat is a unit within a scene that has a beginning, a middle, and an end. Each beat is determined by finding each change within each scene, such as the entrance or exit of a character, a new objective or obstacle, that changes the subject under discussion.

3. The analysis of the beat (action and objective) depends on the analysis of the lines within the beat. The actions of the lines, linked together, determine the action of the beat.

4. What is the transitional line between beats? One beat does not necessarily stop suddenly and another begin, but often something or someone ties one to the other, such as the entrance of another person or a new circumstance.

C. Scene Analysis

1. Follow outline for line analysis.

2. In finding the scenes, use script scene designations to begin with.

3. The analysis of the scene's action and objective depends on the analysis of the beats within that scene. The actions of beats, linked together, determine the action of the scene.

4. Find the character traits you will try to blend with each of the important or emphasized elements (beats) in the play.

D. Act Analysis

1. Follow outline for line analysis.

2. The analysis of the act depends on the analysis of the scenes within that act. The actions of the scenes, linked together, determine the action of the act.

3. By linking all these together you can determine the overall objective, or super objective, of your character in the play.
4. Select the most important elements (usually beats) you will emphasize in performance. These are the ones most directly linked to your super objective in the play.

Why is scoring the role important?

Scoring is important for the complete involvement of the actor and the audience. Scoring allows authentic projection of the character. When audiences see this deep layering, its attention becomes mesmerized.

■ FINAL PROJECTS

1. *Score a Progressive Exercise.* This exercise relates to the previous ones in chapters 1–4, so you have the same partner.

   EXERCISE 5: An empty restaurant. Two years have passed. You and your partner are intensely related. The exercise is scored in three beats.

   Beat 1 begins as you each play an opposing objective, action, obstacle, and inner image. Begin the scene in silence, with each engaged in a physical activity. Then begin the verbal conflict.

   Beat 2 begins when a second couple enters. Objectives, actions, obstacles, and inner images shift.

   Beat 3 occurs when still another couple enters, and a new conflict erupts. (Note: If the class is small, couples from the entire class can ultimately enter the conflict of the scene.) Hand in written background and score the elements of all three beats.

2. *Score a Scene.* Rehearse a scene from a play (see Appendix E). Determine the opposing objectives, your super objective, overall action, obstacle, and inner images. Ask yourself,

"Is my interior monologue related to the same stream of consciousness as the character's? Am I journeying through the same life experience?" Do a line-by-line score of the scene.

3. *Score an Article.* Choose an article from a magazine or newspaper. Score the article as a monologue, deciding who it is addressed to and noting line-by-line actions, objectives, obstacles, and inner images. Perform the monologue in class.

4. The following is a preliminary score for a scene. Go through with a thesaurus to see where you might strengthen the verbs.

IF I COULD PAINT THE RAIN BY ROSARY HARTEL O'NEILL

Scene 1

Setting: A spacious garden room. There is a luxuriously cushioned day bed with an empty bird cage like a Chinese house. Vivid landscape paintings are placed about. The effect is of a boy's dream, the actual furniture being less important than the wonder created.

At Rise: SOUND: It is raining quietly, one of those late- afternoon showers that New Orleans is famous for. ROOSTER DUBONNET, a young man, late twenties, dark-haired, gaunt, almost emaciated, lies in bed in silk pajamas. If he were not so sick and pastylooking, he could be handsome with strong features, thick hair, and broad shoulders. Even so, there are kindness and nobility in his face.

Rooster: I'm cold. Maybe the rain makes me that way. (ROOSTER *closes his eyes.* MONICA FALCON, *a stunning nurse, twenty-eight, arrives.* [1]*She pauses at the doorway,* [2]*removing her cape. She is dressed simply but impeccably and holds a satchel under her arm.*)

Monica: [3]Hello, [4]hello . . . [5]anyone there? [6]I'm Monica Falcon, [7]the new nurse.

Rooster: What? (*Calls out*) Ma.

[8] [9]Monica: [10](*Puts thermometer in his mouth*) [11]Are you in pain?

Rooster: No. (*He pulls out the thermometer, leans to an intercom.*)

Monica: [12]You sounded as if you were in pain.

Rooster: (*Into the intercom*) Ma, pick up.

Monica: [13]Everyone's gone.

Rooster: Unlikely. (*Into the intercom*) Pick up, I said.

Monica: [14]The house echoes quiet.

Rooster: (*Into the intercom*) Ma. They sent a woman.

Monica: [15]You've a wonderful house. . .

Rooster: (*Into the intercom*) I asked for a male nurse.

Monica: [16]It's like a hotel.

Rooster: (*Into the intercom*) You're not my guest. I'm not lying about half-dressed with a woman. [17](MONICA *checks about for lights.*)

Rooster: Don't.

Monica: [18]Do you live in darkness?

Rooster: Best way to survive in the Garden District.

Monica: (*Looks at her feet*) [19]These shoes looked good before I walked through water.

Rooster: Click your heels and go back to Oz.

Monica: [20](*Retreats to window.*) [21]We can catch the last rays of the sun.

Rooster: You're not staying. (*He sits up, reaches for his robe, but is still weak and has to breathe a few moments. [22]She looks out the window. He reaches for the phone.*)

Monica: [23]The light feels good. [24]Cold bracing sunshine, right behind the rain. [25]That'll keep you awake.

Rooster: (*Into the receiver*) Is this the Parker Agency?

Monica: [26]I love a bright afternoon sky.

Rooster: This is Rooster Dubonnet. I requested a male nurse.

Monica: [27](*Reaches for the phone*) [28]Give me that.

Rooster: (*Stretches phone away, panting, talks into it.*) I'm not paying for this woman.

Monica: [29]What do you have against women?

Rooster: (*Into the phone*) I was nice to those rejects you sent. She can't be the only nurse who'll come.

Monica: [30](*Takes out a blood pressure kit*) [31]I'll take your blood pressure.

Rooster: (*Into the phone*) You said you had 200 nurses. (*Into the phone*) I don't want this woman. (*Into the phone*) Tell her to leave.

Monica: [32](*Takes phone. Speaks into it.*) [33]Everybody's fine. [34](*Hangs up. To* ROOSTER) [35]One, two, three. . . up. (ROOSTER *sits up, very weak, wraps his robe limply over his silk pajamas.*)

Rooster: Stay away. I'm warning you. (*He reaches for the phone,* [36]*but she grabs it and* [37]*puts it in her pocket.*)

Monica: [38]I'll change those sheets. (*He stumbles to his feet. He is panting for breath, totters, and grasps onto furniture. He stops for a second.* [39]*She watches him from the corner of her eyes* [40]*and goes to make the bed.*)

Monica: [41]You can do it?

Rooster: I can do it. (*He presses a hand alarm which blares.* [42]*They struggle for the alarm.*)

Monica: [43]What's that? [44]Turn it off.

Rooster: Not likely.

Monica: [45]Give it over.

Rooster: No.

Monica: [46](*Pulls alarm from his fist*) [47]You think you can get rid of me?

Rooster: You're the roughest. . .

Monica: [48]My landlord's evicted me.

Rooster: Toughest. . .

Monica: [49]Called me at five a.m.

Rooster: This is not a hotel.

Monica: [50]I've no friends or relatives here.

Rooster: That's the first good news about you.

Monica: [51]Can you do it alone? (*He walks, but stumbles.* [52]*She calls out as he moves cautiously along.*)

Rooster: Uh-huh. If I push myself I can. I'll be right back. (*He walks carefully. Reaching the window, he calls out, "Police! Police!" then turns and sets off a strobe light siren. [53]She runs over. They struggle for it.*)

[54]Monica: [55]You crazy. . . [56]Out of my way! [57]Stop. [58]Nobody's going to bail me out. [59](*She turns the siren off. He staggers to a chair and leans over the back coughing.*)

Monica: [60]Have you had anything to eat? [61]Or drink?

Rooster: Not today.

Monica: [62](*Hands him water.*) Take a few sips.

Rooster: No, thanks. Have you ever heard of the nurse who poisons the emperor? This emperor so feared assassination, he only ate ripe figs from a tree.

Monica: [63]Drink.

Rooster: In the night, his nurse injected them with poison.

Monica: [64]Just a little.

Rooster: In the morning, the emperor ate one and died. (*He pours water on a plant. She speaks continuously, overlapping him.*)

Monica: [65]Since you won't let me help you, [66]may I ask you some questions?

Rooster: What's that?

Monica: [67]I'm studying astrology. . . [68]on the side.

Rooster: It's amateur night in Dixie.

Monica: [69]I looked you up. [70]You've got a tenth house, [71]Pluto in Leo.

Rooster: [72]Fortune tellers. They're everything I'm running from—

Monica: Which means you're gifted. . .

Rooster: (*Breathing fast*) The whole specter of charlatans—

Monica: [73]At being able to. . .

Rooster: That haunt artists' history.

Monica: [74]Translate archetypal energy. . .

Rooster: I'm three times more likely to die from the flu. . .

Monica: [75]Through the power of the personal image.

Rooster: Than to speak to a student astrologer. Y'all are the psychos of the science profession.

Monica: [76]I know you're a famous artist [77]from a well-to-do family. . .

Rooster: Why do people pursue me?

Monica: [78]May I ask you some questions? [79]It would make my job easier.

Rooster: You haven't a job with me.

Monica: [80]You're so. . .

Rooster: Difficult? Some artists don't do interviews, and thank God they don't do them. I don't want to be the entertainment.

Monica: [81]And you're not. (ROOSTER *rises with effort, crosses to the bird cage, whistles "Dixie."*)

Rooster: My parrot, Commander Butler, just flew in.

Monica: [82]Where?

Rooster: He died but sometimes he visits. He's my very special house ghost. The two things Butler does best are scream "Where's the maid?" and whistle "Dixie." Calling the maid is so passé.

Monica: [83]What's your diagnosis?

Rooster: (*Pause*) Are you from the South?

Monica: [84]Delaware.

Rooster: Y'all like to eat on paper plates in halls covered with graffiti. What do you have going for you?

Monica: [85]My husband was from Jackson.

Rooster: There's a touch of Mississippi in your family? What does Mr. Falcon do?

Monica: [86]My. . . [87]I. . . [88]Oh Lord. . . [89]I mustn't let. . . [90]Where're my Kleenex? [91]You think I'd be here if I. . .

Rooster: Don't start the sadness machine.

Monica: [92]It happens frequently. [93]It's not professional. [94]Your bed is ready. (*Rain pours around the sides of the room.* [95]*She removes the thermometer, writes something on her chart. He pulls a sketch pad from behind a seat.*)

Rooster: I've not stopped painting because I wanted to. This morning I said, I'm going to paint, if my energy holds out. . . Soon as it's warm and the sun's shining. . .

Monica: [96]Well?

Rooster: (*Rain begins whistling around. He rubs the armrests.*) My energy didn't hold out. . . Listen to that rain blowing, 'round outside.

Monica: [97]It sounds neighborly.

Rooster: Coming right through the sun.

Monica: [98]I love to hear it when I'm inside.

Rooster: Oh, but it's cold walking into the rain. (*Begins to shiver.*) Look at me shake? The thought of rain and I start to shiver.

Monica: [99]Try to nap. [100]Would you like another blanket?

Rooster: (*He lies back slowly. [101]She covers him.*) That does feel good.

Monica: [102]I told you. (*He has closed his eyes and gone to sleep. [103]MONICA watches over him as the lights are brought down.*)

IF I COULD PAINT THE RAIN BY ROSARY HARTEL O'NEILL

Score for Monica Falcon, Scene 1

Super objective: to save the patient

Spine: to champion

Major obstacle: He is dying

Main action: to support

Scene tag: subduing the patient

Inner problem (that doesn't come up in scene): My husband recently died of a similar illness.

OBJECTIVE	ACTION	OBSTACLE	INNER IMAGE
BEAT I: FINDING THE PATIENT			
1. to pull self together	to breathe deep	terrified	Mel Gibson stuffy Carrollton
2. to preserve a calm exterior	to cool self	heat flashes from nerves	cave
3. to warm patient	to call out	lateness of day, dark, patient's disarray	patient's pajamas
4. to wake someone	to insist	patient's death?	bathroom nude

OBJECTIVE	ACTION	OBSTACLE	INNER IMAGE
5. to contact someone	to overcome silence	dark, emptiness, eerie house	burglar
6. to get help	to identify	quiet, dullness, huge house, smelling of death	Bultmar's Mortuary
7. to get respect	to classify	helplessness of being an outsider	Bultmar's Mortuary
8. to find patient	to follow voice	darkness, quiet, hostility in air	Waveland, Dad mad

BEAT II: ASSESSING THE PATIENT

9. to assess his condition	to identify feeble man	his rudeness, disinterest	Terry in Santa Monica
10. to assess his condition	to use medical instruments	darkness, can't see his features	Terry in Santa Monica
11. to determine seriousness of his condition	to inquire	insecurity, first patient, his detachment	Deb wisdom teeth
12. to comfort	to confirm	silence, rudeness unnerve me	silence
13a. to comfort him	to overrule	his irritability, darkness	RPO cottage door

BEAT III: CONTROLLING THE PATIENT

13b. to control him	to overrule	his irritability, the darkness	RPO cottage door
14. to control him	to demonstrate	servants, his family arriving soon	spooky lamps

15. to relax him	to distract	his withdrawal, darkness	tranquility at night
16. to relax him	to flatter	his rejection, time running out	small quarters and life, Paris garret, Georges Z hotel

BEAT IV: CHEERING THE PATIENT

17. to cheer him	to brighten room	his moodiness, violence, my strangeness	Dad: exclusive-ness, Waveland
18. to cheer him	to discourage	his sullenness, strangeness	Dad, sign of ferventness
19. to get him to laugh	to point out my failure	his distance, ignorance of deluge outside	Dad at Fon-tainebleau café
20. to get him to enjoy me	to cover hurt		
21. to lift his spirits	to change subject	lateness of hour, his disinterest	hospital, me by window
22. to lift his spirits	to cover hurt	lateness of hour, time running out to win him	2140 upstairs window
23. to cheer him with the fight	to bask in sun	his depression	Waveland, water often storms
24. to cheer him	to describe landscape	his indifference	light sparkle over gulf
25. to cheer him	to applaud its strength	his distance from window	coffee, double espresso
26. to cheer him	to champion the air	he can't see the sky	expectant blue sky, Waveland

OBJECTIVE	ACTION	OBSTACLE	INNER IMAGE
BEAT V: REPRIMANDING THE PATIENT			
27. to punish his coldness	to shut off phone	his rudeness, violence, my intrusion	G. Nix and her phone, lifeline
28. to punish him	to demand phone shut off	danger of offending him and losing the job	G. Greham
29. make him apologize	to defy	losing my job	Bob—rigid freedom
30. to get his statistics	to show my competence	he's my first patient, inexperience with kit	Dale first day Bolleview
31. to calm him	to describe what I am doing	his resistance	Ma's wacky blood pressure kits
32. to stop him	to disrupt	his money, power with agency	Dick 7th St.
33. to reassure agency	to contradict	their disbelief, his money	RPO—whacky
34. to dominate Rooster	to defy	his moodiness, belligerence	
35. to distract from phone	to lift	his phone habit	flying plane
BEAT VI: ORDERING THE PATIENT			
36. to dominate him	to defy	his slyness, belligerence	GN phone habit
37. to control him	to guard phone	his unreliability, moroseness	
38. to refresh him	to straighten bed	old, dirty sheets, his detachment	plastic sheets with Bob, NYC

#				
39.	to see how bad off he is	to observe him	his pride	Barret, flashes of temper
40.	to get him to rest soon	to repair bed	his desire for me to leave	unsure what to get and dirty sheets
41.	to give him confidence	to champion	his disbelief, his feebleness	Ma to go to bathroom, Fountainebleau

BEAT VII: RESTRAINING THE PATIENT

#				
42.	to keep away police	to grab alarm	he is bigger, knows alarm	
43.	to keep away police	to interrogate	time—he'll grab it again	door alarm NAC
44.	to keep away police	to order it off	noise	
45.	to keep away police	to demand for it	his house, noise	
46.	to keep away police	to yank out alarm	his painful hands, noise	
47.	to intimidate him	to dare	harder, his boldness	RO arrogance
48.	to intimidate him	to defy	his disinterest, doesn't rent	Jim Lanza query
49.	to dominate him	to rebuke	he's angry, not listening	Denise bedroom phone
50.	to dominate him	to demonstrate my prowess	his friends and relatives, he could oust me	Defiance Road
51.	to protect him	to assist	his feebleness	Mame walking
52.	to protect him	to guard	his pride	Mame walking
53.	to keep away police	to stop	noise	house alarm, Fountainebleau
54.	to get the alarm	to badger	his strength, his illness, noise	bucky nails, Fountainebleau

OBJECTIVE	ACTION	OBSTACLE	INNER IMAGE
BEAT VIII: DOMINATING THE PATIENT			
55. to contain	to demean	his anger, determination	B.—Tulane
56. to contain	to push aside	noise	B.—Tulane
57. to contain	to halt	his mental agitation	
58. to contain	to call for sympathy	my tiredness	Tulane ward
59. to contain	to deactivate	cops patrol this dangerous, wealthy neighborhood	Burglars on Carrollton
BEAT IX: FORCE FEEDING THE PATIENT			
60. to pacify him	to find out if hungry	his coldness	Brooke Skinny
61. to pacify him	to find out if thirsty	his silence	Brooke Skinny
62. to protect him	to encourage him, to eat	his indifference	Brooke Skinny
63. to protect him	to suggest	his stub-bornness	
64. to protect him	to encourage water	his stub-bornness	Bob no eat morning
BEAT X: BARGAINING WITH THE PATIENT			
65. to release him into revealing himself	to bargain	his brittleness	ITO moodiness
66. to release him into revealing himself	to propose	time running out	Veleka—cards
67. to get his cooperation	to explain	his ignorance	Taro-Maria

68. to get his cooperation	to qualify	he's misunder-standing	Dale chest
69. to get his cooperation	to bypass slur		Veleka reading
70. to prick his interest	to name his state	his derision	Leo—July born Tulane med center
71. to prick his interest	to denigrate further	his derision	Pluto—good night in gallery
72. to lift his spirits	to describe	fear he'll snap	gifted ones near crazy
73. to lift his soul	to keep young	darkness, he's mounting tension	
74. to lift his soul	to specify his uniqueness	his withdrawal	D. F.— archetype class Cornell
75. to lift his soul	to clarify method	his ignorance	painting, personal mood B. H.

BEAT XI: EXPOSING THE PATIENT'S HISTORY

76. to expose his history	to identify his emptiness	his coldness, fragileness	Mel Gibson
77. to expose his history	to identify his lineage	his coldness, fragileness	Anderson, Ocean Springs
78. to uncover his problems	to stop theatrics	his fearfulness	Brer hostility
79. to uncover his problems	to qualify	time, his coldness	Brer hostility
80. to make him feel guilty	to retaliate	his wall of defense	JFP South Monica
81. to win his sympathy	to correct	this misunder-standing	Pockard temperament

OBJECTIVE	ACTION	OBSTACLE	INNER IMAGE
82. to use the birds as a clue	to search	darkness, no sounds, fear of birds	Bambi starved

BEAT XII: CONFRONTING THE ILLNESS

OBJECTIVE	ACTION	OBSTACLE	INNER IMAGE
83. to confront the illness	to get back on track	his resistance, eccentricity, my husband's death	BAM. Tulane jail students
84. to create a bond	to appease	his isolation	murky dullness of Westchester
85. to create a bond	to concrete	his ignorance of feeling for Mississippi	four hours from New Orleans
86. to hide my desperation	to collapse	deep pain of missing Bob	emptiness at funeral parlor, Kleenex boxes
87. to hide my desperation	to explain	one month husband dead	Carrollton Avenue House
88. to hide my desperation	to retreat	brittle feelings	Dad in coffin
89. to hide my desperation	to excuse tears	guilt, anger at his death	borrowed white shirt
90. to hide my desperation	to search for box	my bills	his belt on bathroom, gold belt buckle
91. to hide my desperation	to attack Rooster	my eviction from apartment	pictures of me on his dresser
92. to shut him up	to shirk off	my loss of all goods, bankruptcy	the cork paperweight
93. to shut him up	to apologize	tiredness	cold shoes
94. to shut him up	to distract	brittle emotions, hungry	empty wallet, bounced check

| 95. | to confront his illness | to focus on medical procedure | my feelings for my husband | Sweetie's girl |

BEAT XIII: BONDING WITH THE PATIENT

96.	to perk his spirits	to prod	my depression	Renoir paintings
97.	to perk his spirits	to praise	my depression	
98.	to boost his morale	to glorify	his depression from not painting	Ohio garret
99.	to get him more hopeful	to console	his depression, rain, isolation	rain on Mama's casket
100.	to prevent a chill	to warm him	his nervousness, shivering	symptom of fever
101.	to get close to him	to drape him	his sickness, fever is worse	103-degree fever
102.	to get him to rest and live	to conform	his high fever, chills	
103.	to keep him quiet	to guard		Dale wisdom teeth

6

CHARACTER
Who am I?

This chapter deals with character—the distinguishing features of an individual. Who you are affects how you act.

Unless you use your text to advantage you cannot act. Preliminary study is seeking to learn the facts about your character. You have to go to your author to get these. His words cannot mean anything unless you get his meaning behind the words. Creating a character is like building a house. You have to accumulate the material with which to build it.

Charles Jehlinger, founder of the American Academy of Dramatic Arts

■ WHAT IS CHARACTER?

Character is the distinguishing features of a person—looks, feelings, and actions. It is the "how" of action. How we do something depends on who we are. After we know what we are doing onstage, we must discover how we do it. We must become the character.

What is becoming the character?

Becoming the character is developing the physical and psychological traits of the role. Each of you in life plays a character and does things in a certain way. So linked are you to your own character that when you are out of sorts, you may be surprised when others remark, "You're not yourself today." Observation helps you identify distinctions necessary to becoming the character.

Sometimes in my classes, I will assign each actor to come to class like a fellow actor. The actor must wear the same clothes and act exactly like that other person. I then come to class like another teacher and behave totally differently—soft spoken, cautious, slow moving. The actors keep asking me whether I'm mad or sick. The point is that in order to play someone else, you must adjust how you behave.

When you look at the character you're to play you must ask yourself, "Who am I?" Using the "I" will help you identify with the character. Your aim is to give yourself a new background, to embrace all the elements of the new you. You begin developing the new you through observation and reflection. You observe the inner and outer worlds of others, attempting to grow into the part.

■ OBSERVATION

Genius is the talent for seeing things straight . . . without any bend or break or aberration of sight, without any warping of vision.

Maude Adams, American actress, 1872–1953

What is observation?

Observation is the acting technique of being aware of yourself and others offstage. Zoom in on details of dress and physical behavior. Look around you and try to notice someone with an interesting body and voice, or someone behaving in a special way. Study that person's gestures, body movements, tones of voice, posture, and clothes and imagine yourself becoming that person.

What is an observation exercise?

An observation exercise is one in which you notice and record another's behavior and restage it in class.

Begin by observing the physical traits. As you move into the creation of a character's thoughts and feelings, you will identify and copy the more subtle actions of the soul.

CLASS GAMES

1. *Giant Exercise.* Think and act like a giant, like somebody big. Say your name as loudly as you can to startle your partner.

2. *Character Description.* Sit in a circle and describe in detail your father, mother, or best friend. Use precise words: "She speaks in measured tones; has long, red, perfectly manicured nails; prefers black or navy accessories" and so forth. Anyone who uses a grunt or a generality such as "very," "kind of," "sort of," "really," "you know," "you see," "you understand," "maybe," or "like" is thrown out of the circle.

3. *No Hands.* Play the character description game while sitting on your hands.

4. *Expressive Body Positions.* In groups of two to six, demonstrate different ways to do the following:
   a. sit in a chair
   b. lounge on the floor
   c. lean by a door

   The interesting group wins.

■ CHARACTER ANALYSIS

What is a character analysis?

Character analysis is an evaluation of the play for the sum of your character's experiences, training, or education. Apply an understanding of the play to developing your role. First and foremost, your character must fit into and advance the play. Reread the script to discover tidbits of information.

The character must not change the play's overall direction and meaning. The character must work for the play. Some characters are aggressive, self-centered, blindly ambitious, or savage, with few redeeming features. The actor must expose the breadth of negative traits that works for the play.

The audience can recognize those traits. Watching them performed, the audience obtains greater self-knowledge, a relief, or catharsis. You need to dig for the truth, whether or not you personally like the traits that are unearthed.

How do I study a script for character?

Look for facts about your character. Start by simply trying to understand the language. As the lines become clearer, search for clues to your character. Ask yourself, "What is my character's function in the play? When and why do I enter a scene? What do I and others say about my character?"

You must discern from deep study of the play facts about your family, rearing, education, friends, well-being, talent, and hobbies. Look for your character's main desires, what thoughts your character leans upon, your subconscious needs.

In studying the character, you may need to face certain traits you don't like about yourself. Perhaps your character is healthier, in better shape, more educated than you. These are areas you will need to work on to grow into the character.

■ PHYSICAL TRAITS

What physical traits should I look for?

You begin any character analysis with a study of physical traits. These are the easiest to grasp and will lead to an understanding of your character's psychological traits. The physical is the most obvious level of characterization because it reveals external traits: sex, age, size, color, health, fitness, vocal quality, physical quality (fast or slow). Sixty percent of what you reveal to the audience about your character is how you comb your hair, how you gesture, how you dress.

Think about yourself right now. Are you tall, short, shapely, a bit overweight? Are your eyes blue, is your hair brown, is that your natural color? How old are you? Do you look your age? Would you describe yourself as attractive—do others see you as such? Are your clothes stylish? Are you dressed for class or for work? Are you healthy? Is your lifestyle active or sedentary?

Imagine your character's physical life. Were you a healthy child? Are you athletic? Were you in the service? Do you like the outdoors? What is your work background?

Note the physical differences between the two brothers Eugene O'Neill describes in *Long Day's Journey into Night*, act 1, scene 1. These facts are taken directly from character descriptions in the play.

LONG DAY'S JOURNEY: CHARACTER DESCRIPTIONS

JAMIE	EDMUND
Physique	
Broad-shouldered, deep-chested physique; is an inch taller than his father and weighs less, but appears shorter and stouter because he lacks bearing and graceful carriage	Looks taller than Jamie; thin and wiry; more like his mother
Coloring	
Fair skin is sunburned a reddish, freckled tan	Sunburned a deep brown, but with a parched sallowness
Age	
Thirty-three	Twenty-three
Face	
Good-looking, despite marks of dissipation; never been handsome; resembles father; fine brown eyes; hair	*Big, dark eyes* are the dominant feature in his long Irish face; hypersensitiveness; high forehead; dark brown

is thinning, and already there is an indication of a bald spot; nose, aquiline without sneering	hair, sun-bleached to red at the ends, brushed straight back; nose like his father's
Hands	
Sunburned, a reddish, freckled tan	Exceptionally long fingers; nervous
Health	
Lacks vitality; signs of premature disintegration are on him	Nervous sensibility; in bad health and thinner than he should be, with feverish eyes and sunken cheeks
Clothes	
Dressed in an old sack suit; wears collar and tie	Dressed in a shirt, collar, and a tie; no coat, old flannel trousers, brown sneakers

To play Jamie, or any role, you must decide how each physical trait affects your action. For example, Jamie is described as lacking vitality. Imagine what causes this. Jamie the character is based on O'Neill's brother. Several symptoms could cause Jamie's listlessness. But as you read the play you discover that alcoholism is the cause.

Identify real problems to deal with onstage. Is Jamie protecting his gruff voice already scratched from too much shouting in bars? Does he lumber along awkwardly because he's a bit high? Practice various choices. With your director's help, pick the interpretation that works best for you.

Does my character have a handicap?

Some characters operate with a permanent disability. If your character has a handicap, you will need to spend time researching and making it real for yourself. If you are the blind Helen Keller, practice the scene (under careful supervision) blindfolded. Experiment at home with getting dressed or eating when sightless. If you are lame like Laura, wrap part of your leg in a bandage. Use a stone in the bandage for a soreness, a real metal brace for polio, and so on. Test possible physical ailments and adjustments.

Some conditions, such as an epileptic seizure or drunkenness, may be temporary. Identify that sensation and what it does to the body. Let that lead you to the adjustment to overcome it. For drunkenness, a thick tongue (sensation) makes you enunciate (adjustment). Instead of simply being "drunk," determine the specific site of the discomfort (tongue won't move, so you must overarticulate). Rehearse the scene first normally, then add the adjustments.

What is my character's profession?

The profession of your character may affect how you act. Although both in their sixties, James Tyrone (the actor) and Willy Loman (the salesman) have been handicapped by different professions. James Tyrone seems taller because of his theatrical bearing. His voice is remarkably fine, resonant, and flexible. His speech, movement, and gestures reveal a studied acting technique. Willy is dressed quietly, slouches, and talks to himself. He heaves a sigh and flinches his sore palms, the effect of years of lugging heavy sales cases.

Does my character act like an animal?

You can use traits of animals and objects to expand your characterizations. Is your character like an animal, machine, or object? Do you lumber like an old stag? Dart about like a mouse? The traits of animals are graphic and communicate immediately with an audience. Think of how expressive the movement of a monkey, crane, or tiger can be. Going to the zoo can stimulate your imagination. Watch a hippopotamus snort, a monkey fidget, a bat flutter, an elephant swagger. Listen to a pig and a seal; they squeal differently. Observe how an animal defends itself: A parrot shrieks, a peacock fans its tail, a lizard hides.

Some writers cite animals for certain characters, as in the films *Beauty and the Beast* and *Wolfman* and the plays *The Lion in Winter*, *The Elephant Man*, and *Cat on a Hot Tin Roof* (the lead, Maggie, even refers to herself as a cat). Through *observation*, become aware of how expressive animals can be.

Does my character act like a machine?

Close your eyes and listen to the rhythmic sounds of machines around you (humming clothes dryer, clicking computer, screaming doorbell, grinding alarm clock, straining car, shrieking phone). What if you clicked your teeth like a metronome or groaned like an industrial vacuum? The traits of machines can add an exciting dimension to your role. In some roles, mechanical traits predominate: Robocop, C3PO, the Tin Man.

How should I rehearse physical traits?

Attend rehearsals dressed hat to shoes in character. If you are practicing in tennis shoes, whereas your character would really be wearing spike heels, you're wasting your time. Wearing the appropriate clothes helps you experience the necessary changes in posture, breathing, and speech from the beginning.

The best costumes lead to a revelation of character. For example, if your character is a glutton, which coat do you pick? How about practicing with a coat that's too tight? Or a coat with a seam split out?

Refer to your character as "I" rather than as "he" or "she." Say "I am doing this," not "He is doing this." By uniting yourself with your character, you begin imagining his actions.

EXERCISES

1. *Physical Trait.* Play the action "to pack a suitcase," "to fix breakfast," or "to rearrange the room." Use one of the following handicaps: crippled, obese, blind, surgery patient, arthritic, pregnant.

2. *Imaginary Garment.* Wear an article of clothing (such as high heels, back brace, straw hat) that restricts your behavior. Do a task. Then do the same task not wearing the garment but using it as an imaginary influence.

3. *Different Uniforms.* Create an improvisation in which you and a partner imitate two waiters. Find the differences between the two. Now switch roles.

4. *Character Tasks.* Demonstrate the following tasks as two different characters: (a) to enter a room; (b) to stand on a chair; (c) to remove your shoes; (d) to kneel; (e) to leave the room. Do not change the order of the tasks.

■ PSYCHOLOGICAL TRAITS

What are psychological traits?

Psychological traits are the emotional and intellectual aspects of character that inspire action. Education, social background, religion, and type of work are significant here. Childhood environment, class background, and work experiences all affect your thought. Your character's dominant attitude (positive/negative), beliefs, and moral and social class all influence thought and psychological traits. These can be strengthened by knowing your character's inner motive forces, feelings, mind, will.

How do inner motive forces work?

The first, and most important master (is) *feeling* . . . unfortunately it is not tractable. . . . Since you cannot begin your work unless your feelings happen to function of their own accord, it is necessary for you to have recourse to some other master. . . . Who is it? The second master is the *mind*. . . . Your mind can be a motive power in . . . your creative process. Is there a third? . . . If longings could put your creative apparatus to work and direct it spiritually . . . we have found our third master—*will.* Consequently we have three impelling movers in our psychic life. Since these three forces form a triumvirate, inextricably bound up together, what you say of the one necessarily concerns the other two. . . . This combined power is of utmost importance to us actors and we should be gravely mistaken not to use it for our practical ends. . . . Actors whose feelings over-balance their intellects will, naturally, in playing Romeo or Othello, emphasize the emotional side. Actors in whom the will is the most powerful attribute will play Macbeth or Brand and underscore ambition or fanaticism. The third type will unconsciously stress, more than is necessary, the intellectual shadings of a part like Hamlet or Nathan the Wise.

It is however necessary not to allow any one of these three elements to crush out either of the others and thereby upset the balance and necessary harmony. Our art recognizes all three types and in their creative work all three forces play leading parts in shaping psychological action. (*Stanislavski Handbook*, pp. 82–83)

Why are psychological traits challenging?

Psychological traits are every bit as important as physical traits but are less tangible. In Tennessee Williams's *Cat on a Hot Tin Roof*, Brick has a broken leg; he wears a cast and uses a crutch. His physical handicap is obvious to the audience. Brick is depressed, tormented, but sexually appealing. What kind of choices can Brick make to communicate these feelings to the audience?

What do you do when you feel depressed? Do you withdraw, shut the door to your room, and crawl into bed? Do you overeat? Do you snap at people who try to befriend you? Do you neglect yourself physically—not combing your hair, not tying your shoes?

Onstage you must convey your depression to your audience immediately and dramatically. You may decide to investigate what you have to subtract from and add to your action to expose and sustain your depression as Brick.

How should I rehearse psychological traits?

Test instinctive choices. What is your immediate response to impersonating a snob? Think of snobs you have known. What did they do? Keep their distance? Wait for people to approach them? Speak in a measured tone? Hold their head high? Dress better than everyone else? Smirk at others' failures? Try those choices and keep the ones that work for you in the scene.

Watch children at play. When you see kids on a playground, and their imaginations are racing, if one says, "Okay, I'll be the fairy princess, and you be the wicked witch," the other doesn't respond, "Give me ten minutes to get in touch with my wicked witch." She responds automatically from a sense of truth, and so should you.

How do impulses relate to my character?

Discovering your character's impulses grounds truthful interpretations. You must learn to connect with the appropriate reactions for the character. The more you can arouse the necessary feelings in your heart and body, the more you can channel your spirit into the role. A big part of acting is creating the environment for the strongest impulse-based reaction. What is your character sensing at this moment? Do you feel confused, uplifted? How is that emotion located in your body? What are you going to do because of that impulse? We live in a highly sophisticated technological society. Yet, in art, it is often the primitive, intuitive reaction that provokes interest.

A vital part of actor training is to nurture through spontaneous exercises the identification and personal involvement required in creating a role. You must discover and (most important of all) learn to trust impulses as the authentic raw material of acting.

How can playing games help me develop my impulses?

Contact is arguably the trigger for impulses. Develop the habit of really connecting with another actor, with another part of yourself, with the audience. Playing games can help you make contact with others and get in touch with your impulses. In every game, as in every sequence, you act spontaneously, and you play to win. Play games to loosen yourself up and relax: number games, word games, face-feels, where everybody tries to recognize one another. Provoke a gale of laughter from a partner.

Play games and enact fairy tales that fire you to behave preposterously for a goal. Onstage, you move and speak almost twice as much as in life. Games prepare you for this intensified activity by sharpening your instincts. Fairy tales emphasize the glamour of largeness and offer condensed images that open Pandora's box.

You can invent as many types of improvisations as there are games. Your improvisations can have one or numerous guidelines. You can also use improvisations as a spot-check of principles studied in class. There are many types of brief extemporaneous exercises that you can do alone or in groups to heighten your technique. When doing them, employ real objects to trick your impulses into full involvement.

EXERCISES

1. *Calling Qualities.* Play the action "to straighten the room." Adjust your interpretation as your teacher calls out, "You are lazy, shrewish, depressed, angry," and so on.

2. *Emphasizing Traits.* Interpret a scene two ways by emphasizing different personality traits. Possible adjectives to implement include *lazy, outgoing, hyper, shy, determined, pensive, violent.*

3. *Clothes Swapping.* Come to class dressed like someone other than yourself. Have classmates guess who you are.

■ WHAT IS A LIFE SCRIPT?

How does the past shape the present?

Twentieth-century psychology has illuminated our understanding of the past's influences on the present. Remember two important principles: (1) The brain functions as a high-fidelity tape, recording the feelings associated with past experiences. (2) Recorded experiences and the feelings associated with them are available for replay today in their original vivid form and largely determine the nature of today's transactions. The breakthrough discovery is that an event and the feeling produced by it are inextricably locked together in the brain. One cannot be evoked without the other. We record not only past events in detail but also the feelings—sensations, emotions, sensitivities, tolerances, excitabilities—associated with them. The following report by the pioneering psychologist Carl Jung in *Man and His Symbols* illustrates the way present stimulations evoke past feelings:

> A forty-year-old female patient reported she was walking down the street one morning and, as she passed a music store, she heard a strain of music that produced an overwhelming melancholy. She felt herself in the grip of a sadness she could not understand, the intensity of which was almost unbearable. Nothing in her conscious thought could explain this. Later in the week she phoned me to tell me that, as she continued to hum the song over and over, she suddenly had a flash of recollection in which she saw her mother sitting at the piano and heard her playing this song. The mother had died when the patient was five years old. I asked her if the recall of this early memory had relieved her depression. She said it had changed the nature of her feelings; there was still a melancholy feeling in recalling the death of her mother, but it was not the initial overwhelming despair she had felt at first. It would seem she was now consciously remembering a feeling which initially was the reliving of a feeling. In the second instance, she remembered how it was to feel that way; but in the first instance, the feeling was precisely the same feeling which was recorded when her mother died. She was at that moment five years old.

Some psychoanalysts, such as Eric Berne, say your life script determines your outlook. Are you "waiting for Santa Claus" or "waiting for rigor mortis"? A life script reflects a character's expectations—often unmet by the scene.

Writing your character's life script should help you uncover the early decisions your character made unconsciously as to how life should be lived. L. S. Kubie wrote in the *Journal of Mental Science:*

> Early in life, a central emotional position is frequently established which becomes the affective position to which that individual will tend to return automatically for the rest of his days. This in turn may constitute either the major safeguard or the major vulnerability of his life. . . . Whenever the central emotional position is painful . . . the individual may spend his whole life defending himself against it, again using conscious, preconscious, and unconscious devices whose aim is to avoid this pain-filled central position. Your life script, formed in early childhood, may have gone through various "rewrites" as you grew up, with the plot and imagined ending remaining essentially unchanged.

How does my life script dictate my actions?

Your character acts not according to what things are really like, but rather according to his life script, which gives rise to mental images of what he perceives things to be. In *A Layman's Guide to Psychiatry and Psychoanalysis*, Eric Berne claims that "everyone has images of himself, the world, and others and behaves as though those images, rather than the objects they represent are the 'truth.'"

Your life script—how you see the world—creates the action. If you are waiting for Santa Claus, and your action is to get dressed, you might hum, dance into your stockings, put on bright clothes. If you are waiting for rigor mortis, you could slam off the alarm clock, curse, break your nail as you zip up your drab pants. Your outlook, which is formed by your experiences, actually determines what you do and how you do it. You are so allied to your own life script that you act spontaneously from it. You do certain things because of it. Wed yourself to your character's history, and you will choose specific actions appropriate to the character.

Berne observed, "What is called 'adaptability' depends on your ability to change images in your life script to correspond to a new reality. Most people can change some images but not others." Many characters cling to certain pictures and sensations that they refuse to discard.

■ REMARKS

I am the very slave of circumstances and impulse—borne away
with every breath.

Lord Byron, Sardanapalus, act 1, scene 2

What is the perfect role?

Many actors search for the "perfect role" that fits like a glove with their own selves. But you should strive to play a number of roles and spend a lot of time on varied traits. Any transformation, such as the development of a butterfly from a cocoon, involves many minuscule adjustments. Daily alterations (in rehearsal and in study at home) help you expand your body and mind into the character's. The extent of that metamorphosis depends on your talent as well as your commitment to research and practice and to justify everything your character says and does.

What is "living the part"?

The Stanislavski system is based on living the part, as he explained so clearly to his students:

> The art of living a part asserts that the main factor in any form of creativeness is the life of a human spirit, that of the actor and his part, their joint feelings and subconscious creation. . . . What we hold in highest regard are impressions made on our emotions, which leave a lifelong mark and transform actions into real, living beings. . . . Aside from the fact that it opens up avenues for inspiration, living a part helps the artist to carry out

one of his main objectives. His job is not to present merely the external life of his character. He must fit his own human qualities to the life of the other person, and pour into it all of his own soul. . . . An artist takes the best that is in him and carries it over on the stage. The form will vary according to the necessities of the play, but the human emotions of the artist will remain alive, and they cannot be replaced by anything else.

Therefore, no matter how much you act, how many parts you take, you should never allow yourself any exception to the rule of using your own feelings. Salvini said: "The great actor . . . should feel the thing he is portraying . . . not only once or twice while he is studying his part, but to a greater or lesser degree every time he plays it, no matter whether it is the first or thousandth time."

Always act in your own person. . . . You can never get away from yourself. The moment you lose yourself on the stage marks the departure from truly living your part and the beginning of exaggerated, false acting.

Spiritual realism, trust of artistic feelings . . . these are the most difficult achievements of our art, they require long, arduous inner preparation.

The difference between this art and that practiced by others is the difference between "seeming" and "being." (*Stanislavski Handbook*, pp. 90–91)

■ CHECKLIST

This checklist should help you explore exciting details about your character. Answering these questions should encourage a vigorous approach to characterization.

1. How does my character develop the play?

2. What are my distinctive psychological traits?

3. What physical traits affect the way I speak and move? What are my character's age, weight, height, speech characteristics, walking/sitting/standing patterns, mannerisms or peculiarities, nationality, health, and level of vitality?

4. What is my character's life script? How does it shape my point of view onstage?

■ FINAL PROJECTS

1. *Progressive Exercises.* Throughout the next few chapters, you will do a second series of related progressive exercises. Each shows you how the background element of that chapter interrelates with your entire performance. Each exercise strengthens a new area of your knowledge. Rehearse each sequence at least three times with your partner.

   EXERCISE 6: Part one. A spa or ski lodge. Pick a new partner. You are strangers with opposing traits. For example, one is neat, and one is sloppy. Your character traits affect all you do throughout the scene. Begin the exercise with opposing objectives, each of you performing an action in silence; then one of you begins a verbal conflict.

   Part two. Interrelate an understanding of history with your action as the character. A desolate cliff. You are the same character, but two years have now passed, and you have developed an intense relationship. Develop a detailed biography for yourself, a common history, and an abandoned cliff bristling with memories. Begin the sequence with two minutes of silence, with each performing a physical task. Then a conflict erupts. Bring in objects loaded with meaning to support your task.

2. *Autobiography.* Write a life script for a role that you have recently played or want to play. Create this script from the point of view of the character at a given age (growing up, before marriage, working).

   Optional: *Operative Word.* Based on your life script, decide which words are the operative or most important ones in a scene. In rehearsal, touch your partner on those particular words. Stage the sequence for class.

3. *Nightmare.* Stage a sequence for a nightmare your character might have had. Write from your point of view as a helpless adolescent. You are driven into and must submit to overwhelming circumstances. Relax as you pursue a series of extreme actions. Rehearse using objects from your own past.

4. *Character Analysis.* Analyze a character in a scene for physical and psychological traits. Use a play from Appendix E or F or one your teacher suggests. Stage a short sequence.

7

SETTING
Where am I?

This chapter deals with establishing the scene's time and place, which allows you to respond sensitively to your action.

The weight of this sad time we must obey; Speak what we feel, not what we ought to say. The oldest hath borne most: we that are young Shall never see so much, nor live so long.

Shakespeare, *King Lear*, act 5, scene 3

■ WHAT IS THE SETTING?

Why do I need to study setting?

Setting is the time and place of a scene. When you walk onto a stage, you are always walking into a specific setting. In real life, you never forget the time and place. Onstage, in a make-believe setting, you need to keep contact with that vacant park at dusk, that waiting room at dawn, or that stifling noonday apartment. A vivid setting is central to today's stage productions and films. Some directors, like Joseph Chaikin, preconceive no spatial characteristics but work with designers throughout rehearsals to develop the environment with the performances.

■ THE TIME

What is time?

Stage time is a special period in which your character's action occurs. When it is influences what you do. Just as in real life, time onstage stimulates action. When you move onstage, you are doing so for a timely reason. You are getting a cup of morning coffee, answering the door for the noon mail, waiting for a seven o'clock date. So at 8 A.M., June 1, 2005, you might be getting dressed for work in a linen suit or watching the TV news, whereas at 6 P.M., November 1, 1943, you could be raking leaves, reading news about the war, or listening to the radio. Your words come forth from a context of time.

How many of us would not dress and deal with a brisk Sunday morning in a different way than with a sticky, humid Monday at dawn?

But how do you create a Sunday morning quality? You ask yourself what you would wear and do on a Sunday morning. For example, you might wear a kimono, sip coffee, and loll around the patio table with a newspaper. On a Monday at dawn, you might slip into a business suit and eat breakfast on the run as you pack your briefcase. Most plays sketch out the time, and you the actor must complete the details.

How do I rehearse for time?

As you practice, keep examining the question, "What would I be wearing and doing at this time?" Evaluate your costume. Are you pulling on a heavy winter coat, muffler, and cap, or are you lounging in your silk pajamas? Ask yourself, "What rituals—answering phone calls, responding to mail, getting my hair done—are particular to this special day, this Monday as opposed to this Saturday?" For example, if your scene is set on a noisy Friday in a dorm room, start running through activities like answering the phone, leaving messages for your roommate, sorting out clothes to wear Friday night. Conversely, the activities for a teacher then might include packing up books, erasing the blackboard, storing charts.

Imagine what details each of your senses is responding to while doing the activity. For instance, if you are getting dressed at 6 A.M., you might hear the ignition of a neighbor's car, smell bread from a nearby bakery, see the sunlight filter through the blinds.

How do I create a different era?

Looking like a person in a different era also depends on your clothing and behavior. You must understand the era to choose convincing actions. Watch films, listen to music, read historical novels to experience an earlier time. For example, how might you act after an evening banquet in the first century A.D.? What would you be wearing then at midnight? Imagine yourself cast as the young Syrian in *Salome* by Oscar Wilde. How would you respond to a milieu of soldiers, pages, slaves, Jews, and Nazarenes at the Palace of Herod? What would a Syrian of that era be doing—gossiping about the palace, watching veiled dancers, drinking at the cistern, socializing at banquets?

The boldfaced words in the opening scene from *Salome* show information about time to be evaluated.

SALOME: TIME CLUES

*A great terrace in the Palace of Herod, set above the **banqueting hall**. Some **soldiers are leaning over the balcony**.* To the right there is a gigantic staircase, to the left, at the back, an old cistern surrounded by a wall of green bronze. **Moonlight.**

The Young Syrian: How beautiful is the Princess Salome tonight!

The Page of Herodias: Look at the moon! How strange the moon seems! She is like a woman rising from a tomb. She is like a dead woman. You would fancy she was looking for dead things.

The Young Syrian: She has a strange look. She is like a little princess who wears a yellow veil, and whose feet are of silver. She is like a princess who has little white doves for feet. **You would fancy she [the moon] was dancing.**

The Page of Herodias: She is like a woman who is dead. She moves very slowly. **(Noise in the banqueting hall)**

First Soldier:	**What an uproar! Who are those wild beasts howling?**
Second Soldier:	The Jews. They are always like that. **They are disputing about their religion.**

Actor's notes: *It appears to be late at night after a wild banquet. The soldiers are supporting themselves on the balcony. Maybe they are tired from overeating? Could they be drunk? Why is the moon so peculiar? Does it portend evil, unnatural disturbances ahead? Perhaps the Jews are drunk and are disputing about religion into the wee hours. You must do some research into the moon and into the first century to fully evaluate the clues of the text.*

What should I emphasize in creating an era?

Onstage, you should emphasize the physical action of your character. In particular, you might explore the physical activities of a different time. A few select physical details can capture the reality of another period. Note the tasks an actor has jotted down for Richard in O'Neill's *Ah, Wilderness!*, set in a Connecticut beach town in 1906. The underlined activities are ones actually performed in the play.

AH, WILDERNESS!: RICHARD'S NOTES

Clothing: slacks, long-sleeve shirt, black leather oxfords, straw hat

Activities:

Indoors: dominoes, cards (war, fish, old maid, solitaire, poker, wishing aces), <u>poetry books</u>, rubber ball, <u>letter writing</u> with an old-fashioned pen and inkwell, tic-tac-toe, checkers, dice, crossword puzzles, diary writing, <u>piano</u>.

Outdoors: tennis, volleyball, biking, pebble throwing, swimming, fishing, <u>throwing a straw hat</u>, swinging from a tree, folding newspaper boats, tracing names with a stick, flying a kite, playing badminton, "light my candle," hold fast all I give you.

Beach: What could I do while waiting on the shore? Feel the murky water, throw second-rate pebbles, shake my unkempt hair in the breeze, trace names with a flimsy stick, search for whitened shells, dump sand from my itchy shoes, wade in the glowing water?

How does knowing the period allow me to think like my character?

By experiencing certain activities, you begin to think like your character. For example, if you're playing Richard in *Ah, Wilderness!* you might read books on Victorian manners and wonder why a teenager would follow these rules. Is Richard ignoring these rules? Why does he go to so much trouble to meet his girlfriend Muriel secretly on the beach? You might imagine Richard's family dinner table. What was the family like back then? How many children lived to their adolescence? What were his siblings like? Their health? Their values? You might study why parents behaved so rigidly at the table.

You could think about Muriel. Is her father an old dragon? Yes, except he's about forty, forty-five maybe, at the oldest. He knows that when unmarried girls get pregnant, they lose all their worth. You might ask yourself, "Where's Muriel's mother? Why are the women not controlling these youngsters?" Well, women weren't voting, driving cars, or even working back then. Note that Lily, the maiden aunt, still helps with the dinner and lives with Richard's family.

Then you might wonder why Richard's mother likes to sew and complain. She says things like: "If you don't stop talking Fourth of July—! To hear you go on, you'd think that was an excuse for anything from murder to picking pockets!" (act 3, scene 2).

You will find out that these Victorian parents are clinging by their fingernails to a very formal, cautious lifestyle, but the Goths are at the gate, so that's why they're so uptight. When your way of life is threatened, you either change or you clamp down and do it better. Suddenly, you might see behind the scenes where Richard slips away for the night, a bored teenager baffled by his parents' rules.

How do I rehearse another era?

To rehearse another era, test out your character's clothing and physical behavior. For example, the way Richard in *Ah, Wilderness!* moves is not something that you imagine. It's you on the beach with this damp straw hat, these conservative slacks, and these turn-of-the-century shoes and socks. You must duplicate what happened back then, obviously, with a contemporary sensibility. If you want to look carefree, like Richard, begin practicing with his shoes and clothing.

Knowing how people dressed and behaved in a certain period will help you choose specific actions. For example, leaving the Belle Reve plantation in the 1950s in *Streetcar*, Blanche is likely to act out of place in Stanley Kowalski's tiny slum apartment on the fringes of the French Quarter. Note Williams's poignant character descriptions, suggesting a clash in activities of the two main characters. Observe the details of the period: the paper-wrapped package from the local butcher, the bowling jacket (a big item in the 1950s), and the white gloves and hat worn by upper-class women when going anywhere in that decade.

STANLEY *is about twenty-eight or thirty years old, roughly dressed in blue denim work clothes. He carries his bowling jacket and a red-stained package from a butcher's. He stops at the foot of the steps to his apartment, hollers for his wife, heaves the package at her, then starts back around the corner. . . .*

BLANCHE *comes around the corner, carrying a valise. . . . She is daintily dressed in a white suit with a fluffy bodice, necklace and earrings of pearl, white gloves and hat, looking as if she were arriving at a summer tea or cocktail party in the garden district. She is about thirty. Her delicate beauty must avoid a strong light.*

Should I establish a season?

Whether they are described in the text or not, your character has thoughts, feelings, sensations, and ideas related to the time of year. Imagine now the differing sensations of stepping out on an icy winter's night, an autumn afternoon, a spring morning, a noontime summer day. Events are inextricably tied to specific seasons: fall classes, a June wedding, spring break, summer vacation. Seasons affect your well-being, for example, Guinevere (in Lerner and Loewe's *Camelot*) is itchy to flee the castle for the May woods, Ratso (in the film *Midnight Cowboy*) has succumbed to a freezing winter's virus, Shannon (in Williams's *Night of the Iguana*) is boiling from a bus ride in the Mexican tropics in September.

The season dictates what you wear and anticipate. Walk outside. How does the air hitting against your cheek make you feel? Oppressed or energized? What greenery do you see? Miles of lush forests or one barren tree? You will recoil if you walk out of your New York City apartment and it's 100 degrees in the dead of winter.

Note how the season affects Anne Frank stuck inside the attic in the following sequence from act 2, scene 2 of *The Diary of Anne Frank* by Frances Goodrich and Albert Hackett.

Thursday, the twentieth of April, nineteen forty-four. Invasion fever is mounting every day. Miep tells us that people outside talk of nothing else. For myself, life has become much more pleasant. I often go to Peter's room after supper. Oh, don't think I'm in love, because I'm not. But it does make life more bearable to have someone with whom you can exchange views. No more tonight. P.S. . . . I must be honest. I must confess that I actually live for the next meeting. (*Work light off.*) Is there anything lovelier than to sit under the skylight and feel the sun on your cheeks and have a darling boy in your arms?

How does weather affect clothes and behavior?

You are dressed now for the weather. Indoors, you adapt to chilly conditions by grabbing a coverlet, pulling on a sweater or warm slippers. Outside, you respond to rain, snow, sleet, sunlight, wind, lightning, thunder, fog, humidity. Onstage, weather conditions may erupt suddenly: thunder cracking, winds howling, lightning striking.

Weather intensifies action. For example, the blizzard in Horton Foote's *Tomorrow* heightens the actions of each character, and it makes the scene more exciting by adding suspense:

A young woman, black-haired, poorly dressed, thin, gaunt, almost emaciated, comes in R. She is pregnant. Her clothes are patched and worn and no protection at all against the cold. She gets as far as the boiler room, and she faints. FENTRY *starts outside to wash the dishes when he hears the woman moan in pain. He steps outside the door, and he goes over to her and gently rolls her over on her back. He sees how cold her thin arms and legs are and takes his coat off and puts it over her. He feels her pulse, watches her for a moment longer and then shaking her gently, he tries to rouse her.* Lady. Lady. (*She opens her eyes slowly.*)

How do I rehearse for weather?

To respond to a dripping rain, freezing wind, or broiling sun, imagine the weather condition, then work against its effect on your body. For example, for heat, you could recall the sensation of lukewarm perspiration beading up on your forehead, then wipe those beads with your fingertips. For snow, imagine thin flakes trickling down on the crown of your head; scrunch your shoulders forward to minimize saturation. Notice different places where a weather condition touches your body. For example, rain hits the nape of the neck and gives you a chill between the shoulder blades. As you try to overcome the sensation, you (and the audience) will begin feeling the rain.

Remember to adapt to the weather slackening or intensifying, because weather may dull interest if it is too consistent. Work a scene first without weather conditions, then add a mounting or lingering rain, wind, fog, snow, throughout the scene. Fabricate weather early on in rehearsal by incorporating technical effects (lights darkening or brightening, candles glowing, etc.) to work against.

Is the day of the scene significant?

Besides using the season and weather, many playwrights set a scene on a particular day, such as Christmas, New Year's Eve, a birthday, wedding, or reunion. *Ah, Wilderness!*, whose beach scene we have been studying, takes place at the climax of summer, the Fourth of July.

Smart actors emphasize the theatrical significance of the day. They know that actions that characters might ordinarily stomach repel them on special occasions like Thanksgiving Day. If someone begins cursing at your Thanksgiving dinner, an expectation for people to act lovingly will probably increase your distress.

Ask yourself, "Is this the first day of the week, a weekday, or a weekend?" Sometimes the day itself promotes a crisis onstage. Note how upset the family members are because they can't figure out what day it is as they await the Nazis in their attic hideout in act 2, scene 4 of *The Diary of Anne Frank:*

Dussel: Something has happened, Mr. Frank. For three days now Miep hasn't been to see us! And today not a man has come to work. There hasn't been a sound in the building!

Mrs. Frank: Perhaps it's Sunday. We may have lost track of the days.

Mr. Van Daan: (*to* ANNE) You with the diary there. What day is it? (ANNE *closes the diary so he cannot read what she is writing.*)

Dussel: (*coming up to* MRS. FRANK) I don't lose track of the days. I know exactly what day it is! It's Friday, the fourth of August, Friday, and not a man at work! (*He rushes down to* MR. FRANK *again, pleading with him, almost in tears*) I tell you Mr. Kraler's dead. That's the only explanation. He's dead and they've closed down the building, and Miep's trying to tell us!

Mr. Frank: She'd never telephone us.

Dussel: (*frantic, indicating ringing telephone*) Mr. Frank, answer that! I beg you, answer it!

Should I keep a journal?

Keeping a journal can help stimulate your imagination. Studies have shown that 80 percent of what you learn each day you forget. Note how the time of day affects you in real life. Watch the changing of the seasons, the way people adjust to weather, to light, how time influences even the way people breathe. By recording these observations, you broaden the sources for expanding your imagination.

How do I rehearse time passing?

One of the quickest ways to establish time passing is through change: a switch in clothing, hairdo, or behavior. For example, in scene 1, it's Saturday morning at the dormitory. You, a freshman, have been sleeping in your jeans because you were up most of the night. You start picking up pretzel bags and Coke cans scattered around the room. In scene 2, it is two years later in the same dormitory. You are dressed in a blue pinstripe suit, eating sliced fruit, and scanning the *Wall Street Journal*. The changes in your clothing, hairdo, and behavior reveal that time has passed since your freshman days. Recent advances in computerized lighting and sound effects can clarify subtleties of time onstage. For example, with lights you can create a palpable difference between dawn and 11 A.M. Sometimes you can add these technical elements in rehearsal to heighten your concentration.

EXERCISES

1. *Listing Activities.* Write out activities appropriate to 2 A.M. for Jim or Mother in this sequence from act 3, scene 1 of Arthur Miller's *All My Sons*. Jim, a friend of the family, is warning Mother to stop waiting up for her son. Stage the sequence.

   Two o'clock the following morning, MOTHER *is discovered on the rise, rocking ceaselessly in a chair, staring at her thoughts. It is an intense, slight sort of rocking. A light shows from upstairs bedroom, lower floor windows being dark. The moon is strong and casts its bluish light.*

   Presently JIM, *dressed in jacket and hat, appears from the Left, and seeing her, goes up beside her.*

Jim: Any news?

Mother: No news.

Jim: (*gently*) You can't sit up all night, dear, why don't you go to bed?

Mother: I'm waiting for Chris. Don't worry about me, Jim, I'm perfectly *all* right.

Jim: But it's almost two o'clock.

Mother: I can't sleep. (*Slight pause*) You had an emergency?

Jim: (*tiredly*) Somebody had a headache and thought he was dying. (*Slight pause*) Half of my patients are quite mad. Nobody realizes how many people are walking around loose, and they're cracked as coconuts. Money. Money-money-money money. You say it long enough it doesn't mean anything. (*She smiles, makes a silent laugh*) Oh, how I'd love to be around when that happens!

Mother: (*shakes her head*) You're so childish, Jim! Sometimes you are.

Jim: (*looks at her a moment*) Kate. (*Pause*) What happened?

Mother: I told you. He had an argument with Joe. Then he got in the car and drove away.

Jim: What kind of an argument?

Mother: An argument, Joe . . . he was crying like a child, before.

Jim: They argued about Ann?

Mother: (*slight hesitation*) No, not Ann. Imagine? (*Indicates lighted window above*) She hasn't come out of that room since he left. All night in that room.

Note: The scene continues for several pages. For an extra incentive in class, try doing the *entire* scene.

2. *Passage of Time.* Stage a sequence involving your normal routine at a specific time. For example, you're returning home from work. Note your work dress. What routine items do you deal with—mail, the refrigerator, recorded phone messages?

Restage this sequence set two years later or at 4 A.M. Allow for change of hairdo, clothing, and behavior to reveal a different time.

3. *Social Context.* Biff and Happy Loman in Miller's *Death of a Salesman* are living in a society experiencing declining morality in post–World War II America. They are feeling mounting anxiety in personal issues, a queasy fear in relationships, a collapsing self-esteem, and the dissolution of family life. In class, discuss how the brothers are lost in their careers in the late 1940s and how their outlooks have changed from when they were boys.

4. *Clocking Time.* Observe how many rooms in your house have a clock or other timepiece. Jot down whenever you look at one over a twenty-four-hour period and why. Determine when you are most dependent on time.

What is urgency?

Go, sir, gallop, and don't forget that the world was made in six days. You can ask me for anything you like, except time.

Napoleon Bonaparte

Action onstage happens within a compact time frame. What your character is doing you must accomplish at this moment. Urgency heightens a scene's interest. The more important your action is to you, the more involved you will become in it. In fact, the audience's experience of time depends on your attitude toward your action. If you throw yourself wholeheartedly into what you are doing, time appears critical.

How do I rehearse for urgency?

Tardiness, hurrying, weather, time of day, holidays, work hours may all put pressure on your character. Are you so late that you must perform actions quickly? Do you need to concentrate to get this demanding action done? Does a holiday spirit fire you to try a difficult feat? Discover why you are under pressure each second.

Find your way of creating urgency from the outset. Imagine time pressuring the initial moments of each scene. For example, ask yourself in rehearsals, "Does my character want to be in this house? How long do I imagine this situation should last? Should I try to exit after entering or to leave early?"

To stimulate urgency, some actors imagine a time bomb concealed in their pockets, which will go off if they don't get what they want in a scene. Others stick to urgent tasks. A critical activity gives you some place to put your concentration, so if you don't buy what the other character is doing, you have the option of going back to your activity. Furthermore, your life can continue if that character never enters. Some actors like to rehearse using an urgent, independent activity from the outset of the scene. For example, you are writing a chapter that you have to finish in the next fifteen minutes. Your assistant is waiting to type it. She's going to lunch in a half-hour. But you have to deal with someone knocking at the door to ask something that has nothing to do with this.

Why is "time running out" important?

If you cannot determine the urgency of a scene, you can always add the element of time running out. For example, in *The Glass Menagerie*, Amanda corners her son for ten minutes before he goes to work at the warehouse. Their scene begins with the ringing of an alarm clock. Amanda insists that he continue his dead-end job in order to provide for his sister, Laura. Similarly, in Peter Shaffer's *Amadeus*, Salieri desperately pleads for help as the clock winds down.

SCENE 2
Salieri's Apartment
November 1823. The small hours

Salieri: (*a clock outside in the street strikes three*) I can almost see you
in your ranks—waiting for your turn to live. Ghosts of the Future!

Be visible. I beg you. Be visible. Come to this dusty old room—
this time, the smallest hours of dark November, eighteen hundred
and twenty-three—and be my confessors! Will you not enter
this place and stay with me till dawn? Just till dawn—merely
six o'clock!

(*he peers hard at the audience, trying to see it*)

Now, won't you appear? I need you—desperately! This is the last
hour of my life. Those about to die implore you! . . . What must
I do to make you visible? Raise you up in the flesh to be my last,
last audience?

To some degree, all characters struggle against time to get their
needs met. Even in comedies, characters confront pressing
situations. In the following sequence from James McLure's
Laundry and Bourbon, note how Hattie makes a futile effort
to control the chaos her children are causing at her mother's
house.

Hattie: Figure I better check on the kids. No telling what devilment they've
gotten up to. (*Dialing*) Everything gonna turn out fine you'll see.
(*On the phone*) Hello? Cheryl? Cheryl dear, this is Mommy . . .
Mommy . . . your mother. (*Aside*) Child needs a hearing aid.
What's that dear? Vernon Jr. threw a rock at you? Well, throw one
back at him, honey. Show him who's boss. Cheryl, Sweetheart, put
Grandma on the phone . . . Cheryl this week! (*Pause*) Sounds like
they're running her ragged. Hello? Little Roger. Is that you. I don't
want to talk to you right now punkin, I want to talk to Grandma . . .
'cause I want to talk to Grandma . . . yes Grandma does have
baggy elbows. Now lemme talk to her . . . what's that? Honey of
course Mommy loves you . . . I love you all the same. . . . Do I love
you more than who? Fred Flintstone. Yes. More than Paul New-
man no, but Fred Flintstone yes. . . . It's a grown-up joke, Honey.
Now put Grandma on. . . . She's what? Tied up! You untie her you
hear me? You want a switchin'?

Time is the thief you cannot banish.

Phyllis McGinley, "Ballad of Lost Objects"

■ THE PLACE

What is place?

Place is the specific location (building, neighborhood, state, country) of the action. What can be done to create an interesting place in a few months, weeks, even days of rehearsals? Begin by examining the play's set description. Some playwrights detail each item. If the playwright does not localize a scene, start posing questions. If you are playing a witch in *Macbeth*, ask: "What is the layout of this open heath in Scotland? Do thunder and lightning provoke me?" and so forth.

Stage truth happens on a ground plan that is an arranged reality. Visualize the colors, shapes, textures, and the arrangements suggested. Your stage designer may have made particular interpretations of the writer's suggestions. After you understand the setting, and the purpose of its angles and colors, you will automatically start to adapt to the place. If you establish a particular neighborhood, a specific room with doors in it, with ordinary exits, with characters coming and going, sitting at tables, peering out windows, that place will influence the way you interact.

How do I build on the floor plan?

Take time to create a well-laid-out space for a scene. Walk around the floor, adjusting movements, testing doors, lounging in furniture. To fill in a ground plan, look for what you are doing onstage besides talking. Stop, fantasize, build the space surrounding the action. Even when the space inhibits you, it provides expressive possibilities. You need to choose actions to overcome it. For example, the chilly beach at night—pebbles, brush, light beams—could hinder Muriel's dash down the shadowy path to meet Richard in act 4, scene 2 of *Ah, Wilderness!* If Richard is killing time, strolling, daydreaming, what objects might distract him—an old bottle, a wrecked boat hull, a cold puddle?

(RICHARD *starts to stroll around with exaggerated carelessness, turning his* *back on the path, hands in pockets, whistling with insouciance "Waiting at* *the Church."*)

(MURIEL MCCOMBER *enters from down the path, left front. She is fifteen,* *going on sixteen. She is a pretty girl with a plump, graceful little figure, fluffy,* *light brown hair, big naive wondering dark eyes, a round dimpled face,* *a melting drawly voice. Just now she is in a great thrilled state of timid ad-* *venturousness. She hesitates in the shadow at the foot of the path, wait-* *ing for* RICHARD *to see her; but he resolutely goes on whistling with back* *turned, and she has to call him.*)

A theatrical place furthers the conflict. Think of how theatri-cal the following situations might be: (1) to escape from a com-bat zone; (2) to sleep in a sewer; (3) to exercise in a china shop; (4) to laugh in a morgue; (5) to blow up a museum.

CLASS GAMES

1. *A Childhood Room.* Visit a room from your childhood and encounter, through each sense, its uniqueness. Record your impressions. In class, map out the room. Use chairs, tables, and other items available in the acting area. Visualize furni-ture, objects, and their location for the audience. See if you begin to remember how you felt in that room at that time.

2. *Diagramming the Place.* In a group of two to four, develop your own romantic beach. Link the make-believe shoreline, sea, and path to landmarks onstage: crevices in the floor, objects, curtains, lights. With the other actor in the scene, diagram the stage floor for an outdoors scene at a beach. Ask, "Where does the coastline run across the set? Do any trees create a pathway? From which direction does the tide gush in? Does it churn up the waves and sand or spray foam? Is a moon or sun beaming down?" Explore the entire ground plan for rehearsal objects such as items in a skiff, un-der a sand pile, behind driftwood. Even on an empty beach something—a perfumed letter, some rotting fish, the springy

sand, your busted hat, a ripped towel, a dirty bucket, a cracked bottle—could forward your action.

■ OBJECTS

How do I find privacy onstage?

Acting with privacy means acting as if no one is watching you. When you are truly private onstage, you are relaxed and totally comfortable. You act as if no one is observing you, much as you do when you are alone, at home. In most scenes, you must discover what you do when you feel completely relaxed, comfortable, and unobserved. You find this privacy through associating the place with your own activities and things. Most important is your relationship to the objects around you onstage.

Learning how to use objects helps actors experience life on the stage, which is different from but analogous to real life. Dealing concretely with objects gives you a real sense of belief in the stage place. For example, an actress hung a portrait of her real-life father on the set when she played a father-dominated alcoholic.

Fabricate a believable environment for yourself through association with your personal objects. Imagine decorating your character's childhood room. Use objects from your own life: your books, sapphire marbles, rock albums. When you replace these for the final production, you will have experienced an investment in personal objects. Ask yourself, "What toys did I fight over? A shiny piggy bank, a one-eyed teddy bear? What childhood treasures, like racing car stickers, Christmas photos, college pennants, might kindle memories of my mother, father, and friends?"

Continue your exploration at rehearsal by roaming around the room. Claim your bed, your books. Suggest connections by asking, "What objects did I leave in my old room?" or "What room have I felt touched by in a movie or book that resembles this place?" or "What mementos do I long to take away with me?" Transforming the set into a place that you inhabit encourages interesting actions. Imagine activities you could engage in, such as "checking out the old room" or "getting ready for bed."

How should I endow props?

"To endow" means to deal with a false object as if it possesses real qualities. Imagine handling a ragged rug like a plush oriental, a bottle of water like an exotic perfume, an empty teakettle like a boiling one, a scrap of paper like an ardent love letter. Endowment is critical for hazardous objects onstage such as a razor blade, knife, and gun.

To endow false props with qualities they don't possess, use sense memory to recall the qualities of real things you own. Sense memory means remembering the physical sensation of objects. You can practice with your own real objects that have certain sensual qualities of touch, taste, smell, sight, sound. Then you act as if the stage prop has the same qualities by adjusting the way you handle it.

How do I practice physical endowment?

Practice endowing objects at home and in rehearsals. When you smell the salt breeze, your nose contracts in a certain way. Capturing that one adjustment can stimulate a whole series of unconscious thoughts and feelings. Note how one actor has jotted down certain physical sensations connected with the lines of the beach scene from *Ah, Wilderness!*

LINES	SENSE MEMORY (sight, hearing, touch, smell, taste)
RICHARD (*Thinking aloud*): Must be nearly nine.	What do I see to make me think it's nearly nine? Do I see my watch, the clock, feel the wind getting cooler?

I can hear the Town Hall clock strike,

it's so still tonight.

Gee, I'll bet Ma had a fit when she found out I'd sneaked out.

I'll catch hell when I get back, but it'll be worth it. . . . if only Muriel turns up . . . She didn't say for certain she could . . . gosh, I wish she'd come!. . .

Am I sure she wrote nine? . . .

(*He puts the straw hat on the seat amidships and pulls the folded letter out of his pocket and peers at it in the moonlight*)

Yes, it's nine, all right.
(*He starts to put the note back in his pocket, then stops and kisses it—then shoves it away hastily, sheepish, looking around him shame-facedly, as if afraid he were being observed*)

Does the clock chime, gong, how far away is it? Am I counting chimes?

What do I hear? A distant ship. Feel? No wind on my cheek.

Do I hear Mother calling "Richard"? See her checking my bed covers?

Do I feel Dad's belt strap? Taste having no dinner for two days? Should I grab the letter again? Should I hear her voice, feel the touch of her cheek?

Grab the letter.

What does the straw hat I bought to make an impression feel like after two hours on the beach? Damp, sandy? Do I rip at the straw?

What does the crinkled letter smell like? Rose perfume? Do I reread it? How does it taste when I kiss it? Salty, musty from my pocket? Do I fondle it?

To improve his sense memory, this actor rehearsed the activities outdoors at night on an abandoned skiff. He also got ideas from observing pictures and films of lovers on the beach at night.

Why do all objects need an emotional life?

Some objects won't need physical endowment (for example, you may deal with a letter as a letter), but all objects need psychological endowment. Recall the way you handled a cherished teacup, your fashionable senior ring, or the bear-claw patchwork quilt Grandma sewed. If you spent your last twenty-five dollars on a bright blue picture book and then dropped it in the gutter, you would salvage it with gusto.

In one performance, when the maid said, "Oh, you dropped your book, Sir," the actor lost at least three moments because he just picked it up. Had he fully endowed this book, he might have played a moment where he dusted it off, checked it out, retrieved his place. You may think, "Maybe he didn't need those moments," but his cursory treatment of the book and other objects ultimately resulted in an unconvincing performance.

What is a fourth wall?

Most sets provide you with three walls. To complete your world you will need to imagine objects on a fourth wall behind the audience. Concoct a fourth wall containing points to focus on when you look out toward the audience. Facing forward is the most powerful position for the actor, but controlling concentration from this vantage point is the most difficult.

To control your focus, create the fourth wall as a part of the script's particular location. Identify on a fourth wall behind or between audience members five to seven places that you can spot from where you are positioned onstage. For instance, in a blackened auditorium, you may still spy (without seeing audience members) a red exit sign, a lighted aisle, a lacquered doorway.

If you are sharing the scene with other actors, determine your fourth wall together. Lay out together the same imaginary objects at certain spots on the fourth wall—a blue sailboat, a treacherous wharf, a leaning post. Take as much time to assign fictional objects to these spots as you would to arrange real stage furniture.

When working in an outdoors scene or on an arena stage, you must often create four walls surrounding you with objects of primary importance such as a little village with a few white steeples way down at the bottom of the hill, or crashing surf on the reef next to you. Explore your emotional relationship to these objects and to their distance from you.

What are a primary and a secondary fourth wall?

Using a primary fourth wall means dealing directly with something on that wall. For instance, you might point out something there, such as the moon. Pick a spot in the auditorium to look at; then adjust your body—especially head and shoulders—to the correct tilt they would have if the spot were miles away, like the moon. Using a secondary fourth wall means dealing indirectly with the wall behind the audience. You rely on the wall as a backdrop. If you're looking in a mirror five inches away, you might focus on the exit sign and adjust your body accordingly. For example, as you read this, you are trusting a secondary fourth wall. Now look up and imagine talking to a friend. You will look at that person, but your eyes will also take in the fourth wall backdrop behind her. When you sit in the yard, you spontaneously include the fourth-wall view. You are not focusing on the fourth wall but are including its presence behind whatever you see. Trusting in your fourth wall helps you relax and perform freely, that is, act with privacy onstage.

EXERCISES

1. *Physical Endowment.* Stage a scene in which you use three of the following objects. Endow each object with strong physical qualities, such as a *boiling* teakettle, *dripping* ice cream, *bitter* cough syrup:

shoe polish	mascara
teakettle	cough syrup
ice cubes	nail polish
razor	ice cream
gun	

2. *Psycho-Physical Endowment.* Restage the preceding exercise by endowing the same objects with psychological traits, such as a *magical* teakettle, *forbidden* ice cream, or *poisonous* cough syrup.

3. *Primary Fourth Wall.* Stage a monologue or scene in which you use the fourth wall in a primary way.

4. *Secondary Fourth Wall.* Stage a phone conversation in which you use the fourth wall in a secondary way. When you talk on the phone, allow yourself to automatically gaze at different spots on the fourth wall as you focus on the listener.

5. *Re-Create a Telephone Conversation.* Relate to the subject matter or content, not to the sound of the person's voice.

■ ATMOSPHERE

What is atmosphere?

After you have determined the floor and the walls of your scene, imagine what its atmosphere might be. "Atmosphere is the emotional sphere enveloping the space," wrote Michael Chekhov, Russian actor and disciple of Stanislavski, in *The Actor's Eye*.

Chekhov said that when you enter a place, certain elements around you — sounds, smells, sights, temperature conditions — stimulate your thoughts and feelings, and you react in a certain way. The atmosphere of the place excites your personal reaction. A vast cathedral with a grave atmosphere evokes pity from some but silence from others.

How people react to the same atmosphere may differ dramatically. Observe how the atmosphere around you right now evokes certain body sensations, thoughts, or feelings influencing your actions.

In real life, we are unconsciously affected by the rattling of the wind, the groaning of the sea, the tolling of chimes, the cawing of a lonely bird. We notice the bug on our sock, the rusted fishing pole, the seashell on the ground. A film actor, through the magic of a sound track or special effects, is sometimes able to hear the rustle of leaves, to battle real drafts piercing through a flimsy shack, or to feel rain dripping down from the skies. Onstage, you must use sense memory to fashion your own reactions to the elements of nature.

Besides physical elements, atmosphere embraces the emotional conditions attached to a place. You *can* sense the tranquility, sadness, emptiness in a room. When you enter a gloomy scene, you can feel the sorrow in the air. You often work against the atmosphere. When you see someone crying, you say, "Don't cry! Things will get better!"

How can I create atmosphere?

Creating atmosphere involves both experiencing something in the air and adjusting to that sensation. We do this automatically in life, so it will be easy to do onstage after you become aware of atmosphere's importance. First, get into the habit of noticing atmosphere. When you enter rooms, streets, buildings, conscientiously observe their atmosphere so you will notice dynamic ones. Next, study the creation of other atmospheres in art: in films, pictures, and books.

Stanislavski said that when standing before a painting, you should squeeze yourself into the frame of the painting in thought, try to enter into it, so as to become infected with its mood and become physically accustomed to it, not from without, but from within. When creating atmosphere for a particular scene, reread the script and imagine yourself inside its world, in that flea-bitten basement or marble palace. Use Stanislavski's "Magic If" phrase to grapple with those objects and people and unlock your particular responses. In rehearsal, experiment with moving in harmony with a particular atmosphere. For example, imagine a sadness in the air; observe what sensations and feelings arise. Or imagine the air permeated with smoke. How do you react to that? Because it's easier to envision the room loaded with smoke than with sorrow, next conceive sorrow as a real weight in the air that you work against.

CLASS GAMES

1. *Harmonious Atmosphere.* Move in harmony with the following atmospheres:

   fresh aroma of a florist shop

   uplifting air of a cathedral

   serious mood of a library

   cold air of a tomb

2. *Sorrowful Atmosphere.* Conceive sorrow as a weight in the air that you work against.

3. *Sweet Atmosphere.* Imagine yourself in the mountains of North Carolina in June. Breathe the crisp air, smell the sweet woods, sense the bright sky, feel the refreshing greenery.

4. *Your Present Atmosphere.* Close your eyes and allow yourself to experience the atmosphere around you right now. Then open your eyes and move harmoniously within it.

5. In groups of two or more, identify the visual and aural atmospheres called for in the following scenes. Improvise/perform your scene for the class.

Tennessee Williams, The Glass Menagerie, *Scene 4*

The interior is dark. Fading light in the alley. A deep-voiced bell in a church is tolling the hour of five as the scene commences.

   Tom appears at the top of the alley. After each solemn boom of the bell in the tower, he shakes a little noise-maker or rattle as if to express the tiny spasm of man in contrast to the sustained power and dignity of the Almighty. This and the unsteadiness of his advance make it evident that he has been drinking.

   As he climbs the few steps to the fire-escape landing, light steals up inside. LAURA appears in the night dress, observing TOM'S empty bed in the front room. Tom fishes in his pockets for door-key, removing a motley assortment of articles in the search, including a perfect shower of movie-ticket stubs and an empty bottle. At last he finds the key, but just as he is about to insert it, it slips from his fingers. He strikes a match and couches below the door.

Ketti Frings, Look Homeward, Angel, *Act 1, Scene 2*

The Dixieland Boarding House. The night is sensuous, warm. A light storm is threatening. Long, swaying tree shadows project themselves on the house. (Seated on the side veranda are JAKE, MRS. CLATT, FLORRY, MISS BROWN, and MRS. SNOWDEN. MRS. PERT is seated in her rocker, BEN on the steps beside her. They are drinking beer. MRS. PERT measures the socks she is knitting against Ben's shoe. JAKE CLATT softly plays the ukulele and sings. EUGENE is sitting on the side door steps, lonely, yearning.

JAKE (Singing) "K-k-katy, K-k-katy! Etc. (as JAKE finishes. FLORRY gently applauds. Jake starts softly strumming something else.)

Henrik Ibsen, Hedda Gabler, *Act 4*

The same room at the Tesmans. It is evening. The drawing-room is in darkness. The back room is lighted by the hanging lamp over the table. The curtains over the glass door are drawn closed (HEDDA dressed in black, walks to and fro in the dark room. Then she goes into the backroom and disappears for a moment to the left. She is heard to strike a few chords in the piano. Presently she comes in sight again, and returns to the drawing room. BERTA enters from the right, through the inner room, with a lighted lamp, which she places on the table in front of the corner settee in the drawing-room. Her eyes are red with weeping, and she has black ribbons in her cap. She goes up to the glass door, lifts the curtain a little aside, and looks out into the darkness. Shortly afterwards, MISS TESMAN, in mourning, with a bonnet and veil on, comes in from the hall. HEDDA goes toward her and holds out her hand.)

How do selected details create the space?

Developing your place is like redoing a room. You begin with the floors (ground plan), the walls (the fourth wall), objects (endowment). Then you move into more intangible areas—the atmosphere (feeling of a place). Add new elements after you have mastered old ones. An exciting place evolves from an infusion of details.

■ CHECKLIST

This checklist should help you explore exciting details in your place. Answering these few basic questions should encourage a vigorous response to the setting.

1. What is my emotional response to this setting?
2. What is the weather like?
3. What experiences have I had here or in a setting like this?
4. What am I dressed for? Why?
5. What must I do in this setting?

■ FINAL PROJECTS

A friendly reminder: There is no right or wrong way to do any of these exercises. Their purpose is to help you discover the influence of the setting. Let your teacher guide you in the ways most beneficial to you.

1. *Progressive Exercise.* EXERCISE 7: A empty church or temple. Use the same partner from the previous progressive exercises. Two more years have dramatically changed your relationship. Reveal time's passage for this scene through changes in clothing, hairdo, behavior, profession, or health. It is now four years since you initially met in Progressive Exercise 1. Establish the weather conditions, the events of the day, the outdoor neighborhood, and the world inside the train. Plan where you will place furniture and objects for certain activities.

   Now each of you should play conflicting objectives and action. For example, one of you is studying, and the other is doing vocal exercises.

Begin the sequence with each of you performing a task in silence; then one of you begins a conflict.

2. *Privacy.* Re-create one action in a place where you feel at ease, totally unobserved. Use objects to experience the stage as a "real" setting. For example, you might make a salad in your kitchen at noon or get dressed in your bedroom at dawn. Your mounting involvement in the action should lessen your sense of being watched, so you act as if you are in private.

3. *Childhood Setting.* Create atmosphere for a scene. Re-create objects from a similar room from your past, for example, the red plaid bed covers, scratched maple desk, yellowed university catalogues from a childhood room.

   Stage a conflict with two characters. Examine what you might have done together in the past. Establish objects—phone, schoolbooks, and so on—that will help you create an old routine together. Now perform a new routine in which your actions conflict.

   Optional: Put a clock in your pocket and set the alarm for one minute before you expect the sequence to end. Pretend the clock is a bomb that will explode if you don't get what you want *right now.*

4. *Atmosphere.* Incorporate a tense atmosphere into a scene set in a bedroom. Close your eyes and remember a time when you were surrounded by an anxious atmosphere. You and your partner had repressed your feelings, and a hostility existed between the two of you. Relax your eye muscles behind your lids and imagine what you did at that time. Imagine in detail all the physical elements of that place from your own life, similar to the setting in a play. In rehearsal, demonstrate these special elements to your partner and collaboratively re-create a sense of atmosphere. Hand in a description of the place: ground plan and atmosphere. Stage the scene.

8

GIVEN CIRCUMSTANCES
What is my life situation?

This chapter evaluates how previous, present, and future events and conditions affect your character's actions.

Life cannot wait until the sciences may have explained the universe scientifically. We cannot put off living until we are ready. The most salient characteristic of life is its coerciveness: it is always urgent, "here and now," without any possible postponement. Life is fired at us point blank.

Jose Ortega y Gasset

■ WHAT ARE GIVEN CIRCUMSTANCES?

This expression means . . . the story of the play, the facts, events, epoch, time and place of action, conditions of life, the actors' and director's interpretation, the mise-en-scene, the production, the sets, the costumes, properties, lighting and sound effects— all the circumstances that are given to an actor to take into account as he creates his role. (*Stanislavski Handbook*, p. 67)

Your circumstances—previous, present, and future situations—control much of what you do. For example, your character, Pete, enters the stage. He is coming home from work after a fourteen-hour shift at the railroad. He is expecting to be embraced by his mother and sister. His mother has promised to cook him a marvelous roast, like she did for his birthday, and his sister should be practicing his favorite tune on the piano.

These circumstances affect how you, as Pete, greet your mother (your first action upon entering).

Given circumstances are the physical, emotional, and social conditions spelled out by the playwright. You must connect with them emotionally and fill in the blanks in those circumstances that are implied. You must also find a framework of associations from your life to activate you onstage. After you begin anchoring your lines with these associations, you will find yourself having more commitment to even the smallest actions.

Circumstances can influence your conflicts, fuel your motivation, and shape your action. Our circumstances can never be studied enough.

How do I find my circumstances?

Picture an actor living in the year 2091 portraying you. What vital circumstances would she have to unjumble about you to interpret your actions? You would expect the actor to spend time observing your best photographs, studying your relationships at work, empathizing with the tensions, concerns, and issues permeating your home, understanding your circle of friends.

Similarly for any character you play you must search for clues. You can sensitize yourself to circumstances by looking at other plays. Similar tensions unite the works of many playwrights. Witness the strain between father and son in many of Arthur Miller's plays.

Study related works—recordings, films, books. If, for example, you are impersonating Lorraine Hansberry (the first black woman playwright to be produced on Broadway), listen to her taped interviews. If you are playing the voluptuous Marilyn Monroe type in Arthur Miller's *After the Fall*, investigate the many films of Monroe (Miller's ex-wife), the cult books on her, and the photographs. In the play itself, you must comb stage directions about time and place as well as dialogue and what's hidden under the words. You have to understand not only what happens in the play but also the circumstances under which it happens.

How do I evaluate the play for given circumstances?

Begin by examining the plot. Each play has its skeleton of events. Answer the question "Without what occurrences would there be no play?" Reread the play to experience the progression of circumstances. Jot down flashes of similar experiences from your life. A plot summary of *The Glass Menagerie* by Tennessee Williams reveals the key circumstances.

> Tom Wingfield, alternating in the roles of narrator and participant of the "memory play," evokes the home in St. Louis which he left years ago: the drab reality of the little flat in a dark alley; his monotonous job in a warehouse from which he escapes by writing poetry; his mother, a former Southern belle who tried to govern her two grown children by the constantly recalled standards of her girlhood; his sister Laura, a shy, slightly crippled girl who found refuge in the imaginary kingdom of her glass animal collection; and Jim, a friend from the warehouse whom Mother, determined to find a "gentleman caller" for her daughter, had forced Tom to invite, and who for a moment falls under the spell of Laura's dream world. Tom, too, flees from his mother and sister, but he cannot banish the thought of their fragile, helpless existence. The play has the delicate twilight atmosphere of time remembered, "truth in the pleasant disguise of an illusion." (from Van Cartmell, *Plot Summaries to 100 Plays*)

Substituting and particularizing circumstances are a key part of your work. You look at plot for the circumstances that change during each scene for the progression of circumstances and changes between scenery and acts. What are circumstances around your life at home, at work, on vacation, in love?

How do other characters' circumstances affect me?

You will learn much about your character's situation from observing the circumstances of the other characters. At a quiet time, jot down impressions of their predicaments from your character's perspective. Imagine playing Tom in *The Glass Menagerie*, set in the 1930s. Note how the same circumstances influence you and your mother, Amanda, differently.

For example, she cheers and you regret having the Gentleman Caller to dinner.

THE GLASS MENAGERIE: CIRCUMSTANCES

CHARACTER	CRITICAL CIRCUMSTANCES
Father: (*absent*)	Charming ways, his records, postcards, picture, his love for long distance, and abandonment of the family
Jim: (*Gentleman Caller*)	Charming ways, his go-getter attitude, his money ethic, his love for dancing, his interest in sports, his "secret" engagement, his success at the warehouse, his concern about the future, his obsession with television, his scholarship, his failures after high school
Tom:	Thirst for adventure, the boredom in St. Louis, the tiny apartment without privacy, his cot in the living room, his obsession with writing, his disgust with the shoe warehouse, his drinking and movie watching, his attraction to the Merchant Marine, his function as the provider for the family
Amanda:	Her enormous girlhood popularity and social standing, her exaggerated storytelling, glamorizing past boyfriends, her money-success ethic, the limited opportunities for women in 1939, her total dependence on Tom, her previous attempts to get Laura a boyfriend, her fun at church socials and with her friends, her love for both children as her *whole* life, her abandonment by men
Laura:	Her peculiarities: her limp, her shyness, her withdrawal with glass toys, her love for Tom and her mother, her worship of Jim, her failure at high school and business school, her lying to her mother about typing, her visits to the penguins, her obsession with the Victrola and her father's old records

■ THE SCENE BREAKDOWN

What is a scene breakdown?

Fire up your imagination by doing a scene breakdown for circumstances, evaluating the play scene by scene for key conditions. Sometimes actors will note who's in the scene, the number of pages, location, key event. If the play is not broken down by the playwright into scenes, your director may do this and explain how she views the sequence of key scenes. Note how provocatively one actor has assessed circumstances by scene for *The Glass Menagerie*.

THE GLASS MENAGERIE: SCENE BREAKDOWN

This dream play flashes onto the stage a memory: Tom's recurring nightmare about saving his sister Laura from a complete breakdown. Each scene reveals Laura's inability to cope: make a living, marry, adapt in the real world. Each character tries to save Laura, but then physically or emotionally abandons her.

Scene Tag (Key Action, Emotional Experience)	Setting (Spot Creating Circumstance)	Characters (Others Experiencing Problems)
1. Saving the old maid (tragic and comic)	Fire escape landing Alley apartment interior	Tom, Amanda, Laura

A winter's evening in an alley apartment in St. Louis, where Amanda is urgently trying to teach her grown children manners, style, and the right attitude for a winning marriage. Amanda pretends that a caller could come any minute in the hopes of encouraging some responsiveness from Laura and Tom. Amanda acts as if she is still a belle on a plantation. Laura exposes her dread of being abandoned as an old maid, a state akin to starving in 1939.

2. Using the keyboard	Interior	Amanda, Laura (tragic)

Another freezing twilight. Laura pretends to practice typing, but Amanda, returning home from the business college, and not the D.A.R., reprimands Laura for never having attended her typing classes. Laura has been visiting penguins and tropical flowers in glass houses at the zoo. Laura reveals a secret high school crush, and Amanda, realizing a business career for Laura is impossible, desperately encourages her to cultivate charm to offset her crippled condition and attract a husband.

3. Attacking Tom Fire escape Tom, Amanda, Laura
(tragic and comic) Interior

An evening in late winter. Getting a gentleman caller has become an obsession for Amanda. Turning into a nagging witch, she attacks Tom for his moping, doping, and coming in late each night. Hurling his coat at her, he jars the glass menagerie where Laura, terrified, is observing them, then he flees.

4. Escaping the coffin Fire escape Tom, Laura
(tragic and comic) Interior

The next morning, 5 A.M. booms from a bell in a nearby church tower. Laura greets the drunken Tom and quiets him to bed. Laura experiences his desperation as Tom compares his plight as provider for her and Amanda to being alive in a nailed-up coffin.

(Three more scenes complete the play.)

How does a scene breakdown reveal circumstances?

A scene breakdown usually includes a scene tag, the setting, and the characters. A scene tag underscores the key action and serves as a reminder of where you will be focusing attention. For example, if the key action in scene 1, "Saving the Old Maid," is "warning Laura about old maidship," then you'll probably ask yourself, "Why was spinsterhood dreaded? What did it mean to be an unmarried woman in the 1930s? How would she survive? What would she do?"

The setting and characters of the scene signal your circumstances. Scene 1, "Saving the Old Maid," takes place on the fire escape and interior as Tom vacillates between abandoning his sister and remaining trapped in a two-room apartment. If you are playing Tom, you might speculate, "How can I escape being trapped in an impossible situation at home? Have I ever lived in close quarters for any length of time? How did it make me feel?"

In scene 1, Amanda is concerned about Laura's spinster status. Why? Do you have someone in your family whom your mother is concerned about? What doom do you fear for this person? How do other relatives' outlooks about this person differ from yours? What tensions could develop because of different sensitivities over the same situation?

How can a scene breakdown help my acting?

An actor usually knows from the outset whether the play is a comedy or tragedy, but a study of the scene breakdown will clarify *how* it is comic or tragic. The circumstances in a comedy cause frustration and in a drama, sorrow. For example, if you couldn't get your sister to stop daydreaming, you might feel frustrated. If you couldn't save your sister from a mental collapse, you would feel devastated. The seriousness of the circumstances differs, but the frustrated character is as determined as the dramatic one about achieving his goals.

Although drama usually has a sad ending and comedy a happy one, many plays (even Shakespearean tragedies) contain funny as well as sad scenes. Depending on which circumstances you choose to support the scene, you will lean toward a comedic or a dramatic interpretation.

A scene breakdown can help your acting in smaller, more specific ways by illuminating details of your situation, which enrich your interpretation of each small piece of the scene.

How can I feel the part?

Now that you understand the given circumstances of the play, you will need to experience them. Begin by looking up key words in reference books. By opening up windows into the words, you prick your curiosity about what you want to do with them. An intriguing definition, an imperceptible shade of meaning, can reveal your character's thoughts.

For example, if you are playing a hysterical alcoholic, you could begin with the obvious dictionary definition of "alcoholic": "suffering from a diseased condition due to the excessive use of alcoholic beverages." You might then pursue a richer encyclopedia description. Books on human behavior can yield information about addiction. You piece together your character's alcoholism from a variety of sources: dictionaries, psychology books, medical books, and reference books.

What is the "Magic If"?

Imagination! Imagination! I put it first years ago, when I was asked what qualities I thought necessary for success upon the stage. Imagination, industry, and intelligence—the three I's— all indispensable to the actor, but of these three, the greatest is, without any doubt, imagination.

Ellen Terry, British actress, *The Story of My Life*, 1908

The "Magic If" is a method for surrendering yourself to the character's circumstances. Stanislavski said that you must imagine yourself as the character by using "if." If you were in the character's situation, and if you had the same needs and values, and if you made the same choices, you would become the person. Each of us has a vast subjective potential to be a nun, a murderer, a thief. To embrace these circumstances, use the "Magic If" as the starting point.

To use Stanislavski's "Magic If," say to yourself, "If I were the character in these circumstances, what would I do?" Using the "Magic If" helps actors step into the world of memory. You remember various experiences and imagine certain conditions, then you mentally put yourself there. For example, you picture a train wreck you saw in life or in a film, then you imagine yourself there. You sense how you might feel and act in that situation. You leap into the scene emotionally, through this mental connection of "what if."

Next, you picture yourself as the *character* in the circumstances. You imagine, "What if I were in a train wreck and I were an IBM executive, not myself, then what would I do?" You picture the lifestyle of that executive, and you fantasize how her actions might differ from yours in the scene. Use the "Magic If" to expand your expressiveness as the character. When you mentally see yourself as the character in the circumstances, you discover exciting possibilities to experiment with. Appropriate action leaps to mind.

What is subtext?

Subtext is hidden information you use below the line to strengthen meaning. As you work on each scene, you'll find places where you'll need to fill in the blanks with specific associations. If you're playing Blanche in *A Streetcar Named Desire*, you will have to contact Blanche's feelings about teaching school. Determine when she taught, say, 8 A.M. to 3 P.M. (six sections of honors English)—and the hourly routine. Was she respected by her colleagues, admired by her students?

Because most characters are jolted awake by extreme circumstances, find those moments of trauma. Trauma—an injury, wound, mental shock—creates a violent collision in the mind. Observe the confrontation here, the juicy word there, and the deathlike pause somewhere else. Fill in these spaces with vivid subtext. Note the sore spots italicized in Blanche's opening scene in *Streetcar*.

A STREETCAR NAMED DESIRE: BLANCHE'S SUBTEXT

Eunice: I think she said *you taught school* [Trauma—I lost my job]

Blanche: Yes.

Eunice: And *you're from Mississippi,* huh? [Trauma—I got kicked out of there]

Blanche: Yes.

Eunice: She showed me a picture of your home-place, *the plantation.* [Trauma—I lost it]

Blanche: Belle Reve?

Eunice:	*A great big place with white columns.*
Blanche:	Yes . . .
Eunice:	A place like that must be *awful hard to keep up.* [Trauma—It's being demolished]
Blanche:	If you will excuse me, I'm just *about to drop.*

Any confrontation requires more unspoken information, or subtext, than dialogue. Words are like a veil. What lurks behind them out of sight, concealed, repressed, tinges the veil with significance. That mass of hidden experiences creates meaning onstage.

For example, you will have to evoke a stream of crises to activate Blanche's lines. Her bankruptcy, degeneracy, and her dependence on her only sister all pressurize her present action "to find a haven at her brother-in-law's cramped apartment."

Erotic memories, premonitions, fantasies flash beneath different lines. Expand on her impressions and phobias to support your stage action.

CLASS GAMES

1. *Fairy tale.* In groups of two to six, improvise a fairy tale situation. Stage the sequence first realistically, then in an exaggerated way, as if in a nightmare. Have other class members guess the circumstances.

2. *Current Circumstances.* In pairs, tell each other your worst current circumstances, for example, if you're broke, your mother is ill, you have just gotten divorced, or you have just been robbed. Note what associations pop into your head as you speak and listen.

3. *Physicalizing Circumstances.* Communicate one of the following circumstances through what you do physically. Your suitcases are heavy. You are tired, your clothes are dirty. You are freezing; your hair is falling out. You are broke. Discuss some of the most interesting behavior choices.

4. *Worst Circumstances.* Describe to another the worst circumstances you have experienced. Remember how they made you feel, for example, terrified in a bank holdup, cautious in a job interview, cowardly at a traffic accident.

What is "living the role"?

"Living the role" means providing yourself with a direct experience of the character's circumstances. Some actors go a great distance to do this. For example, if your character was raised on a plantation, you might spend a day at a plantation, read about leisure class life, see southern films. You could prime yourself to experience the thoughts, sentiments, and sensations of life there. Gradually, you will begin acquiring a sensitivity, a cognizance. Meryl Streep is reported to live the circumstances of the character outside rehearsals—reading, eating, doing only things her character would do.

More often, actors find indirect experiences to correspond with their characters' circumstances. They weave their own memories and fantasies into their characters' thoughts. Compelling actors associate every person, place, and thing their characters talk about with a personal experience.

What are previous circumstances?

Previous circumstances are anything that has happened recently to your character that affects you right now onstage. Jim, the Gentleman Caller in *The Glass Menagerie*, is lonely for his fiancée, so he flirts with Laura. Previous circumstances predispose you to pursue the character's action.

If you are playing Jim, find the circumstances that make you lead Laura on. Ask yourself, "In my life, what person so worshipped me that I encouraged her?" Did you approach her with disdain, with relish, with tension? What were the circumstances? She lived next door, was friendly with your younger sister, used to watch you play baseball, grinned at you. Contact your own past so that Jim's past affects your present actions.

Experiencing previous circumstances can help you expand the expressiveness of your initial actions. Practice what happened before your character enters. For example, if you have been traveling all night from one grimy bus station to the next, your legs will feel cramped as you enter. Experiment with the slowness of your gait. How might your shoulders slump from hauling heavy luggage? Try dragging luggage onstage. Work on the previous circumstances for the first moment. If you are specific and believable, you are laying the groundwork for the truth of the scene to evolve naturally.

What are present circumstances?

Present circumstances are conditions hitting you as you enter the stage. Look for physically expressive choices that can be read by the audience. For example, if your character has been stuck with a busload of complaining women in 100-degree Mexico, you might drag yourself into the hotel, you might wipe your brow as you say hello to the hotel manager. Or you might gulp down some water, unbutton your shirt, remove your hat, and dry the inner hatband. You do specific things to make that heat real for yourself. If you can capture the truth of one circumstance—you really feel hot (and adjust to that heat) as you enter—that will stimulate truth in other parts of the scene.

Consider during the rehearsal process what you can convey to the audience. To give your character dramatic bite, rehearse active information, such as your back hurts, your feet are sweating, you are fighting a stuffy nose. Test a range of choices to find the most active. Sometimes after performing a rather flat scene, an actor might say, "If you only knew the story I made up—" and I'll respond, "Look, if it doesn't come across in your actions, you won't get the chance to explain." When acting goes well, you affect the audience with the same emotions that you are undergoing. Physical choices clarify what you are experiencing and immediately trigger audience response.

What are future circumstances?

Onstage, there are two types of future circumstances: the real (what actually will occur) and the expected (what the characters imagine). Expectation—the fiction that your character imagines—is what you play. You long for the opposite of what appears. Interweave expectations, the mental pictures, thoughts, and conditions you want with your character's actions.

For each scene, ask yourself, "What positive future might I imagine?" Expectations are vital to a riveting performance. Each moment you are actually working for something you don't get. Train your imagination to expect the improbable! When you are constantly surprised by what occurs, your expectations are working.

EXERCISES

1. *Investigating Circumstances.* Underline all circumstances you would need to experience if playing a character in one of the following scenes.

   Oscar Wilde, *The Importance of Being Earnest,* Act 1

   (LADY BRACKNELL *and* ALGERNON *go into the music room;* GWENDOLEN *remains behind*)

Jack:	Charming day it has been, Miss Fairfax.
Gwendolen:	Pray don't talk to me about the weather, Mr. Worthing. Whenever people talk to me about the weather, I always feel quite certain that they mean something else. And that makes me so nervous.
Jack:	I do mean something else.
Gwendolen:	I thought so. In fact, I am never wrong.
Jack:	And I would like to be allowed to take advantage of Lady Bracknell's temporary absence . . .

Gwendolen:	I would certainly advise you to do so. Mamma has a way of coming back suddenly into a room that I have often had to speak to her about.
Jack:	(*nervously*) Miss Fairfax, ever since I met you I have admired you more than any girl . . . I have ever met since . . . I met you.
Gwendolen:	Yes, I am quite aware of that fact. And I often wish that in public, at any rate, you had been more demonstrative. For me you have always had an irresistible fascination. Even before I met you I was far from indifferent to you. (JACK *looks at her in amazement*) We live, as I hope you know, Mr. Worthing, in an age of ideals. The fact is constantly mentioned in the more expensive monthly magazines, and has reached the provincial pulpits, I am told; and my ideal has always been to love someone of the name of Ernest. There is something in that name that inspires absolute confidence. The moment Algernon first mentioned to me that he had a friend called Ernest, I knew I was destined to love you.
Jack:	You really love me, Gwendolen?
Gwendolen:	Passionately!

Eugene O'Neill, *Ah, Wilderness!,* Act 3, Scene 2

SCENE—*Same as Act I—Sitting-room of the Miller home—about 11 o'clock the same night.*

MILLER *is sitting in his favorite rocking-chair at left of table, front. He has discarded collar and tie, coat and shoes, and wears an old, worn, brown dressing-gown and disreputable-looking carpet slippers. He has his reading specs on and is running over items in a newspaper. But his mind is plainly preoccupied and worried, and he is not paying much attention to what he reads.*

MRS. MILLER *sits by the table at right, front. She also has on her specs. A sewing basket is on her lap and she is trying hard to keep her attention fixed on the doily she is doing. But, as in the case of her husband, but much more apparently, her mind is preoccupied, and she is obviously on tenterhooks of nervous uneasiness.*

LILY *is sitting in the armchair by the table at rear, facing right. She is pretending to read a novel, but her attention wanders, too, and her expression is sad, although now it has lost all its bitterness and become submissive and resigned again.*

MILDRED *sits at the desk at right, front, writing two words over and over again, stopping each time to survey the result critically, biting her tongue, intensely concentrated on her work.*

TOMMY *sits on the sofa at left, front. He has had a hard day and is terribly sleepy but will not acknowledge it. His eyes blink shut on him, his head begins to nod, but he isn't giving up, and every time he senses any of the family glancing in his direction, he goads himself into a bright-eyed wakefulness.*

Mildred:	(*finally surveys the two words she has been writing and is satisfied with them*) There. (*She takes the paper over to her mother*) Look, Ma. I've been practicing a new way of writing my name. Don't look at the others, only the last one. Don't you think it's the real goods?
Mrs. Miller:	(*pulled out of her preoccupation*) Don't talk that horrible slang. It's bad enough for boys, but for a young girl supposed to have manners—my goodness, when I was your age; if my mother'd ever heard me—
Mildred:	Well, don't you think it's nice, then?
Mrs. Miller:	(*sinks back into preoccupation—scanning the paper vaguely*) Yes, very nice, Mildred—very nice, indeed. (*Hands the paper back mechanically*)
Mildred:	(*is a little piqued, but smiles*) Absent-minded! I don't believe you even saw it. (*She passes around the table to show her* AUNT LILY. MILLER *gives an uneasy glance at his wife and then, as if afraid of meeting her eye, looks quickly back at his paper again.*)
Mrs. Miller:	(*staring before her—sighs worriedly*) Oh, I do wish Richard would come home!
Miller:	There now, Essie. He'll be in any minute now. Don't worry about him.
Mrs. Miller:	But I do worry about him!

2. *Associating Memories.* Close your eyes, relax your eyelids, and imagine the circumstances your character is experiencing in the first exercise. Remember a time when you were worried about a proposal or waiting for a missing relative, then stage the *Earnest* or the *Wilderness* sequence.

3. *Associating Facts.* Jot down initial associations for the following facts about Blanche in *A Streetcar Named Desire*. Read the first three scenes of the play.

FACTS		ASSOCIATION
where you live	208 Esplanade	John's apartment
whether you are married	widow	breakup with John
whether you have children		
whether you be-have yourself		
whether you are underpaid		
whether you are disciplined		
whether you are healthy		
whether you are meticulous		
whether you are aggressive		
whether you are critical		

How can I tell whether my circumstances are effective?

Consider whether the circumstances lead you to the most dramatic choice. A French production of *The Winter's Tale* by Shakespeare immediately visualized the agony of Paulina. The actress playing Paulina, when discovering her queen's death, acted with abandon. Bending over at the waist, she tossed her long black hair like a mask over her face. Then she encircled the king as she yelled curses at him for killing his queen. When on the edge of despair, individuals often dare extreme choices.

Onstage, highlight the astonishing aspects of your character's circumstances. Imagine yourself in a fantasy or dream. Riveting choices like those in a dream inspire the audience to greater self-knowledge. "Nowadays more and more people, especially those who live in large cities, suffer from a terrible emptiness and boredom, as if they're waiting for something that never comes," Jung wrote in *Man and His Symbols*. "Movies and television, spectator sports, and political excitements may divert them for a while, but sooner or later they have to again face the tedium of their everyday lives."

To enter the "dream," the actor allows herself to be completely driven by circumstances through a series of occurrences. Even the tiniest circumstance seethes with significance. The actor must completely trust the other characters and audience to succumb to an almost selfless experience. The actor expands beyond the self and truly becomes someone else.

■ BACKGROUND

How does background affect your circumstances?

Background triggers your circumstances. The more you can experience the predicament of your character, the more you'll respond intuitively each moment. Fill in the blanks about the character's world so that you can react impulsively. You can never know too much background. Your character's background directly affects your feelings about each situation.

What is a history?

A history is your character's background or back story. Histories for each scene can influence the conflict by making real (1) the who, the character; (2) the time, including century, year, season, date, minutes; (3) the place, including country, city, neighborhood, house, room, and area of the room; (4) the immediate surroundings, including animate and inanimate objects that influence the character's life onstage; (5) the given circumstances, the past, present, and future, and the events influencing the scene; and (6) the relationship, the character's relationship to other characters and objects in the scene. When actors don't make decisions regarding these six areas, their choices onstage may be too general. You may need to suggest areas in developing your history that should be explored or expanded.

A working actor might use the following approach in creating a history:

> What I do is to read the show five or six times before I even start to work on it. (1) What does he say about himself? It doesn't necessarily mean that he's telling the truth, but what my character says will inform me about who he is. (2) What is said to him, which gives me the perspective from the other characters. (3) What he does is often the most important question. (4) What is done to him? These questions give an idea of where a character is at a particular time in his life because a play is really a little window through which we see the character's life. After that storyboard, I've got to fill in the blank spaces. Is there a clue in the script that will tell me what happened immediately before the play? I start to work way back, as far as I can go drawing from the play—then I start to work forward as far as I can go, giving a logical conjecture of what is going to happen next. I then start to invent it, but a lot of that invention will be as a result of the way people are reacting to me, my character, in rehearsal.

How do I write background?

The following backgrounds show areas to be evaluated to excite your impulses. A student actor wrote this character sketch as homework, although he spent some time in class determining which facts (such as setting, circumstances) were common to his character and his scene partner's. Whenever possible, these questions should be answered for every scene you do.

Note how the background connects with the overall action, "to stall Nancy," so she can get a cheaper room. Whether improvised or scripted, dramatic action must be supported by this sensory framework. These elements are the center of any role. Incorporate them early on, and you're on your way to an exciting performance!

1. Who am I? (Chapter 6: Character)

I am Kit. I am twenty-four years old. I used to live in New Orleans and work as an accountant for an import/export business that is now bankrupt. My professional handicap is that I am meticulous about saving money. This obsession has escalated into a sickness after Hurricane Kartrina.

I was born in Pascagoula, Mississippi. Rumor is my mother was knocked up at Keesler Air Force Base, and then my dad split the scene. My mother died when I was two. I was raised in a foster home by her distant cousin, a widow with three daughters. I mowed grass, worked as a waiter, and then as a bookkeeper to put myself through public college. I am determined never to be poor and dependent. My wizardry with accounting landed me a fabulous job with an export company, but . . . [This biography can be fleshed out further.]

2. Where am I? (Chapter 7: Setting)

I am with Nancy in the waiting room, sixth floor, west wing of the chic Laurel Canyon General Hospital near Beverly Hills, California, U.S.A. What is around me?

There are mauve chairs, a table neatly stacked with *Baby* and *Glamour* magazines, ashtrays, a dispenser of mineral water, and a big plant. Over the intercom system, doctors' names are being paged. It smells sterile and sweaty at the same time. I am unfamiliar with the place, since I have never been to this hospital before.

What time is it? November 23, 2005, 4 P.M., a sunny and bright California afternoon. It is four years since I first met Nancy. We are in the media/machine generation of videocassettes, calculators, films, air travel, high-tech finance. Computer science, communications, and business (once considered trade fields) are dominant majors on college campuses. George Bush is president. My hometown, New Orleans, is undergoing a severe economic depression. Hospitals are bankrupt because of Hurricane Katrina.

3. What are my circumstances? Past, present, and future events (Chapter 8: Given Circumstances)

My dearest friend, Nancy, whom I met in Audubon Park in New Orleans four years ago, moved to California to escape her parents, got married to her therapist, and is now pregnant. Her husband, John, on a three-day assignment, has asked me to come to California to be with Nancy in case she goes into labor. Though he paid my way to California for his own comfort, I feel obligated to save him money. I am totally obsessed!

Nancy is getting tired of me. She was hoping for pampering and fun, but I have been obsessed with saving money, so much so that I went grocery shopping and bought generic food items. She is rich and doesn't need me to do this. I feel guilty because I was excited to come to California, when I am only supposed to be here for Nancy's benefit. Instead of allowing myself fun, I am punishing myself by trying to save John money.

I want Nancy to stay in the waiting room because there are only private rooms available costing almost twice the daily rate of double rooms. If Nancy goes into one, she would pay over $1,437.75 for the first two hours. Since she would probably end up staying in that room, escalating the cost, I am not paying attention to Nancy's labor pains, although her contractions are getting closer together. I have to go back home to my job in two days. John, Nancy's husband, will be back tomorrow.

4. What am I doing? (Chapter 2: Action)

Main objective: to stall Nancy
Immediate objective: to calculate savings
What are the steps to this action?
Silent activity: I am calculating from a figure table how much it would save John if we could wait until a double room is available in two hours. By waiting here for two hours it will save them $778.56. And, overall, for the duration of the stay, depending on the days (one day in double

occupancy is $1,587.56, two days $3,175.12, and three days $4,762.68), a week would save almost $10,000 (if there are any complications like Down syndrome, incubation, fetal heart murmur, jaundice, or surgical procedures the stay could be longer).

Whereas for an improvisation you fabricate the most interesting facts, for scripted material you must enliven facts in the text. As you read through a script, note in pencil information about the following questions:

1. Who am I? (character)

2. Where am I? (setting)

3. What are my circumstances? (circumstances)

4. What is my action? (action)

SAMPLE BACKGROUND FOR SCRIPTED SCENE

Role: Martha in Edward Albee's *Who's Afraid of Virginia Woolf?*

1. Character

What way do I speak and move? What part of New England am I from? Is my parents' mother tongue English or German, French, Russian? Do I speak with a mixed melody pattern because of having lived different places before my father became college president? Did my father, the college president, use certain slang expressions? Do I imitate these? Did I pick up certain gestures from a peer group, especially around puberty? What are my major traits?

How can I fill in the following facts with memories, sensations from my life? (Note substitutions in parentheses.)

I was born fifty years ago tomorrow, the only daughter of wealthy, highly educated parents (my mom went to Radcliffe). My dad, a renowned college president, gave me the best private education (St. Martin's Episcopal), including four years at Wellesley (Wellesley alumni house). Ever since earliest childhood, I have been the little star (applause of teachers) at faculty parties (dinners on the Cape). As an only child (visits to Grandma's), I was often lonely and played with make-believe friends such as a pet mouse (my dog Brownie). Later I began drinking (college football weekends). I married right out of college (hot sex) and hoped to have four sons—all college presidents. I have no children (two miscarriages). [Biography needs to continue, expanding on details indicated in the script.]

2. Setting

What is my feeling about this living room? When did we buy this house? Why do we live on the campus of a small New England college? Where did I get certain objects, the old bookcase, the sofa, Daddy's picture, the liquor chest? How does this history professor's house differ from my childhood home as the college president's daughter?

How does the fact the play moves from 2 A.M. Sunday until dawn affect the rowdiness and final slowdown of my actions? How do I feel about the first faculty party of this year?

3. Circumstances

How did I meet George? What did we do together? What's the basis of our fascinating persecution of each other? More important, am I obsessed with my father? Why is my mother never mentioned?

What did I consume at the party we're returning from? Whom did I long to see or not see there? What was featured in the college paper today? Why do I do the following: pick up new faculty, insult my husband, stumble home drunk from a party, set up seduction scenes, enjoy lewd dancing, discuss my "son's" birth, plan impromptu cocktail parties, and disguise my barrenness?

■ WHAT IS A HISTORY?

You can document a character's history by making a written record of the events and feelings in the character's life. This written history includes all the factors affecting your stage action. In real life, you are the consequence of all history preceding this moment. And you will be the consequence of all history following this moment. A person's history is so significant that many cultures identify individuals by their forefathers, parents, neighborhood, and address. You can never ignore, nor make too much of, your character's history. Understanding the past leads to specific action in the here and now of the performance.

That's why good actors write down their character's history. They invent emotional experiences that prompt a flood of memories, thoughts, and sensations. These experiences create a stream of consciousness for the actors onstage and shape the course of their actions. Through conscious means, they are expanding their imagination to embrace the unconscious: the spirit of their character.

Many actors keep a daily journal of observations about their character's background, which they refer to when writing the history. Recording pertinent details helps them integrate their role with real-life observation.

A word of advice: Whenever writing a history, always consult your director. You want to compose a scenario that works with his or her vision of the play. A production with all of the actors writing histories supporting that vision can possess an unusual focus.

How does the history influence my stage actions?

Imagine yourself making a serious decision with no sense of your past and you will experience how vapid a performance is without a history. You are so close to your own history that you take it, like your shadow, for granted. You speak, think, act, dream from your memories.

The history affects each action. If you feel melancholic, you might retreat to your room, call a friend, or aggravate a neighbor, depending on your history—what kind of person you are. A strong history of your character that is grounded in your own experiences and fantasies will stimulate you to choose actions appropriate to the character.

What is the emotional value of the history?

The history's emotional value lies in how it weights your stage actions. In writing the history, you are finding feelings to fill moments onstage. Evoked recollection is not the exact photographic or phonographic reproduction of past scenes or events, but rather a reproduction of sensation: of what you saw, heard, felt, and understood. These palpable experiences can be both recalled and relived. I not only remember how I felt, but also I feel the same way now. Loading all you say onstage with your thoughts, feelings, and sensations from the past generates convincing action.

A history prepares the way for the climax, the unconscious explosion that will erupt onstage. For instance, in your character's day-to-day life your first priority could be to act like a loving wife. But your history (your parents' oppressive insistence on obedience and perfection, for example) may ripen you for the terrifying action of seducing your husband's best friend.

In writing the history for such a character (a character present in Harold Pinter's play *Betrayal*), you might create the mind-set of a "good wife" who is keenly aware of daily duties but blind to the dangerous tedium in her marriage.

■ DISCOVERING THE HISTORY

Why is my character's childhood important?

The "good old times"—all times when old are good—are gone.

Lord Byron

The mental and moral qualities of an individual are shaped by childhood, the most impressionable stage. Each human being is largely the product of her earliest experiences. Your capacity to govern your destiny is limited, to a much greater degree than you are ever conscious of, by patterns laid down sometimes even *before* birth.

Ask the following questions about your character: What were your parents' attitudes toward having children? Did they really want you? Why? Did one parent wish for a boy and the other a girl? Were they disappointed? How healthy were they physically? How stable emotionally? How sound is your genetic inheritance? How ideal were the environmental conditions in your mother's womb? What were the obstetrical circumstances of your birth? Which childhood events may account for some of your behaviors now? How do you feel about where you came from, what your upbringing was like, what your parents were like? What people did you know as an adolescent? Who influenced you to become the person you are now?

EXERCISES

1. *Yearly Diary.* Remember a significant emotional experience for each year of your own life, starting at your present age and moving backward. Do this exercise daily between practice sessions. Keep a journal and fill in events for each year as a resource for your roles.

2. *Treasured Object.* Bring in a treasured object from a historical period, such as a doll from turn-of-the-century Britain, a pilot's helmet from World War II, a fan from the 1950s. Use your affection for the object to tell us something about a character in a particular play.

3. *Histories.* Create two different, but explosive, histories for a character in the waiting room of a hospital. Based on these histories, stage two different interpretations of the action "to stall."

■ WRITING THE BIOGRAPHY

How do I write a history?

The actors in most professional training programs write two kinds of biographies—a subjective one and an objective one. A subjective biography is what the character knows. An objective biography is what the actor knows. I prefer the subjective biography because in writing it, you submerge yourself in the thoughts, feelings, and sensations of the character.

As you develop your character's history, use rehearsals to invent more facts. Obviously, the way the actress playing your wife touches you should suggest what the marriage is like because the two of you are working on that story. The way your brother and you argue should suggest your character's childhood. Acting is behaving as if the situation is real. Rehearsals with your fellow actors should suggest your common history.

Why do actors who add nothing to the lines bore us? Because the lines are lifeless. What you invent gives the role vitality.

How do I use my own history?

To find a history that wakes up your inner self, that makes you *very aware* of each moment onstage, you must bring your own personal past into the character's present. Massage your mind with memories so that your interpretation of the events automatically suits the character. The more specific images you recall that are suited to the character, the more details and nuances of feeling will emerge in your performance. If you can find nothing in common with your character, you may have to expand on a few general experiences and use your memories of films, books, and other people's lives. By the age of eighteen, we all have experienced love, jealousy, rejection, ecstasy, loss, disappointment, fear, anger—and all characters, no matter how much they differ from you, experience some of these emotions as well. If you enter the stage tuned into your own particular emotional life, you will create a believable character and truthful action. (See Chapter 4, "Inner Images," for further discussion of this concept.)

It's one thing to tap experiences in ourselves and another thing to "live" a specific sequence of thoughts, feelings, and sensations throughout two hours. Although you should never risk a dangerous choice that might throw you out of control, to re-create the edges of human experience you will have to explore your own memories. You will bring the reality—raw and bold—of who you are to a role.

■ CHECKLIST

The following checklist highlights how circumstances imbue the role with weight and meaning.

1. How does each line of the play affect my character?

2. How do I feel about my previous, present, and future circumstances?

3. What key events affect my character onstage?

4. What experiences can I associate with these events?

■ FINAL PROJECTS

1. *Progressive Exercise.* This exercise builds on the previous progressive exercises. Use strong circumstances to anchor your action as the character.

   EXERCISE 8:   A bumpy airplane. Use the same partner from the previous progressive exercises. Your relationship has intensified as you have shared many experiences. (Be sure to incorporate different hairdos, costumes, and behavior.) You may elect to use a handicap if you like.

   Together work out a scene in a bumpy airplane that is loaded with circumstances. Each of you enters the stage with a troubling circumstance that never comes up in the scene. Although the circumstance bothers you, you never mention it. It simply adds weight to your character. Each of you does a task in silence for two minutes before one of you begins the conflict.

2. *Final Progressive Exercise.* Write a complete background for a final progressive exercise. This might also be considered a very structured improvisation.

EXERCISE 9: An empty courtroom. You are with the same partner from Progressive Exercises 6–8. Two more years have passed, and you have further developed your relationship. (Be sure to include different hairdos, costumes, and behavior.) Since your appearance in Exercise 1, eight years have passed.

Pick an empty courtroom loaded with atmosphere. Include time running out and an inner problem that never comes up. Start an action in silence; then one of you starts a conflict. The new factor is that two couples—and two beats—are involved. The sequence begins with a conflict occurring in each couple. Then, five minutes into that action, a conflict erupts between the two couples.

3. *The Offstage Event.* Choose a play in which a pivotal offstage event dramatically influences a character's action. Do an improvisation on that encounter, then present it in class. For example, in *The Cherry Orchard* by Anton Chekhov, the offstage auction of the orchard affects the final departure scene of brother and sister.

4. *Similar Circumstances.* Choose a character with circumstances like yours. Research everything that is said about these circumstances in the play, compare carefully all the information given by other characters. Note whether you feel they are reliable or lying. Answer "What are my circumstances?" in the most powerful way for your character. Hand in your research. Then stage a sequence from the play.

■ FINAL CHECKLIST

1. Am I playing strong objectives?

2. Who or what is blocking them?

3. Are my relationships personalized?

4. Am I listening to get my objective?

5. Have I broken my scene down into beats?

6. What is my major action?

7. Have I physicalized my actions?

8. Do I have line-by-line actions?

9. What is my major obstacle? Who is doing this to me?

10. What little obstacles are stopping me moment to moment?

11. How are the place, time, and events stopping me?

12. How are the other characters hindering me?

13. Am I contacting exciting inner images?

14. Am I relaxed enough to induce vivid thoughts?

15. What inner monologue is controlling my thoughts?

16. Am I using inner images to make my entrance and exit? To move the other characters?

17. What am I urgently doing and why?

18. How does my character develop the play?

19. What physical traits affect the way I speak and move?

20. What are my distinctive psychological traits?

21. What is my emotional response to this setting?

22. What is the weather like?

23. What experiences have I had here or in a setting like this?

24. What am I dressed for? Why?

25. What must I do in this setting?

26. How does each line of the play affect my character?

27. How do I feel about my previous, present, and future circumstances?

28. What key events affect my character onstage?

29. What experiences can I associate with these events?

9

AUDITIONS
What should I do to get cast?

This chapter evaluates how preparedness and ability affect your success at an audition.

■ WHAT IS CASTING?

The word *casting* comes from the act of casting a mold. To succeed at an audition, you must convince the director that you, like no one else, can fit the mold of the part. To do this, you need preparedness and ability because without them no one works long in the theater. If you think of yourself as needing a 200 percent rating, you will have a good idea of the challenge of auditioning.

Preparedness is key. Even if you become established in the profession, as each engagement ends, the inevitable task of job-hunting begins. The working actor often performs one role while hunting for another, reading the weekly trade papers ("the trades") of the acting business, such as *Backstage, Show Business*, and the *Ross Reports* (for television). For the actor who wants to take some initiative, the *Theatrical Index* and regional guides such as the *Regional and Off-Broadway Theatre Guide* and the *Season Overview* are available. A few actors make the rounds, that is, looking for auditions by going to offices of producers and casting directors, although this is becoming rare. In New York City and Hollywood, you usually need an appointment for theater and film interviews. You can also mail notices and communications to apply for jobs, to thank people for auditions and/or roles, and to notify producers of your performances or of other work in progress.

How do I find auditions?

Write theaters. The fewer words you use in a letter or e-mail, the better the chance that every word will be read. If you must send more than one sheet of paper in an envelope, attach all sheets so they are removed together. The more memorable the letter, the better the chance of a reply. If you have always wanted to play a particular part or have some unique asset that makes you perfect for a part, stress this.

Some years ago one of my students obtained an interview on Broadway in the *Glass Menagerie* through writing a letter to the director. In the letter she stressed how she had similar hang-ups about marriage and dating because she had been reared in a sheltered southern family. She emphasized how she longed to play the role because of its personal significance. Through this letter she got a call from the director's office and a scheduled personal audition.

A "memorable mailing" should include the facts needed for a reply: name, postal address and e-mail address, and fax and telephone number clearly printed on each sheet of paper. (This includes photos, résumés, programs, and notepaper.)

Regional and dinner theater auditions are listed in the trades. Certainly not all of them are cast that way, but it does happen. General auditions are frequently listed, whereas audition notices for specific plays as the season progresses are less frequent.

Write and phone regional and dinner theaters for information you need. If their general auditions are not advertised in the newspaper, an inquiry will get you the required informa-tion. So write or call any theater that you are willing to travel to and try to arrange for an appointment or an audition. Enclose a picture and a résumé (I will describe the format of these later). Be prepared to keep writing if your original letter goes unanswered.

Information on audition patterns may be on a theater's website. Most theaters have fairly regular auditions; some, as often as every month; some, once a season. Choose the right season. The autumn is usually best because regional theaters are earnestly looking for actors then, but lots of general auditions are held in the summer, too. If an actor hopes to do summer stock, early spring, especially March, is the ideal time to seek an audition.

What types of auditions can I expect?

Two types—the prepared scene and the cold reading—and two locations—in the producer's office or onstage—exist for all auditions. For a prepared scene you may be asked to present material of your own choosing, prepared in advance, or you may be requested and given time to work on a scene from a play the director is casting. For a cold reading, you do not see the material until you arrive for the audition.

Auditions for plays are customarily given on a bare stage in an empty theater, with the director, producer, casting director, choreographer, dramatist, or whoever else is concerned sitting out front, usually in the dark. Although these people may not be present for the first reading, many are present for the final call-back.

Conversely, reading for television, film, and commercials takes place in the producer's or casting director's office, with participants sitting in chairs, rather than standing center stage. The office location reflects the time limit involved in meeting the shooting schedule. While auditioning for film, you are not likely to have to read as often as you do for a play; your audition may be taped on a videocassette and replayed instantly or later to the producer or sponsor. A knowledge of camera technique is often an essential.

■ PREPARING FOR AUDITIONS

How can I prepare myself for the audition?

An auditioner wants to cast actors who are easy to work with because such people secure the intelligence of casting, lessen the director's workload, and ensure success of the production.

You must exude confidence, that is, inner trust, acceptance, and knowledge of self. Be professional in a natural, relaxed way. Show enthusiasm. Every director wants to believe that the project in which she is absorbing herself is significant. Be punctual. In professional theater, time is money. In film, several minutes of waiting could cost thousands of dollars because of the overhead in staff and equipment. If you are not on time for an audition, who can say you'll be on time for the rehearsal or performance?

Be considerate. Any theatrical production involves a massive group effort. The director may notice how you treat a secretary, how you relate to other actors, how closely you follow the audition requirements, such as time limits and instructions. I was told of an accomplished actress who, before auditioning, became annoyed because the assistant would not accept a résumé in lieu of her completion of the theater's application card. This actress was rejected for her attitude before she even auditioned.

Your ability manifests itself through proper training and experience. Study acting, voice, and dance; work whenever and wherever you can—in showcases, workshops, and scenes; prepare yourself properly for each audition; continue with your education.

You can never be overprepared because preparation incites confidence and calm. When George C. Scott first determined he wanted to become an actor, he decided to read for the leading part in a campus production. Getting a copy of the script, he memorized the entire part, word for word, before the audition. "They [the auditioners] were flabbergasted," he said, "nobody had ever bothered to learn the part for an audition. I got the role."[1]

You should have material ready for any audition, that is, monologues and prepared scenes with obliging partners who can assist you when needed. Uta Hagen claims, "I have seen actors lose work again and again because, after reading

1. Robert Cohen, *Acting Professionally* (Palo Alto, Calif.: Mayfield, 1995), p. 51.

something for a director, producer, or agent, upon being asked, 'what else can you show me?' the answer was 'nothing.'"[2]

What should I wear to an audition?

Clothing signals your ability. Your appearance as you walk in the door tells the auditioner 75 percent of what he wants to know. You must make a good impression; present a good, confident, attractive look. Wear quality casual clothing that is classic and becoming. Simple clothes that can be kept in condition and colors that blend and do not soil easily are best.

Actresses should groom their hair and wear a simple street makeup. Avoid any clothing that limits your performance or is so novel that it calls attention to its strangeness.

If you have wardrobe items that are generally wearable on the street, as well as perfect for the part, wear them. If possible, look the part without trying to look the part. Master being comfortable in attractive attire.

What should I bring to an audition?

Bring a photo and résumé to every audition. Although producers may have already received these items, producers may have misplaced them. A résumé consists of a simple, typewritten sheet of paper listing the actor's experiences grouped under headings, such as "film," "Broadway," "television," and "commercials."

If your background is more limited, use headings such as "training," "roles played," and "theaters." If you have been in only a few plays but have done scenes from plays in class and know these plays well, list these parts. Although you may be tempted to embellish your past, avoid lying. It's a small world, and getting caught lying will harm your future.

The résumé—the same size as your photo—should be secured to the reverse side of your photo. If it is not, it may get

2. Uta Hagen, *Respect for Acting* (New York: Macmillan, 1993), p. 202.

lost or mutilated in the director's files. Because most casting files are set up for eight-by-ten-inch photos and because standard paper is usually wider and longer than this, you will have to cut the paper down.

Better yet, have your résumé printed professionally. Many agencies in New York City and Hollywood specialize in résumés and sell quantities of 100 inexpensively. More than fifty résumés at a time is a waste because the actor should update his résumé every few months.

Why should a photo and résumé be presented together?

A résumé submitted by itself at an audition has no value and usually gets thrown out; a photo without a résumé is not worth much more. The two must always be presented together. You should select one good eight-by-ten-inch glossy black-and-white unretouched "head shot" that shows your personality and features.

A composite, that is, an eight-by-ten-inch photo with different pictures, is normally useful only when seeking work in commercials. If you must present several photos at an audition, staple them together to keep them attached in a file. Although it's still rare, actors are starting to get color headshots in New York, and it's becoming the standard in Los Angeles.

Whereas you may type your résumé, the photo you submit should be taken by a photographer who specializes in actor's photographs. Many photographers in New York City and Hollywood take such photos exclusively. Several firms there also deal in quantity reproductions of actors' photographs for reasonable prices.

Call Screen Actors Guild or Actors Equity, check the trade papers, or ask working actors to recommend photographers and reproduction agencies in their area. Photographers and agencies may charge less if you let them use your photo for commercial purposes. Also some actors do excellent freelance photography on the side.

Why must photos and résumés be current?

A photo that does not look like you or that you can't look like is worthless. (Even if Mother likes it!) If an acting photograph gets you an interview, and you come in looking like another person, you're wasting the interviewer's time and your own. A glamorous photograph once got one of my students an interview with a top commercial agency in Hollywood; the representative looked at her and said, "Thank you." On the other hand, the auditioners may be looking for someone who does look like the "real" you, and they'll bypass your glorified photo because it's not the right type.

When leaving a photo and résumé, be sure that both list a telephone number that will always be answered during business hours. You or your agent must be reachable by phone at all times.

Why is an agent an asset?

An unknown actor represented by a reputable agent has the edge over one who walks in off the street. The actor sent by an agent will have an appointment to see a particular person. You should have an agent franchised by the actors union because an unfranchised agent may not be reputable. Because an agent claims 10 to 15 percent of income from each acting assignment, the agent usually works for clients who make the most money.

A beginning actor may do best to get an agent who is just starting out and who strongly believes in the actor's work. To get an agent, have her see you act in something or have a producer, casting director, fellow actor, or friend with connections recommend you. No agent needs you, so the fact you have an agent tells the auditioner you are determined and worth representing.

What is a portfolio?

You should also bring a portfolio to some professional auditions, such as an audition for a school or a position with a company. A portfolio is a black leather book of photos, recommendations, and notices from previous shows. If your experience and write-ups are limited, include other professional photos taken by the photographer. Photos in the portfolio should be eight-by-ten-inch glossy, and recommendation letters and notices should be included only if they are from important figures and are ecstatic.

How do I select an audition piece?

For prepared scene auditions, select two short pieces—one from classical theater (drama before 1800) and one from contemporary theater, one emotionally moving, one funny, an offbeat role that is within your age range and a close representation of yourself.

Total audition time should not last more than five minutes. (Note: These requirements are for theater auditions. Straight contemporary presentations are normally preferred in film and television.)

Although I refer to your selection as a "scene selection," for most auditions you will be preparing monologues. Although choosing the right monologues is critical, normally an actor will be asked to do only one piece for an audition unless the part is for a full season or a school. Choose a monologue that is not only right for you, but also right for the part you are auditioning for.

When choosing material, avoid climax scenes, household-word scenes, unproven playwrights, and random cuts. Remember, you need the entire play behind you to work up the emotional pitch for performing the climax. You should give auditioners more to look forward to than what you do at the moment. Find material from good playwrights but avoid resorting to characters of the household-word type, such as Viola from *Twelfth Night*, Richard III from *Richard III*, or Hamlet from *Hamlet*.

One student of mine auditioned at Screen Gems in Hollywood with a scene from *Barefoot in the Park*, which had been used so frequently that the auditioner mumbled the lines along with him. With overdone scenes, directors will usually compare you unfavorably with a memorable performance given by an artist with whom they have worked.

Avoid new, unproven playwrights. Speeches may lack "build," progression, and definite intent. Finally, don't tighten a selection yourself. You may inadvertently edit the scene so that it lacks the dialogue needed for it to build.

Why suit the piece to yourself?

Select a piece suited to your personality and capabilities because your material reflects how you see yourself. Pick the best material you can, material that will sell you as you sell it. Black actors should have at least one solid audition piece from Black Theatre. The selection should be close to your age range. With due consideration to how old you look, choose roles written for persons within a ten-year range of your own age.

Playing wild character roles or those beyond your age types you as an amateur. Remember, old stars usually perform younger roles, so your flexibility agewise will lean more heavily toward looking younger than on looking older.

One of my students lost a part as the lead's daughter on a major TV series because she looked too young. They wanted a twenty-seven-year-old divorcée; she was twenty-seven at the time, but the actresses claiming twenty-seven and competing against her were older.

What is a self-contained piece?

The chosen segment must be self-contained, having a beginning, middle, and end and showing a progression from where you were before the segment began to where you are after the discoveries within the segment are realized. Within the short audition, the material should convey a feeling of completeness.

Self-contained segments can be found in both plays and non-dramatic fiction by established authors. Scenes from the latter make stimulating audition selections because they are infrequently performed.

The segment must be self-explanatory. Before auditioning, you should never have to waste time describing the plot or the characterization you are trying to convey. This process wastes the auditioner's time. At most, say the name of the scene and proceed.

Select flexible material that can be presented anywhere, without the need for a suitcase of production aids. Even if told that a table and chair will be available, you may find, upon arrival, that there is only a bare stage. This happened to a student I coached, and he had considered this situation and had rehearsed for it, so he merely performed his "seated" selection on the floor. If a scene requires props, they should be ones you can bring inconspicuously, for example, a purse, brush and comb, a wallet, a watch, jewelry, or a briefcase. Similarly, articles of clothing (coat, hat, sweater, or shawl) are superb audition aids. All props should be part of your audition attire. The actor should expect to perform his scene anywhere with nothing provided.

The selection must be brief. The auditioner generally gets all the information he wants in the first few seconds; the rest of the time he is possibly thinking of something else or someone else. Leave the auditioner wanting more rather than less. If the scene is brief, the auditioner won't have to cut you off midway through with a "thank you." Be aware that during your brief audition, you are presenting three characters: the real (nonacting) you and the two "yous" demonstrated in the selections. Make all three presentations different, so the auditioner can see divergent sides of your personality. This will triple your chances for success.

How do I rehearse my audition piece?

Rehearse the entire presentation. You should practice each scene's physical setup, (furniture and props), the introduction, your transition between selections, and even "thank yous" concluding your audition. Because time limits usually include your setup(s), introductions, and transition(s), keep these brief. Some auditions give you only one minute.

Always rehearse in audition attire and in a variety of places. Accustom yourself to using your audition clothes and any props that might be part of your attire. Practice your audition at different times. Never depend on any item (clothing, prop, or furniture) that has not been thoroughly worked with before.

Overload your work with images so strong and so personal that they will keep their effect when you are nerve-racked at an audition. Fill your material with enough powerful substitutions from your life that your scene will be successful if only one-quarter of them work.

Finally, have someone whose judgment you respect review your work. With an agent, director, or coach to help you, practice until both of you are satisfied that the audition will show you at your best.

What is an audition interview?

An audition may be preceded by one or two "weeding out" processes, namely, the open call and the interview. The open call or "cattle call" (during which you are evaluated only on physical characteristics) comes first. Actors are lined up across the stage like cattle and are eliminated without a reading because they are too tall, short, fat, dark, and so forth.

An interview (during which the auditioner asks you about yourself) is more humane but offers no opportunity to act. From your response and behavior, an interviewer judges whether or not to let you audition. The interview lets the producer know what kind of individual you are. Because of time constraints for most television shows, films, and plays, producers are partial to the actor whose personality matches the characterization they want.

The interview's structure usually hinges on one statement: "Tell me about yourself." Without fail, describe yourself honestly but positively. Research the producer's plans, select aspects of yourself to emphasize, and be memorable. Have something specific in mind—a role that you think you are right for and that you know the producer is trying to cast. If at all possible, read the play being cast. Broadway producer Richard Barr says, "We are continually annoyed when we ask an actor what part he would like to read for, to find that he is totally ignorant of the play or novel from which the play was originally adapted. Such an approach makes the producer or director doubt the seriousness of the actor applying for the job."[3]

Having knowledge of the producer's plans and play, choose aspects of yourself to display. Relax and let these aspects shine as you describe what you have done and why you feel you might be of value.

Finally, be memorable. Producers see a great many actors when they are casting, so it helps to look, say, or do something memorable. Although this may seem extreme, I heard of a producer who cast an actress because he liked the pin she was wearing. It is generally an asset to be vivacious, friendly, and/or funny (if it's not forced). Any actor can gain an edge by simply remembering names. At the interview you will be introduced to everyone. Memorize names and, when leaving, thank people by name; then go out and write down the names for future reference.

Certain procedures apply to all interviews: (1) Don't smoke unless asked to do so; don't ask where you can get coffee or something to drink; don't drink the office coffee; (2) be brief; don't brag or berate another actor (if you do, directors will feel that you would berate them, too); (3) get a laugh on the way out. If possible, right before exiting, say something clever.

■ STAGING THE AUDITION

How do I set up the audition itself?

When called in for your audition, set up your furniture and props and get into character. Preparation should be simultaneous because all auditions have tight time limits. Any other preparation needed must be left to an off-stage area and done prior to your entrance into the audition room. Don't introduce

3. Ibid., p. 83.

yourself until after you have set your stage, or else you will have to fill your setup time with commentary. Better to give the auditioners a break from the last actor and arrange the stage quickly and quietly.

Examine any furniture or prop that you are using for the first time to assure it works for and not against you. Although you have practiced with your own props and furniture, never take any unexplored item for granted. A shaky chair could ruin the scene.

Most importantly, create the imaginary "fourth wall" of your scene's environment behind the auditioner. Take as much time to place imaginary furniture there as you would to place real furniture on the stage. For example, place imaginary windows, a desk, or a bureau that you might have in your scene's environment at specified spots on the wall behind the auditioner. Doing this will allow you to believe in the fantasy of your environment and will let you feel free to look up and out.

You must be completely comfortable with the full front position, the best one in which to be viewed. A strong belief in the environment facing you will help you avoid gazing up, to the side, or to the floor for most of your presentation.

How do I introduce myself?

Come forward and introduce yourself and your selections all at once. Doing this will save you from repeatedly slipping in and out of the roles of narrator and character. In your introduction, smile and be brief. A smile signals that you are the kind of person whom a director can mold and with whom a director can work easily.

Be succinct and avoid plot outlines. Being verbose runs the risk of "talking down" to a director. It is quite easy to talk yourself out of a job.

Proceed directly into your presentation, which should begin with you in a different physical position from the one used for the introduction. Change of posture captures attention and pinpoints the commencement of the scene.

Why should I stay flexible?

When performing a prepared scene, keep the scene loose, allowing for the size and space of the environment, your specific state of being, and the uniqueness of your partner's interpretation on that day. Flexibility ensures that the scene is spontaneous, exciting, fresh, and new. Never overstructure your performance by aiming for planned effects on given lines or moments. Rather, act fully for the moment, step by step.

The believability of the scene's first moments is crucial. Give yourself fully to the precise thing you are doing during these initial seconds because they establish the level of the scene. If the first moments are emotionally true and full, the rest will build on this, whereas a phony beginning is a surefire indication of disaster. Because you may be cut off before the scene's completion, the impact of the first moments indicates your overall rating.

What are the types of prepared monologues?

The first type of prepared monologue—a person talking alone—is the simpler to stage because you don't have to relate to an absent partner. If you want to be believable, remember that, when people talk to themselves, they are involved in some physical activity.

Real-life observation will reveal that you never enter a room to "talk to yourself." Normally you are involved in some activity, such as searching for keys or putting on makeup, and talk to yourself to help solve a problem or to avoid boredom. When performing this type of monologue, involve yourself strongly in the physical activity before you begin to speak and let the words flow out of and be supported by your physical behavior.

The second type of prepared monologue Uta Hagen classifies as a "duologue" because, according to the script, you are not alone. You are talking to someone else who, in this audition, is absent from the presentation.

Your truthful involvement here is harder because you have to imagine the reactions of your absent partner and respond to

them. The best way to handle duologue with an absent character is to be clear about his location throughout the audition.

When your partner is the audience, never visually confront
the auditioners. They could feel intimidated. Instead, an imagined place should be picked for the audience at specific points
alongside the auditioner.

How do I deal with absent characters?

When your partner is an absent character, give him a specific,
well-thought-out location. Never place him in an onstage chair.
You cannot simultaneously concentrate on your involvement
and on the imagined person's dimensions. If these shift in
location, the stage reality will be broken. The imagined person's
head could sink from six inches above the chair to six inches
below it at another.

Never walk downstage and deliver a speech upstage to no one.
When imagining someone behind you onstage, "anchor" the
partner to a specific location, then find justification for playing
out front and avoiding the need to look back as much as possible.

In addition to "anchoring" the absent character you might
have another actor stand in for the character when the audition
is for a film or school. Be sure that your stand-in can be relied
upon for honest responses. Put the stand-in in a three-quarter
position with his back mostly turned to the auditioner. Place
yourself in a commanding frontal position that assures that you
have focus.

How should I approach a cold reading?

A cold reading, in which you have no opportunity to look at the
material, is the riskiest audition. Make every effort to skim the
script. If you are industrious you can sometimes get the script
the day before. If not, try to read it prior to the audition, perhaps in the office or waiting room. At the minimum, ask politely
for a chance to study the scene for a few minutes before reading the part.

If you do not get to skim the script (this has never happened to anyone I know) or if your character's basic intentions, age, and characteristics are not evident in what is read, ask one inclusive question. A good question might be, "Is there anything important about the character that's not evident in the script?" or, more simply put, "Is there something in this scene that I should know about?" Besides leaving the auditioner free to talk as little or as much as he wants, asking this prods him to reveal any particular way he wants the part to be portrayed. Usually, the auditioner's answer will be brief. Never bore the auditioner by needling for more information, such as a recount of the plot.

Although you sometimes may be asked to read with another actor, you may be asked to read with the stage manager, casting director, or director's assistant. Endow that person with the living substance needed to serve the scene. You must credit that partner with the traits of the character in the play. Doing this requires a strong imagination because often the stage manager or assistant will not be remotely similar to the character called for in the script.

Why pick a strong objective?

Attack the scene. Pick one strong objective (something you want from your partner) and throw yourself into the scene. Go out on a limb. Head for your objective with improvised actions that are as real as possible. Aim for a full performance. The director wants to see the play come alive and to believe that you are really saying what you are reading for the first time.

Suggest a different cold reading if the initial one doesn't work. Most cold readings are terminated by the auditioner when she has found out what she wants to know. Sometimes, however, she may seem uncertain. She doesn't ask you to leave but does not seem entirely satisfied either. She is making up her mind.

This is a good time for you to ask a question that might lead to a different reading. A question such as, "Do you think the character should be more antagonistic?" could evoke a little direction and a chance for another reading closer to her idea of the part. You may even get the role.

■ ENDING THE AUDITION

How should I follow up the audition?

Thank your auditioner by name for her time. If an assistant has received you, thank her by name. Wish luck to any fellow actors who have auditioned with you or who are auditioning after you. Within forty-eight hours you should write a personal note of thanks to the auditioner and mention a "thank you" to the assistant. Establish yourself as a caring person they will want to use.

Keep in touch with the people you have met. If you didn't get the part, try to find out why, then go see the production and drop the director a note congratulating her. Write letters (such as one telling the auditioner of a show you are in) and make occasional pertinent phone calls. If you are in the area, drop by occasionally and repeat your name often, so that it is attached to your appearance in the auditioner's memory. Keep your visits brief unless the auditioner asks you to wait. One of my students once got a part on a major television series through such a follow-up procedure. The star of the series saw him in a show and liked his performance. The student expressed an interest in the filming of the series, and the star agreed to let him visit the set to watch. The student visited the set frequently for short intervals. The first time the student went, the star couldn't recall who he was. After three weeks, the star got the student a part in the series.

Remind your agent (when you get one) to follow up on auditions. If you do not get the part, a good agent can often find out the real reason for your rejection. For follow-ups to be fruitful, always be willing to learn from your mistakes.

Any audition technique is only as good as its implementation. You are a warrior. Keep trying, and you will climb the Alps. Remember Hannibal's advice: "We will either find a path or make one." Learn from others and find your own techniques. Your determination is what makes you special. The biggest contribution you make to the theater is bravery.

■ CHECKLIST

Do!

1. Be prepared. Know your audition selection.

2. Avoid overused material—you may be remembered for the originality of your selections.

3. Be relaxed. Space will be provided for warm-ups; use it.

4. Be on time with completed application form in hand.

5. Cooperate with the audition staff.

6. Choose clothing that is simple and allows for freedom of planned movement.

7. Generally, your audition selection should reflect your casting type or potential.

8. Time yourself. You will not be allowed to exceed the two-minute limit.

9. Begin your selection by clearly stating your name and the selection you will perform.

   Hello. I am Jeannie Lancaster. This is Heavenly from *Sweet Bird of Youth*.

   Your introduction is often more important than the audition itself. Take your time.

10. If a musical is being cast, you may have to reserve an additional singing and/or dancing slot. If not, you may include sixteen bars from a song (sung a cappella) as part of your two-minute audition time.

Don't!

1. Don't make noise while waiting to audition.

2. When possible, never use a script.

3. Avoid audition material that requires heavy use of props.

4. Don't look at those auditioning you as you perform the audition selection—find a focus point slightly above their heads to represent your imaginary participant.

5. Don't audition to a chair.

6. Don't name the playwright in your introduction and never describe the scene or provide exposition.

7. If you go blank, try to be charming—don't make excuses. If you must begin again, say so with a smile and do so.

8. Don't use a dialect piece unless it is specifically requested.

9. Don't fail to extend your last moment slightly before breaking out of the "moment."

10. Don't fail to thank those who auditioned you before exiting.

APPENDIX A

FULL-LENGTH SCORE

WHITE SUITS IN SUMMER

Cast of Characters

Blaise Salatich	an actor
Lucille	his wife, a critic
Susanne Dupré	a painter
Ted Clapper	her manager
Scene:	A mansion on Exposition Boulevard, New Orleans. We are in a big, finely proportioned parlor with high ceiling, Oriental rugs, a crystal chandelier. The atmosphere is that of a grand sanctuary, where the landowner can view Audubon Park as a superior. Floor-to-ceiling windows, sometimes used as entrances, open onto a gallery overlooking a wide lawn, which tumbles onto Audubon Park. During the daytime one has the feeling of a semitropical park, and at night of an oak garden, which climbs into the stars.
Time:	The present. Sunshine, already hard on the windows, fills the room with a sharp light.

Act I, Scene 1

Sequence 1

Setting:	A summer day. Noon. The present. Several suitcases line the stage.
At Rise:	LUCILLE, 28 runs onstage. She's very healthy with a mass of hair and deep-set hazel eyes. There is a curious blend of country carelessness and intelligence. Her husband, BLAISE, enters[1], buttoning his shirt. He is handsome, about 26, but his carriage makes him appear older. He is tall, long-limbed with a wide forehead, thick brown hair, and fine sensitive eyes. He wears conservative dark clothes, obviously expensive, and he wears them well. Harsh sunlight falls over the gallery as TED

211

CLAPPER in a rumpled white suit approaches. HE checks back for fear his car will be towed. An effusive businessman, HE's in his twenties, but his face looks older.

Ted: Anybody home? (*crosses to* BLAISE) Teddy Clapper.

Lucille: Who?

Ted: New Orleans Country Club? Southern Yacht Club? Now I'm managing Susanne Dupré.

Lucille: Susanne Dupré. (*screams in delight*) Oh my. Oh God. Oh, no.

Ted: (*searches about*) My glasses broke. I've a second pair.

Lucille: I'll fix them. You know my husband. (*to herself*) Oh my God. Susanne Dupré.

Blaise: [2]Can I help you with something?

Ted: Mom and I want you to host an exposition of Susanne Dupré.

Lucille: (*to* BLAISE) This is the miracle we've been waiting for.

Ted: (*looks out*) They're not giving me a ticket? I double-parked by a fire hydrant, then barged into the curb . . .

Blaise: [3]You should move your car.

Ted: Like I said, we're looking for patrons to do an exposition of . . . (*Phone rings.* TED *searches for phone, gives up when ringing stops.*) Mom might phone. I've rough car trips calling her. She fired the night watchman and bought me a phone. My mother is the sweetest, panicked person on earth. I advanced up to escort when Dad departed this world. . . .

Lucille: I saw it in the obituaries.

Ted: A show on Exposition Boulevard could be an important event. Susanne's a young legend.

Lucille: A practitioner of the—

Ted: Nobler forms.

Lucille: Her show in Berlin left me—

Ted: Ecstatic as did her show at the—

Lucille and Ted together:	Guggenheim in New York.
Ted:	(TED's *cell phone rings. He waves it off.*) We'll ignore that. All Mom's friends are dying, so it's not great for her. (Her two best friends died within weeks) What with her heart surgery and the cataracts . . . (*Phone stops ringing. He searches for the scrapbook and pictures.*) Mom made a scrapbook of your wedding. She keeps saying, "Why couldn't you've married Lucille." (*to* LUCILLE) Every boy at Jesuit High School was in love with you.
Blaise:	(*to* TED) [4]Thanks for the gift.
Lucille:	(*to* TED) Your glasses fixed.
Ted:	Amazing. (*Phone rings.* TED *answers it.*) Hello there. (*to* BLAISE) If I don't respond instantly, Mom calls the cops. (*talks into the phone.*) Yeah, Mom. I gave Lucille the clippings and the . . . no. (*to himself*) Where are those grapefruit spoons? (*checks about. To* LUCILLE) Mom had them replated. (*to* BLAISE) My family's in fine jewelry and heirlooms. (*into phone*) I got them. (*hangs up*)
Lucille:	(*peeking in the box*) Another priceless treasure from Uncle.
Ted:	Mom says y'all have the finest art collection.
Blaise:	[5]He gave it to the museum. (*Phone rings, but* TED *ignores it. Looking for an outlet to recharge it.*)
Ted:	If I'm gone long, she'll find me—hunt me down. My sister came for a month with her kids—wild, exhausting 6-, 7-, and 12-year-olds. After she left, it required weeks of down time to revive Mother.
Lucille:	Wouldn't it be wonderful to have kids 'round the house?
Ted:	Little Lucilles and—
Blaise:	[6]We're not having children yet.
Lucille:	I didn't mean today.
Ted:	Where's that outlet?
Blaise:	[7]With Uncle Gene's illness and—

Lucille:	Blaise's goal is to become a great actor, get fame, start his own production company.
Ted:	(*interrupting, to* BLAISE) Say, weren't you and Susanne schoolmates at—?
Blaise:	[8]Berkeley.
Ted:	Right. I told Susanne a political edge would move her ahead faster. She started her *Triangle* series in Berlin. (BLAISE *guides him to an outlet.*)
Lucille:	Splendid.
Ted:	I organized this smashing opening at the Mary Boon in New York. She constructed and deconstructed Naughty Marieta and the Casket Girls at the Whitney. (TED'S *phone rings.*) Mom gets foggy and keeps calling. (*speaks into the phone.*) I'll pick you up for dinner. (*hangs up. Phone rings again.*)
Ted:	(*throws up his hands.*) Each time, it's an earnest pitch—when can I expect you? Mom's got a housekeeper, a chauffeur, and a cook, but she's essentially alone. Eating out and her poodle, Bootsy, are all that keep her going. Pardon me. (*picks up the phone and talks to his mom.*) Yes, I gave them the—no, no. I'll do it. More gifts—certificates for silver frames for your wedding portrait and invitation, and for baby rattles, cups, brushes, diaper pins, cutlery, and dishes. All to be engraved later.
Lucille:	How extravagant.
Ted:	We've tons of wedding and baby gifts—never bought or returned—and Mom wants you to have them all—in case something . . . She should never have had heart surgery of that magnitude.(*into the phone*) Yes. She's got it. Goodbye Mom. (*hangs up the phone.*) I handle Mom's expenses, the understatement of the year. Time's coming when I'll have to move in—Blaise: (*checks his watch.*) Excuse me.
Ted:	Wait. About the show—
Lucille:	'Course we'll sponsor it. We'll use the side gallery.

Ted:	Excellent.
Lucille:	Uncle will contribute. I've got great ambitions for Blaise.
Ted:	Is that a meter maid out there? What?
Lucille:	Don't leave.
Ted:	No, I thought you said . . . Three shapes of them are ticketing my car. Bat women from hell. (*to* LUCILLE) I'll be right back.
Blaise:	[9]Take your time. [10]I'm going for a smoke. (*Exits.*) (*Moments later.* LUCILLE, *high-strung, turns up a baby minder, a ritual she deals with continually. Sound:* UNCLE GENE, *moaning upstairs.* LUCILLE *speaks into the machine.*)
Lucille:	Nurse? Can't you ease Uncle's pain?
Nurse:	(*offstage*) I've got a call in to the doctor. (SUSANNE, *24, enters, quietly with her portfolio and paint box. She is dressed casually in seductive clothes. Hollows shadow her cheeks and her slender neck. There is a quality of nervous tension, the mental strain of an artist who puts unrelieved pressure on herself.*)
Susanne:	Hi. I'm Susanne Dupré.
Lucille:	Oh my. Oh my lord. You're an absolutely brilliant artist. I'm Lucille, Blaise's wife.
Susanne:	Hello. Ted sent me in.
Lucille:	Anyone in love with painting admires your work. (*looks about*) Where's Ted?
Susanne:	Parking the car. Is this a bad time?
Lucille:	Sorry—I'm in such a tether.
Susanne:	I understand. My challenge is to discern reality.
Lucille:	Ah. To paint things the way they truly are—
Susanne:	Not through false glasses.
Lucille:	New Orleans must be quite an interesting study when—
Susanne:	Viewed as an outsider. (*stares at her*) You're lovely. (*overcome with disappointment*) I don't think I can exhibit here.

It's too—fussy. (SUSANNE *looks out, her face hot and sweating. Music floats in from the Cathedral. Isaiah 6. "Here I am, Lord, / Is it I Lord. / I have heard you calling in the Night, / I will go, Lord, if you lead me. / I will hold your people in my heart."*)

Lucille: Choir practice from Holy Name Church. I can hear them even better from my classroom at Tulane.

Susanne: (*avoiding* LUCILLE's *face*) You teach?

Lucille: Art history. At Tulane.

Susanne: What a view. The sun sifting through Spanish moss. And the park dancing all around. I feel like I'm being reborn, nourished by Utopia. People would be calmer if they lived in beauty. Marvelous house.

Lucille: It's been in my family for generations.

Susanne: And will stay there.

Lucille: These houses are great 'cause they keep memory alive. (*moaning through baby minder.*) My uncle has cancer.

Susanne: Sorry.

Lucille: I use a baby minder. It's sad.

Susanne: With a certain—

Lucille: If you need to buffer entropy, this is a good training ground.

Susanne: My presence feels inappropriate.

Lucille: I adored your Berlin exhibit. *How the Feminist and the Archetype Intersect.*

Susanne: What did your husband think?

Lucille: Right. You met Blaise.

Susanne: Well?

Lucille: He framed my article comparing your painting to Beckett's drama. (*hands* SUSANNE *the article.*)

Susanne: "Apocalyptic Isolation." Some title.

Lucille: You're a prodigy.

Susanne:	People get noticed if they do something unusual and live in New York in their twenties.
Lucille:	You're welcome to stay—
Susanne:	There is motion here, but again—it's not the house I was hoping for.
Lucille:	We could paint the walls, redo some lights.
Susanne:	(*shaking her head*) No.
Lucille:	Blaise needs to meet people in the arts.
Susanne:	It won't work.
Lucille:	He wants to do leads in film and theater, the—whole panoramic portrait.
Susanne:	Not tiny parts, shards in the mosaic.
Lucille:	We can create projects for you both from here.
Susanne:	(*picks up a large white album.*) Your wedding album.
Lucille:	There's Blaise kissing me at the altar, feeding me cake.
Susanne:	You're still newlyweds. Love hasn't changed to respect. (SUSANNE *fidgets with a cigarette.* TED *enters.*)
Ted:	I can't stay. I promised to take Mom to Antoine's.
Lucille:	Don't worry. Susanne and I can discuss the exposition.
Susanne:	If we have one.
Ted:	Don't mind her. (*Whispers to* SUSANNE) You'll do what I say.
Susanne:	I don't know. (*to herself*) Change carries consequence.
Ted:	I'm off. (LUCILLE *ushers* TED *to the door.*)

Sequence 2

(11BLAISE *enters from the park, brushes past* SUSANNE, *walks to get liquor.*)

Blaise:	12Oh, Susanne.
Lucille:	Right. You knew each other. Kiss me, dear. (HE *kisses her.*) We're still honeymooning.

Blaise: [13]Excuse me. (*leaving*)

Lucille: Don't be rude, darling. I need your input on the exposition.

Susanne: Maybe you shouldn't have it, just enjoy the park, and—

Blaise: [14]Can I get you a drink? [15]Every Southern home has a recovery shelf. (*to* SUSANNE)
[16]A Bloody Mary?

Susanne: Perrier. Might as well drink with class.

Lucille: You'll let us host you?

Susanne: Not sure. I feel mostly good about what Ted and I are doing—It's simply a desire for a real home—that the other galleries can't fulfill.

Blaise: Maybe this need is invalid.

Susanne: I think not—([17]BLAISE *wipes his forehead, which has broken out in a sweat.* LUCILLE *chuckles in the embarrassed silence and passes condiments.*)

Lucille: (*to* SUSANNE) Your use of *triangles* intrigues me. We must include "Shakti's Heart"—your triangle symbolizing—the Hindu Goddess.[18]

Blaise: [19]It's too Gauguin for me. Actually, that piece depresses me the least.

Lucille: Blaise!

Blaise: (*to* SUSANNE) [20]Weren't you supposed to search out dark, lugubrious *triangles.*

Susanne: The easy expositions are over, and the tough ones just begun.

Lucille: Showing here will not be as difficult as you think. ([21]BLAISE *starts to exit.*)

Lucille: You're not leaving? Relax, dear. This is for you.

Blaise: [22]I like to pace. [23]If I sit, might miss something.

Lucille: (*clears her throat*) Tell us about your recent work.

Susanne: I've been correcting energy-draining behaviors.

Lucille: That affects your painting.

Susanne:	And life. Confusion won't divert me from seeing reality.
Lucille:	Your paintings are sharper.
Susanne:	Painting is about paying attention in a Buddhist way.
Blaise:	[24]That's hard to do.
Susanne:	I slip into the skin of people I see—even if it hurts.
Lucille:	You paint "fruitful blank spaces" which life fills in.
Susanne:	When I smile . . . I'm thinking of something enticing.
Lucille:	You're smiling now? Isn't she, honey?
Susanne:	You can use art to heal, to face a part of yourself you hate.
Lucille:	Go on!
Susanne:	In my last *triangle* series, I saw myself in the colors and mended my ways.
Lucille:	(*to* SUSANNE) How do you know when a painting is finished?
Susanne:	(*to* BLAISE) When you love it. (*A moan through the baby minder. A bell rings.* LUCILLE *rises to leave.*)
Lucille:	Uncle calls every five minutes.
Blaise:	[25]Nurse is there.
Lucille:	Yes, but he waits for me. (*to* BLAISE) Darling, get Susanne's press agent, mailing lists. Talk strategy.
Susanne:	I don't know.
Lucille:	We'll give you two an outrageous reception: jazz band, oysters étoufée, mint juleps.
Susanne:	But does the world need another show?
Lucille:	'Course. Artists make dreams.(*to* BLAISE) Kiss, kiss, love bug. (LUCILLE *adjusts the baby minder and flutters off.*)

Sequence 3

(BLAISE *gives* SUSANNE *a hard look.*)

Susanne:	Love bug.
Blaise:	[26]When did you move to New Orleans?
Susanne:	Before your wedding.

Blaise:	[27]You came to our wedding?
Susanne:	(*removes newspaper notice.*) I sat in back of the church. Didn't make the reception.

(*Doorbell rings.*)

Maid:	(*offstage*) The prescription. I've got it, Miss Lucille. (BLAISE *turns down the baby minder.*)
Susanne:	Lucille is, like a mother . . . You think about California?
Blaise:	[28]I recall lots of dead things. (*starts to leave.*)
Susanne:	After your wedding, I slept all day. I felt like a part of me was melting—
Blaise:	[29]Now you've seen me and I've seen you.
Susanne:	Why did you move here? For the?
Blaise:	[30]Restaurants—You can be a starving artist in your teens, but in your twenties you like to dine out occasionally.
Susanne:	When I started painting, I didn't worry about sales.
Blaise:	[31]As long as you work for your soul, it's great.
Susanne:	Sometimes I can't—sleep.
Blaise:	You need to—
Susanne:	I'm not taking pills or fooling around.

Sequence 4

(LUCILLE *enters with mail to get a bottle of gin.*)

Lucille:	The mail came.
Blaise:	[32]My headshots!
Lucille:	Why send them? Soon, we'll produce you here. Money's the crucial factor.
Susanne:	And talent.
Lucille:	Persistence. I won't let Blaise fail. (*Pause.*) Uncle wants a Ramos Gin Fizz made of orange flower, water, and gin.
Blaise:	[33]I'll get it.
Lucille:	(*checks the baby minder*) You plan which paintings to hang. (*moaning through the baby minder. She starts to go.*)

Everything's an argument with Uncle. Is there any nutritional value in gin?

Susanne: (*to* BLAISE) Joy and celebration.

Lucille: Mm. I can hardly get one job done when something hits me. (*kisses him boldly.*)

Blaise: [34]I should help you.

Lucille: Give me a kiss, pumpkin. A bear kiss. (*pause*) (*Exits*)

Sequence 5

(*A breeze rises.* [35]BLAISE *gazes at* SUSANNE *so the light from the great porch lanterns catches her face with streaks of brightness. Distant thunder. The gallery is blanketed with a golden coppery light. A hymn floats from the Cathedral, "On Eagle's Wings." "And he will raise you up on eagle's wings. / And hold you in the palm of his hand."*)

Susanne: (*sings*) "And he will raise you up. And he will raise you up. And he will raise you up . . . on the last day." I love rain on an unexpected day. Every pore opens to the wind.

Blaise: [36]Nice.

Susanne: That's what I remember about New Orleans. The music—and the rain.

Blaise: [37]I don't have time for this (*Thunder*)

Susanne: There's a sense of romance about the rain. The sun is around us, but the rain is within us. (removes her sketchbook, draws.) When I got here, the rain seized me. Mind if I draw you?

(SHE *moves closer, drawing him. Footsteps inside.* BLAISE *calls out.*)

Blaise: [38]Who's there?

Susanne: I'm putting you in a *triangle*—

Blaise: [39]Lucille? (*picks up a book.*)

Susanne: Using weightlessness to let your image soar.

Blaise: [40]Five minutes is all.

Susanne: You've a wonderful body.

(*With a flickering smile,* BLAISE *clutches his book like a Bible.*)

Blaise:	[41]I read one self-help book a week—
Susanne:	Dressed or undressed—
Blaise:	[42]*The Greatest Salesman Alive,* takes a year to finish 'cause it's—
Susanne:	Self-hypnosis.
Blaise:	[43]You read one chapter three times a day for a month.
Susanne:	What contacts do you have here?
Blaise:	[44]None. [45]I'm competitive with people.
Susanne:	Hold that pose.
Blaise:	[46]I forget how I'm supposed to behave.
Susanne:	(BLAISE *gives* SUSANNE *a hard, silencing look.*) When I saw you in *Hamlet,* you defined the word star. (*Takes out his picture as Hamlet.*)

Sequence 6

(LUCILLE *hurries onstage.*)

Lucille:	We've lovely watercress sandwiches and crab soup. Give me a kiss. (LUCILLE *kisses him.*) Oh lord. She's painting here.
Blaise:	[47]Stay and watch.
Lucille:	Ooh. Uncle won't eat 'less I join him.
Blaise:	(*to* LUCILLE) [48]I'm tired. [49]Let's go nap.
Susanne:	I should let you two alone.
Lucille:	Don't be silly. Uncle cries out for attention. His paper is damp. His milk is warm. There's dust on the floor. The new maid is lazy. She barely came in the month we were gone. Then I've got to prepare the shopping list.

Sequence 7

| Blaise: | [50]Let me help you. |
| Lucille: | No. Sit for Susanne. You know how Uncle treats the maid when I'm not there. (LUCILLE *buzzes off.* BLAISE *follows uneasily, stands in the doorway as the night turns black.* |

SUSANNE *toys with a palette knife. Seeing it,* BLAISE *trembles.* SUSANNE *speaks maliciously.*)

Susanne: You've broken out in a sweat.

Blaise: [51]New Orleans is melting me.

Susanne: How long have you been unemployed? Eight months?

Blaise: [52]Warm.

Susanne: Nine?

Blaise: [53]Warmer.

Susanne: A year? Two?

Blaise: [54]"Regret not the glitter of any lost day." Tennessee Williams.

Susanne: What happened in Hollywood?

Blaise: [55]Nothing.

Susanne: You told Lucille you'd talk—

Blaise: [56]I thought I'd make a bundle.

Susanne: Doing what?

Blaise: [57]Selling chunks of my soul at varying intervals.

Susanne: Did you?

Blaise: [58]I auditioned weekly for months.

Susanne: That's a lot of no's.

Blaise: [59]I was holding on for the word, yes—

Susanne: (*slyly*) To lose yourself in the play?

Blaise: [60]Right.

Susanne: You went to interviews with producers?

Blaise: [61]Yes.

Susanne: Casting directors?

Blaise: [62]So.

Susanne: Ah, Blaise Salatich. You've played all these parts blah, blah, blah.

Blaise: [63]Exactly.

Susanne: Finally, a director of a major picture hires you and he gets fired!

Blaise:	[64]Who told you that?
Susanne:	Did you go back to the old ways?
Blaise:	[65]No.
Susanne:	Numbing yourself with—?
Blaise:	[66]No. [67]I wanted to by God.
Susanne:	But you didn't.
Blaise:	[68]I kept busy, [69]worked out. [70]Ran. ([71]HE *feels for a cigarette*. SHE *takes it out for him*.)
Susanne:	You didn't slip once after so many months?
Blaise:	[72]Never.
Susanne:	So you auditioned for special parts.
Blaise:	[73]Right.
Susanne:	You were a hand model? A parts model? What?
Blaise:	Soft porn is what they call it. So.
Susanne:	What happened on your last audition?
Blaise:	[74]Producer arrives in this enormous barrel-like hat.
Susanne:	He asked you to his hotel room.
Blaise:	[75]Devouring pistachio nuts, telling me his tale of woe. (SHE *hands him a drink*.) [76]Asks me to sit on the bed and [77]unbutton my shirt. [78]*This can't be happening, I thought.* [79]I was anxious, [80]but it was a lead. [81]"I'd like to cast you," he said. [82]So, I took off my shirt. [83]He stared till my ears got hot. [84]*This can't be happening, I thought.* [85]He made me lie on the bed. [86]Then he undid my belt [87]and unzipped my pants. [88]*This can't be happening.* [89]I backed off. [90]There was this screaming, this hotness. [91]He came at me with a knife. [92]Blood everywhere, drenching his shirt, pants, the floor. [93]Looked like he was coming at himself with the knife.
Susanne:	He died.
Blaise:	[94]I'm trashed in California. (SUSANNE *adds ice to his drink. The song "Here I Am, Lord" is heard from the Church*.)
Lucille:	(*Entering*) Uncle wants ice chips for his drink. Your sketch is rapturous. (*Looking at* SUSANNE's *drawing*.)

Blaise:	(*to* LUCILLE) [95]Stay, sweetheart.
Lucille:	Did Susanne agree to—
Susanne:	I do!
Lucille:	Glorious. (LUCILLE *exits.*)
Susanne:	You have an agent here?
Blaise:	[96]She calls herself one. [97]The only help I ever got was from other artists. [98]They taught me how to face guerilla warfare, to be outspoken, aggressive.
Susanne:	You can't be an artist unless you plunge ahead. Courage brings peace. Dream big. Fight back. Nirvana awaits. When you march forward, you stand up for the weak, the old, the silenced poets of the world. (*A car horn toots.* SUSANNE *starts, and crosses to* BLAISE.) I have to go. Ted gets impatient.
Blaise:	[99]I've missed you. (BLAISE *smiles sadly. The car toots again.* SUSANNE *hurries out.*

Sequence 8

(LUCILLE *enters with an envelope.*)

Lucille:	Good news. Uncle's financing the exposition.
Blaise:	(*sarcastically*) [100]Victory is ours.
Lucille:	Ours? Did you drink all this gin?
Blaise:	[101]It's a negotiable indulgence. (*Hands her an envelope.*)
Lucille:	Oh dear.
Blaise:	[102]Why does Uncle send you business letters? [103]You talk all day.
Lucille:	He's a Soniat. Soon as they have an opinion, it becomes a legal document.
Blaise:	[104]Throw it away.
Lucille:	Wait, it's a lien on this house. He didn't mention—
Blaise:	[105]He was annoyed you said—
Lucille:	With your career and our stay abroad.
Blaise:	[106]But he gave us the house.

Lucille:	Before he did—he took out a mortgage—
Blaise:	[107]"You don't have to be rich," he said, "when your relatives are rich."
Lucille:	To pay some of his insurance. (*Doorbell rings.*)
Nurse offstage:	Good evening.
Offstage Male Voice # 1:	Patient's sleeping.
Lucille:	Dominicans slinking about . . . badmouthing you to Uncle. (LUCILLE *fixes the baby minder.*)
Offstage Male Voice # 2:	We brought pictures of the baptistery.
Lucille:	They snuck this folder by his food tray. (LUCILLE *hands a folder to* BLAISE.)
Blaise:	[108]A last will and testament—
Lucille:	They're promising Uncle Heaven.
Blaise:	[109]He believes these hypocrites.
Lucille:	He keeps asking for you.
Blaise:	[110]*You swore when I said he could live upstairs—*
Lucille:	Would it hurt to have a conversation?
Blaise:	[111]I'm not going to be two-faced.
Lucille:	Uncle's slipping.
Blaise:	[112]Live in tight-assed denial.
Lucille:	He says you married me for money, that acting is a profession for—
Blaise:	[113]*For parasites?* [114]He thinks if I can't get a TV show, I should quit. [115]Everyone wants to see a play for nothing. [116]They expect you to rehearse on your own time, at midnight, when you're depleted or at 4:00 A.M. before you go to your real job. [117]Find some way an institution can make money off you. [118]Then we have crappy actors, working for free and alienating a dwindling public.

Lucille:	Can't you say you're also interested in sales?
Blaise:	[119]I'm not getting in that pot. [120]The last man in there got eaten. ([121]Laughs, but SHE doesn't join in.)
Lucille:	Uncle thinks you're narcissistic. Well, you do, do for yourself.
Blaise:	[122]*What in God's name are you talking about!*
Lucille:	I'm just asking you to visit.
Blaise:	[123]He doesn't respect me.
Lucille:	You know he . . . he's . . . sick. That's why he's irritable, and can't be with you more than five minutes. I love him. I remember how he was when I was a little girl. I can't think of life without—He's not himself, now he's dying.
Blaise:	[124]Are we sure? [125]God!
Lucille:	The doctor phoned about the living will. Lord, I can't take it. Poke your head in the door. (*She exits.* [125A]*BLAISE gazes after her, breathes deeply. We hear wind from a summer rainstorm, sweeping over the park. HE picks up the book, and goes inside. Lights fade.*)

Act I, Scene 2

Sequence 1

Setting:	The gallery gleams with wetness from a rain. (Pink, purple, and blue colors shadow the decor.) Dance-hall music plays from the stereo.
At Rise:	[126]BLAISE is rehearsing a dance sequence for an audition. SUSANNE appears dressed in an exotic gown.
Blaise:	[127]My wife's not home. (SHE *smiles*) [128]Don't you have an opening?

([129]HE *wipes his face, swallows water.* SUSANNE *strolls over and drinks from his glass.*)

Susanne:	How are you newlyweds making out?
Blaise:	([130]*Walks out on the veranda.*) [131]Most of the guys I grew up with are still here. [132]Sundays you'll see them running

behind baby carriages in the park. [133]Weekdays the wives race-walk and—

Susanne: Recount their husband's infidelities?

Blaise: ([134]*Observes her with a flickering smile.*) [135]My therapy is not to pursue a sexy woman one day at a time, [136]and to spend time with other recovering husbands and not talk about it. Ha. ([137]HE *resumes practicing a step.* SHE *watches him, her eyes moist.*)

Susanne: Your hair's fallen over your face. Let me get it.

Blaise: [138]Don't. [139]Moses came from the mountain and said, "I bear good news and bad news. The good news is I got him down to ten. The bad news is adultery is still in."

Susanne: That's in the Far East. If you accept a second-rate provincial marriage in the South, it's a sort of burial. (*Dance music swells from the stereo.*) Dance with me. Please. The assumption we'll start with is we're not finished.

Blaise: [140]My wife will be here—

Susanne: Don't you ever think of us?

Blaise: [141]Don't squeeze.

Susanne: Let me enjoy you for a moment—arm's length at a safe distance. (*Her eyes keep darting up and down his body.* SHE *lifts his arms, laughing, stretches them around her, her head near his.* SHE *cradles his face.* [142]HE *freezes momentarily like a deer sensing hunters.*)

Blaise: [143]Shame upon you, Susanne.

Susanne: Undo that button.

Blaise: [144]Remove your hand.

Susanne: I love this shirt. Before you, I knew a kiss was something you did with your mouth, but I didn't know what it was.

Blaise: [145]Stop.

Susanne: Lucille couldn't be a good lay. Her housecoat is so aesthetically offensive.

Blaise: [146]Quiet!

Susanne: Don't walk away. If you're going to say something, say it to my face.

Blaise: [147]I've changed.

Susanne: You haven't.

Blaise: [148]I don't require madness, [149]any serious addiction.

Susanne: I've been dreaming of you—

Blaise: [150]The best way to remember something is to forget it.

Susanne: You're teasing me.

Blaise: [151]You know me better.

Susanne: I know how you felt me in the dark. I saw your face when you walked down the aisle. You loved me then and do now.

Blaise: [152]That's a strange thing to say—

Susanne: I've dreamt of you since you married. I have a sixth sense and your thoughts have flown to me.

Blaise: [153]Get away.

Susanne: I can't wait for dreaming. Now you tell me to tear your memory from my eyes? I can't. (*The veranda lights blink on. Suddenly* SUSANNE *is all nerves and sobs.* SHE *buries her head in his shoulder.*)

Blaise: [154]Ssh, [155]go over there.

Susanne: Terrible night. Dark, moon yellow and slippery. (LUCILLE *pounds on the door.*)

Lucille: (*offstage*) Blaise! Honey? Help me with these bags!

Act 1, Scene 2

Sequence 2

(SUSANNE *rushes off.* LUCILLE *stumbles in, puts down the laundry.*)

Blaise: [156]That was Susanne. [157]Inviting us for champagne after her show.

Lucille: I don't think I can make it.

Blaise: [158]You look exhausted.

Lucille: Uncle's no use for these clothes since he's never—

Blaise: (*rubbing her shoulders*) [159]Don't exaggerate.

Lucille: Getting out of bed. Still he insists I run by the cleaners. . . . Uncle wants me to pick out his burial suit and store it in a plastic box.

Blaise: [159A]Close your eyes.

Lucille: All his shirts are yellowed—

Blaise: [160]Wearing you out with errands—

Lucille: He demands we fire Nurse.

Blaise: [161]When he could hire a driver. [162]Has he mentioned the mortgage?

Lucille: He makes me read him the headlines, check his stocks.

Blaise: [163]Explain why we're paying of his personal loan.

Lucille: I can't bring the subject up.

Blaise: [164]You shouldn't have to.

Lucille: We'll have to economize while I get him to replenish my accounts. It's scary watching him fail. He gets mad when I say you're unemployed. And when I say aunt's dead, he screams, "Nobody told me."

Blaise: [165]His body is shutting down, for God's sake.

Lucille: I know he's dying. Lord, I saw the diapers. Go see him.

Blaise: [166]I can't tell him what he wants to hear.

Lucille: He'll be ruthless if you don't comply.

Blaise: [167]Here's money for the note.

Lucille: You pawned your wedding ring? You said you would never!

Blaise: [168]I'll get it back . . . [169]Summer stock theaters are auditioning.

Lucille: You promised we could live here. I can't go off to god knows where. Leave Uncle. Don't be selfish. Next spring is time enough to start all that. ([170]BLAISE *storms out.* LUCILLE *follows.*)

INSTRUCTIONS

You are requested to finish scoring this act—using the method demonstrated above—to create the most effective interpretation. Your score should fit into the overall play which continues with the ending of Act I.

(*The coach lights on the gallery cast a weird glow.* SUSANNE *returns disheveled.* TED *in a smart white suit, follows calling "Susanne."*)

Ted: Some Latino festival's in the Quarter. I could barely get uptown.

Susanne: We don't need the obligatory traffic update.

Ted: You look like a leftover from Saturday night. Fix up.

Susanne: I'm dressed.

Ted: You been drinking again?

Susanne: I deal with sponsors best when I'm manic.

Ted: I leave you, and you have to get drunk. Sixteen hundred is a lot to sink into a one-time dress.

Susanne: I'm trying to figure out—

Ted: Comb your hair.

Susanne: If I've ever made a fool of myself—

Ted: Change that lipstick.

Susanne: With these people in the past.

Ted: Here's your makeup and purse.

Susanne: I'm not carrying this "going to the dance bag."

Ted: Stuart's coming. You needn't cultivate him if he's cold. (TED'S *cell phone rings.*) But whatever's nice about him, I want you to find. He never risks sweating. Soon as May ends, he's off to Newport. (SUSANNE *exits.*)

Ted: (*answers phone*) Ma. I know about the festival. Don't mention that horror again. Susanne goes out of her way to make things difficult. (*hangs up, paces. We hear a crash offstage.*) Susanne!

Susanne: (*offstage*) I'm okay.

Ted: (*calls to* SUSANNE) Hurry up. It's your big show! (BLAISE *enters in a white jacket with drinks.* TED *confronts him.*) It might be bearable if someone wasn't screwing up her mind. Mother heard you were nymphomaniacs. I'm beginning to understand those red-eye bus trips. The nights Susanne would cry all the way till morning.

Blaise: Have a martini.

Ted: (*slaps it off*) What! No! I don't want a shitty drink. I helped her break through her perfectionism . . . I got her to paint even when she was drinking and walking the floor . . . And she would still be painting if . . . (LUCILLE *enters, dressed in a long gown and carrying a soup tureen.*)

Lucille: Turtle soup from the country club.

Blaise: We're famished.

Lucille: Oh lord. I'm so thrilled about seeing Susanne's show with Susanne.

Ted: Y'all go eat. (*calls*) Susanne! Soup's hot.(*to* LUCILLE) That's what I've been missing—

Lucille: Indulgence (SUSANNE *enters*. BLAISE *looks at her with entrancement*. TED *inspects her to make sure she's dressed properly.*)

Susanne: I can't eat. Thinking of those turtles without their shells—

Blaise: You look like you just arrived from New York.

Ted: Is that's a compliment?

Susanne: I like to dress up fancy. Leave the Poor Clare nun for the designer dress. (*to* BLAISE) Ted's my motivation.

Blaise: I wouldn't have thought you needed motivation.

Susanne: You've an air of heightened Edwardian elegance.

Blaise: It's my look.

Susanne: Well, it's working.

Ted: Honey, put this napkin on. Last time you spilled—

Susanne: I'm not wearing a bib.

Blaise: Please.

Susanne: (*to* BLAISE) You must be thirsty?

Blaise:	Especially for a good sherry. (BLAISE *pours sherry in his soup.*)
Ted:	Water for me.
Susanne:	I'll have a drink of water with my two friends.
Ted:	You only have two friends?
Blaise:	Some people don't have any.
Susanne:	Blaise likes my humor when I'm half-crazed with exhaustion.
Blaise:	Ted. You needn't have worried about Susanne's drinking. (SUSANNE *drops her eyes onto the sherry as if she'll drink it, but she only sniffs it with distaste.*)
Susanne:	I can't believe you didn't trust me.
Ted:	Well, your mind was wandering, and you were brushing your teeth a lot.
Susanne:	You imagined I . . .
Ted:	Was taking these big slugs before I could get to you.
Susanne:	I'm going for a walk. Give me my cape.
Ted:	I'll accompany you.
Susanne:	I don't need mother. I'm about to scream—
Ted:	You can't go in the park. All dolled up with that jewelry.
Susanne:	Don't touch me.
Ted:	Someone will kill you. Leave your purse.
Lucille:	Your show's in an hour!

(SUSANNE *leaves.* BLAISE *picks up a cigarette, follows her. Uneasy,* LU-CILLE *arranges the table, watching* TED *who eats nervously and glances out at the two.*)

Lucille:	Pearl-handled spoons, smooth, from years of eating pleasure. How could one be grumpy with such a spoon?
Ted:	I couldn't.
Lucille:	My aunt had a service for sixty in this pattern. See?
Ted:	An acorn's chiseled at the neck.
Lucille:	She used to count silver after every party . . . demitasse tea-spoons, tablespoons, soup spoons, serving spoons, grapefruit spoons . . . You're not listening.

Ted:	I am. I'm just—of course I hear you.
Lucille:	My aunt had a special drawer for her spoons . . . she took . . .
Ted:	Let me help. You shouldn't have to pick up alone. (Lights fade.)

Scene 3

Setting:	7:00 the next morning. Steamy hot. The sun bathes the scene in gold light, intensified by the dampness.
At Rise:	BLAISE, in a crumpled white jacket, has been fitfully dozing. Looks at his watch. Grabs a journal, pen, writes.
Blaise:	I must be vigilant. Stay honest. (*writes some more*) Better to hammer stone in a quarry like Howard Roark than to sell my soul to the parasites. (*Phone rings.* BLAISE *answers it.*) Hello. . . . You want to buy a . . . No. Susanne has not come back. (BLAISE *hangs up.* TED *rushes in, his suit rumpled.*)
Ted:	Is that . . . Susanne?
Blaise:	The phone is a terrible invention that allows people to enter your home without being invited. Your mother.
Ted:	How could Susanne run off?
Blaise:	I phoned the hospitals.
Ted:	She's a manic-depressive. Takes four pills a day.
Blaise:	I can't spend my day worrying.
Ted:	I'm not sure you worry about anyone but yourself . . . Susanne used to be an addict, smoking pot, sniffing coke; she was an alcoholic. . . .
Blaise:	Coffee?
Ted:	I never drink coffee in the morning. It keeps me awake.

(BLAISE *pours two jiggers. Hands one to* TED.)

Ted:	I've no control over her.
Blaise:	You've more control than anyone else.
Ted:	I think it's going to come to me—how to deal with her—if I keep running my mouth. God knows what it's doing to my system. I'll probably give birth to six ulcers. (*Phone rings.*

TED *answers it.*) Hello, Ma. No, she's not back yet . . . No one's called. I'm not rude . . . Look, I can't talk. I said good-bye. Mom. (*pretends he's talking to someone else.*) I'm coming. (*speaks into the phone.*) I'll call you. (*hangs up the phone. Picks up* BLAISE's *journal.*) What's this? Private concerns—

Blaise: (*grabs the book*) How bad off was she?

Ted: The others stopped drinking about eleven. They were drunk, and didn't want to get drunker.
(checks his watch.) At one, she took her paintings and disappeared.

Blaise: You can't handcuff yourself to her.

Ted: Her life's blood's in that show and the assassins are sharpening their knives.

Blaise: I told her if you're going to invite critics, at least have ones who like you. (*Cell phone rings.* TED *answers and speaks into it.*)

Ted: Mom? . . . I can't talk. No. I can barely hear you . . . God what! I'll call back when I get privacy. (TED *hangs up, exits.*)

(BLAISE *crosses to liquor tray, pours bourbon in his coffee. Picks up a cigarette and walks to the gallery, returns and sits by the phone.* LUCILLE *arrives, lugging a portfolio.* SHE *switches up the baby minder. We hear a moaning.* SHE *turns, her eyes strange, unblinking, taking in* BLAISE.)

Lucille: After Church, the Holy Spirit inspired me. I drove by the Quarter. You won't believe it . . . I found Susanne's paintings.

Blaise: Where?

Lucille: Literally on the pavement. The manager said Susanne drank herself into a stupor. He took her incapacitated body out the bar—(*Lifts paintings.*) Look. It's her new *Triangle* Series.

(UNCLE *moans through the baby minder.* LUCILLE *looks up, nervous.* BLAISE *puts away the portfolio.*)

Blaise: I'll take these till later.

Nurse: (*offstage*) It's Nurse. Your uncle's having difficulty breathing. I've called an ambulance.

Lucille: Oh God. We can't take him to . . .

Nurse:	(*offstage*) Doctor wants him at the hospital.
Lucille:	Yesterday he was his impish self.(laughs nervously.)
Nurse:	(*offstage*) He needs you.
Lucille:	Where's the holy water? And those relics? I keep thinking if he doesn't go to the hospital he won't die. (LUCILLE *exits. Squad car sirens blare.* BLAISE *hides the paintings. Flashing lights brighten the gallery. There are scrambling sounds outside, car doors slamming.*)
Lucille:	(*offstage*) What's that?
Blaise:	A police car
Ted:	(*rushing on*) Was I parked in the wrong zone? (SUSANNE *traipses in, barefoot, with a rumpled newspaper. Her sequined gown is ripped, her hair messed, her eyes glazed. A cape flung over her keeps falling off.*)
Cop:	(*blares offstage*) I'm on a twenty-one flag down with a nineteen. Took her from the VCD to the second district.
Ted:	Who was that?
Susanne:	The city's most prominent policeman. He teaches sailing at the Southern Yacht Club, where he and his family are members. He doesn't put the people he arrests in the police report; they go on the society page.
Ted:	Let me get that cape? There's blood in your hair. A cut on your shoulder.
Susanne:	I always dress wrong.
Ted:	(*exiting*) I'll get something to wash you up.
Susanne:	(*looks at her corsage.*) My flowers are wilted. They were happy earlier, but now they're grieving. Throw them out. (*yanks off petals and mumbles.*) He loves me. He loves me not. He loves me—
Blaise:	Not.
Susanne:	I don't listen to the words.
Blaise:	I'd like to start my day not talking to you. So the first hours aren't spoilt—

Susanne:	Sorry. I was trying to be successful; partially to impress you and partially to get your sympathy if that didn't work out. I'm going to ask for what I want, as soon as I figure out what that is—
Blaise:	Cigarette, maybe? (BLAISE *passes one to her. SHE bursts out sobbing.*)
Susanne:	The trouble with past relationships is they're endless.
Blaise:	Have a smoke?
Susanne:	I'm holding out for as long as I can. I've stopped, but I don't know if I've quit. (*laughs. Holds her forehead.*) Oh, my head.
Blaise:	Let me close these blinds. You don't have to kill yourself. Sleep. (*Choir practice from Holy Name Church resounds the hymn, "I danced in the morning when the world was begun, And I danced in the moon and the stars and the sun. And I came down from heaven and I danced on earth at Bethlehem." She pulls him down on her. They kiss.*)

End of Act I

Act II, Scene1

Sequence 1

Setting:	Parlor, continued. (BLAISE leans over and kisses SUSANNE who looks bruised and delicate[171].) TED enters. He and BLAISE wear the same crumpled white suits from before.
Ted:	(*to* BLAISE) You used to be lovers.
Blaise:	[172]Says who?
Ted:	You're tormenting her.
Blaise:	[173]Please!
Ted:	She can't be creative around you.
Susanne:	It's okay, Ted.
Ted:	No, it's not. You were on the verge of greatness—now look at you. Walking around comatose. Remembering Blaise's comments, and saying your talent's lost. What's he doing to you?

Blaise:	[174]Have you forgotten I'm married?
Ted:	I haven't forgotten your lovely wife, but evidently you have. (*yelling offstage*) WHY DON'T YOU GO TO YOUR WIFE?
Blaise:	[175]Fine. (*Exits.* TED *goes to the bar, seizes a drink.*)

Sequence 2

Ted:	What happened after you left the party?
Susanne:	I was drinking in the Napoleon House. I think I was drinking there. I hope I was—there. Ha!
Ted:	And afterwards?
Susanne:	They say I got in a brawl over some Mardi Gras beads, was beat up. There's this huge gash on my shoulder.
Ted:	What do you remember?
Susanne:	Not much. I forgot my shoes.
Ted:	(*alarmed*) And your paintings?
Susanne:	I left them . . . someplace.
Ted:	Try to recall where.
Susanne:	Wait . . . wait . . . no . . . nothing. It's over.
Ted:	Think now.
Susanne:	The exposition of Susanne Dupré.
Ted:	Think hard!
Susanne:	I don't want to—
Ted:	Why not?
Susanne:	These aren't my people in the stiff suits and straight chairs.
Ted:	WHAT SHOULD I MAKE OF THAT CRACK?
Susanne:	I thought I'd be happy seeing the . . . applause.
Ted:	AND YOU WERE!
Susanne:	How do I hold onto reality? When can I paint?
Ted:	Let's find the paintings you lost.
Susanne:	People say talk about yourself, paint later.
Ted:	I come from a line of Southerners with modest talent.

Susanne:	Oh, please!
Ted:	I wanted to lift you to world class.
Susanne:	You've ten shows this month.
Susanne:	Cancel them.
Ted:	You've spent the money. You know the work it took to get those? You're going to drop your schedule? Become a floating artist? Why are you the talk of the art scene? Because you've got me pushing you and panting ten steps behind. God. I should have seen the narcissist you are. Always sending me to do one more thing. I'm disgusted. You want to cancel things! Fine. Where's my coat? Remember the revenue of the art business is the same as *sausage*.
Susanne:	(*calls after*) You don't mind what mediocrity I paint, long as you can sell it. (TED *exits. Doorbell rings. Offstage, we hear* NURSE *answer and priests enter, whispering and fawning.*) ([176]BLAISE *enters.* SUSANNE *undoes her blouse, exposing a shoulder wound. There is a startling change in* BLAISE'S *manner.* HE *crosses cautiously to her.*) Would you . . . fix this . . . bandage?
Blaise:	[177]You're scary.
Susanne:	It looks more theatrical than it is. (*gestures to the newspaper*) You saw the review in the *Times*?
Blaise:	[178]You remember that book that says you have to pass through stages to evolve? [179]That critic hasn't passed through stage one.

Sequence 3

Susanne:	Take a look. (SHE *hands him the paper.* [180]BLAISE *turns on a silk lamp and reads. A flicker of light, narrow and intense, streams down. Church bells chime seven o'clock.*)
Blaise:	[181]Nasty.
Susanne:	I'm so embarrassed.
Blaise:	[182]Does he have some vendetta against you?
Susanne:	I have to stop reading these notices.

Blaise:	[183]"The event was very organized," he says. [184]"Thank God. I'd hate to think it meant something."
Susanne:	My flesh crawls when I hear that voice coming through the pages.
Blaise:	[185]Never listen to those who demean your gift.
Susanne:	I felt the slaughter coming—
Blaise:	[186]Their motive is envy always.
Susanne:	It happens every now and then, but I was hoping for then and not now.
Blaise:	[187]Art's a bleak world—
Susanne:	I shouldn't let it hurt me.
Blaise:	[188]You're human—
Susanne:	Chaotic moments come but . . . Sometimes I just feel wounded.
Blaise:	[189]Everyone has a broken heart. [190]Everyone has suffered or will suffer incredible loss. [191]Don't budge. [192]Don't bow. [193]You don't have to hide and lick your wounds like the youthful Cezanne.
Susanne:	I hated those paintings. I had sessions with Ted, went away—
Blaise:	[194]Monet refused to show his water lilies—
Susanne:	And came back with something that'd deteriorated.
Blaise:	[195]Fabergé told his artists to dream of golden castles.
Susanne:	I've been dreaming about you—of how hard these months have been—
Blaise:	(*his voice drops.*) [196]They were tough on everybody.
Susanne:	Lucille's made a big splash in the papers. (BLAISE *takes out a cigarette, tosses it aside.*)
Blaise:	[197]You're not going to force me to do something, not in my best interest—.
Susanne:	You like it with her?
Blaise:	[198]Lucille is kind, reliable. [199]She won't run off with—
Susanne:	You've anesthetized yourself?

Blaise:	[200]I'm going to be working in my own theater business.
Susanne:	Where?
Blaise:	[201]Summer stock theaters are starting up.
Susanne:	There's none here.
Blaise:	[202]We'll open one. [203; 204]I'll do it slower than you'd want me to. [205]Timeline one to two years to get running. [206]In my later years I'd like to be back in New York.
Susanne:	Where do we fit . . . together?
Blaise:	[207]You're doing what you need to for your career, [208]and you're making progress.
Susanne:	Not true.(*The morning angelus chimes from Holy Name Church. Sunlight glows over the park.*)
Blaise:	[209]I wish you well. [210]I do, [211]I mean it.
Susanne:	You can't expect me to hang around—watching you two—
Blaise:	[212]It's a *marriage blanc*—
Susanne:	Night after night—
Blaise:	[213]A sexless marriage—(*retrieves the paintings and turns to her with pleading eyes.*) [214]Lucille found your sketches— slightly damaged.
Susanne:	I don't care about the paintings, strangely—
Blaise:	[215]You can repair them. [216]Throw yourself into—
Susanne:	Burn them. I don't want to paint now.
Blaise:	[217]'Course you do.
Susanne:	Are you keeping them to torture me?
Blaise:	[218]Calm down.
Susanne:	No! Ted never could see why some art had to be destroyed. (*lighting a match.*)
Blaise:	[219]They're not your best work. [220]True.
Susanne:	I spent seven months making paintings I despised. I created monsters, and I want them killed! (SHE *thrusts sketches into the fireplace.*)

Blaise:	[220A]God. [221]Don't do that.
Susanne:	I didn't want to hang this. Ted tore it out my hands.
Blaise:	[222]Stop shouting.
Susanne:	The painting is a shroud, and nothing happens till—
Blaise:	[223]Enough!
Susanne:	The spirit returns, and the painter gets back inside. I hate them! Hate! Hate! (*sobs*) Can't you . . .
Blaise:	[224]OK, Susanne.
Susanne:	Burn the paintings for me?
	([225]BLAISE *downs liquor.* [226]*Takes a match to the fireplace.*)
Blaise:	[227]There. I'm burning—
Susanne:	We're burning them!
Blaise:	[228]Right. [229]We're doing it.
Susanne:	Oh yes. Yes. Now people can remember me like I was.

(*Ambulance sirens come louder and louder.* SUSANNE *runs out.* TED *rushes on stage followed by* LUCILLE.)

Ted:	That's the ambulance.
Blaise:	([230]*crossing down and looking out*) [231]It's here.
Lucille:	Oh God, it's time.
Nurse:	(*offstage*) Make way, everyone.
Male Voice #1:	(*offstage*) We're coming through. COMING THROUGH.

Act II, Scene 2

Sequence 1

Setting:	Later that day. The gallery glows in afternoon light.
At Rise:	[232]BLAISE is reviewing a book. LUCILLE enters lugging a man's suitcase, bags, and canes. [233]BLAISE goes to embrace her, but SHE backs off.
Blaise:	[234]Your uncle died?
Lucille:	Lord. Oh. Yes. During the Last Rites, Uncle couldn't breathe; I needed you.

Blaise: [235]Didn't you get my message?

Lucille: Don't. The Bible says honor your relatives—

Blaise: [236]It also says don't lie. (*smiles vaguely.*)

Lucille: Kindness is something your family either taught you or not. You needn't feel nice, but you should act nice—

Blaise: [237]Janus-faced.

Lucille: The service is Wednesday morning, for those interested. Uncle's last words were: "Where's Blaise?" He wanted me to have a real partner. (*fumbles out a plastic bag*) The attorney gave me these trinkets: some spoons. Uncle's rings and his watch, and his will. (*hands BLAISE the will.*)

Blaise: [238]You want to read it?

Lucille: Sure.([239]BLAISE *reads. His face pales.*)

Lucille: What's wrong?

Blaise: [240]I don't know how to—God—

Lucille: (*grabbing the will*) The entire estate goes to the Dominicans except for . . . What's this? He's willing me—these pearl handled spoons?

Blaise: [241]The bastard went through with it.[242]Here I felt . . .

Lucille: I can't . . . believe it—

Blaise: [243]If I stayed away—He might leave you something—-

Lucille: Oh my lord. Mercy. Oh no.

Blaise: [244]You look weak.

Lucille: There hasn't been time to tell you with all the commotion . . . but I took a pregnancy test.

Blaise: [245]It's just . . . I don't feel—

Lucille: The doctor said it's unlikely. We'll have the results later today. Don't be depressed, I can't take it if you are. A woman always fears she'll miss out—Since we've been home you . . . neglect me to share confidences with Susanne.

Blaise: [246]God! Don't talk this way.

Lucille: Are you screwing her?

Blaise: [247]No. [248]You're overwrought.

Lucille: I'm falling apart. Uncle tried to set things straight. He tried and tried to talk to you . . .

Blaise: [249]Don't punish me because your mean uncle—

Lucille: You dawdle with nowhere plans—Why do this to us?

Blaise: [250]I'm going out. ([251]*grabs a cigarette.*)

Lucille: I needed you at the hospital and I need you now. Marriage means being there. (LUCILLE *looks around with dismay.* [252]BLAISE *puts on his tennis shoes.*) You can't just waste hours with some part you may never play. (*picks up the empty portfolio.*) Where are Susanne's paintings?

Blaise: [253]"Disparus," as the French would say . . . [254]I—We burned them.

Lucille: (*horrified*) Not possible.

Blaise: [255]Susanne couldn't bear seeing . . . [256]art she hated.

Lucille: (*stunned*) They were priceless.

(*The phone rings.* [257]BLAISE *answers it.*)

Blaise: [258]It's Blaise . . .[259]Yeah . . .

Lucille: Artists must separate ego from art. Art claims its own life. You can't destroy it because the artist isn't—in the same place— (*irritated*) Tell whoever's calling about Uncle.

Blaise: (*into the phone*) [260]I love the part. [261]They're paying that much. [262]When? ([263]*hangs up. To* LUCILLE) [264]Some friends are starting a summer theater.

Lucille: Where?

Blaise: [265]New York. [266]I want us to go.

Lucille: Now?

Blaise: [267]I don't want to turn into all I've hated. [268]I'd rather do everything bad and get caught.

Lucille: We have to clean out Uncle's place.

Blaise: [269]The Dominicans can do it. [270]There's nothing holding us, sweetie. [271]You can visit anytime, [272]but I'm never coming back—[273]ever . . . [274]You said you'd support—

Lucille: Opportunity, at the right time—

Blaise: [275]Every day I do what I have to and you look sadder.

Lucille: Your talent won't take care of us.

Blaise: [276]I'm beginning to hate the sight of this house—[277]With the big mortgage. [278]Here I'll assign you my interest.

Lucille: I won't live in some rattrap.

Blaise: [279]I never asked that—-

Lucille: I can, could, and probably will leave Exposition Boulevard soon.

Blaise: [280]Good girl.

Lucille: But we don't have to leave it now.

Blaise: [281]I won't let property trap us. [282]I'm an artist.

Lucille: Says who? Sorry.

Blaise: [283]I'm going. (*haltingly*) [284]You'll come?

Lucille: I need to hire a good lawyer. Uncle was out of his mind when he made this will. Undue influence is how it happened.

Blaise: [285]I'm heading back. [286]Eventually something is going to hit. [287]If I keep pushing, I'll keep finding. [288]I've got the drive—

Lucille: You're crazy.

Blaise: [289]I'm not sure [290]but I'll act in my best interest—

Lucille: Self-absorbed—

Blaise: [291]And from that strength.

Lucille: Reckless—

Blaise: [292]I won't be fooled!

Lucille: Uncle was right.

Blaise: [293]This is what it feels like to live. [294]I'll take it. (*Exits.*) (*A bit later, the house phone rings and* LUCILLE *gets it.* TED *enters carrying a large box.* LUCILLE *gasps at his miserably timed appearance.* SHE *hangs up the phone.*)

Lucille: Susanne's not here.

Ted: What's wrong?

Lucille: Uncle died. Blaise's moving. I'm disinherited.

Ted: All in one day?

Lucille:	And I found out I'm not pregnant.
Ted:	Maybe that's a good thing.
Lucille:	I'm by myself now.
Ted:	I need your help. (*lifts one of* SUSANNE's *drawings from the box.*) Do you recognize this?
Lucille:	My eyes are blurry.
Ted:	Discarded sketches. I've retrieved hundreds. Could you organize them? Take over her lectures?
Lucille:	I'm starting to cry . . .
Ted:	You know her work better than anyone.
Lucille:	First, I need to confront this letter. (*hands it to* TED) Read it? After his will, I can't bear to.
Ted:	It's from your uncle.
Lucille:	I'm his only heir and he gives all to the Church.
Ted:	(reads) "Dear Lucille, You and Blaise need to start out on your own."
Lucille:	Nasty!
Ted:	(*reads*) "Still your aunt and I wanted *you alone* to have this bag."
Lucille:	Worthless heirlooms—
Ted:	(*reads*) "Special spoons for a special heart." Uncle Gene.
Lucille:	Rusted silver . . .
Ted:	A few dollars a spoon.
Lucille:	(*opens bag.*) What's this? Oh!
Ted:	A paper?
Lucille:	Heavenly mother! Oh, no?
Ted:	(*takes the paper.*) It's a life insurance policy for—
Lucille:	Six, seven,
Ted:	eight figures.
Lucille:	Oh no!
Ted:	You're the beneficiary.

Lucille: Good lord! There must be some mistake.

Ted: There's your name. The policy is paid in full.

Lucille: It's a miracle! Oh my!

Ted: Fabulous!

Lucille: I'll pay off the mortgage. I can live here like—

Ted: You did before! Great.

Lucille: We'll start a tradition.

Ted: A new artist a month at Exposition Boulevard.

Lucille: Oh my God. Mercy. Yes.

Ted: But can the heiress still do Susanne's lectures?

Lucille: You haven't canceled anything yet?

Ted: No.

Lucille: We'll create a retrospective with Tulane.

Ted: Mother will be delighted.

Lucille: We'll work upstairs, clear out Uncle's quarters.

Ted: Wonderful! (THEY *continue to plan as* THEY *exit. From the Cathedral we hear the hymn, "City of God." "Let us build the City of God, / May our tears be turned into dancing, / For the Lord, our Light and our Love, / Has turned the night into day."*)

Sequence 2

(*Moments later* [295]BLAISE *walks in to pack.* SUSANNE *enters nervously, looks at the park.*)

Susanne: Beautiful night . . . Starry skies. Moon's coming up over the park. It rained earlier and we needed the rain . . .Oh, . . . is that Ted with Lucille?

Blaise: (*looking out*) [296]Who knows? . . . [297]I'm leaving.

Susanne: You work on a short fuse.

Blaise: [298]The essence of flight is immediacy.

Susanne: You're leaving to do a play?

Blaise: [299]Something like that.

Susanne:	I once ran off with a guy who promised me a string of pearls. I did what I was supposed to do, but—
Blaise:	[300]People don't pay you well in the theater I work in.
Susanne:	You owe me pearls.
Blaise:	[301]It pays in the high two figures like an allowance. [302]The smart actor—
Susanne:	I'm dreaming of you—
Blaise:	[303]Makes you buy a ticket to see him.
Susanne:	Your touch—
Blaise:	[304]I can't think of one successful actor with a—
Susanne:	Your body—
Blaise:	[305]Happy home life. [306]One of my friends is in drug rehab—
Susanne:	To me you are—the sound of leaves stirring—
Blaise:	[307]Another jumped off the Mississippi River Bridge—
Susanne:	Water over cool stones—
Blaise:	[308]My most stable friend had a nervous breakdown—
Susanne:	You arouse the dark side of my soul. Say there's room for me, Blaise. Just say—there's room ([309]HE *takes her in his arms. A melancholy refrain from "The City of God" is heard from the Cathedral. "Let us build the City of God, / May our tears be turned into dancing, / For the Lord, our Light and our Love, / Has turned the night into day."*)

The End

Score for Blaise

Super objective: to find a new life
Spine: to make my marriage work
Main action: to rid the past

OBJECTIVE	ACTION	OBSTACLE	INNER IMAGE

ACT I, SCENE 1

SEQUENCE 1

SCENE TAG: AVOIDING SUSANNE

SEQUENCE 1 TAG: DUMPING TED

OBJECTIVE	ACTION	OBSTACLE	INNER IMAGE
1. get rid of intruders	to ignore	Ted's persistence Lucille's love of gossip	PO—T— McClain
2. to get rid of Ted	to confront	his persistence, my wife's enthusiasm, my secret past, racing heart	family at Favre door
3. to chase him out	to terrify	his stubbornness Lucille's love of gossip	T. McClain, K.P. at back door
4. to usher Ted out	to say goodbye	Lucille's enthusiasm, love of gossip business with his glasses. My fear of exposure	T. McClain at door SCH envelopes
5. to cancel his proposal	to close the art subject	my wife is art historian, the family, obsessed with art	Louvre, Renoir, Degas books Degas and V.

OBJECTIVE	ACTION	OBSTACLE	INNER IMAGE
6. to avoid Lucille's illusions	to close kid's subject	Lucille's neediness, this family's lineage, Ted's enthusiasm	blue eyes, birth control pills
7. to get Ted out	to remind of sickness	Lucille has baby monitor, supplies for Uncle Gene, uneasiness with my relationship with Uncle	Bob's mom. Rosary at hospital
8. to move Ted out	to dismiss	passion for Susanne, loneliness, Lucille's coldness	Degas, Germany, D. V. David at UCLA
9. to keep him out	to encourage	his intrusiveness, attraction to my wife, nosiness, his money, class, background	T. McClain. Maybe someone will keep him outside
10. to terminate further talk of	to distance	it's Lucille's house, no privacy, Uncle Gene's throat cancer	need for caffeine, Marlboros

ACT I, SCENE 1

SEQUENCE 2

SEQUENCE 2 TAG: DUMPING SUSANNE

OBJECTIVE	ACTION	OBSTACLE	INNER IMAGE
11. to get rid of Susanne	to ignore	my passion, her fame, Lucille's a fan Susanne is stubborn	Rory my selling car
12. to humiliate	to berate	her fame, instability control	T. Chase, explosiveness

13. to distance Lucille with Susanne	to duck	Lucille's house, she's in control	Friendship diary
14. to encourage her to cancel	to salute	she was an alcoholic	T. in S.M.
15. to threaten Susanne with exposure	to belittle	her temper flares, addiction	T. with Pam in S.M.
16. to expose her addiction	to tempt	Susanne's temper, drinking	B.M. in N.O. at Columns
17. to squelch the event	to contradict	her persistence, Lucille is enamored of her	Bob's house in Defiance
18. to win her sympathy	to reveal nerves	she's cold and Lucille's blind Lucille likes threes	Friendship D. and B.'s selfishness
19. to keep her from pursuing triangle	to insult painting	Susanne likes threes. Lucille likes three	Larry C., David and G, Joe W.
20. to repulse Susanne	to insult all painting	she is hardheaded, a sex maniac	triangles at UCLA
21. to kill her plan	to leave	L. & S. seem in collusion me. It's her house.	fleeing Fontainebleau
22. to punish Lucille	to insist	She is dense, doesn't hear me. It's her house, don't want to be with her.	SCH at Favre
23. to warn Susanne	to correct	She is hardheaded, fierce, and determined. It's late	D. V. at NYC

OBJECTIVE	ACTION	OBSTACLE	INNER IMAGE
24. to kill further philosophy	to refute	Susanne's intelligence. My desire for it, boredom with Lucille.	B. on tractor
25. to avoid being alone with Susanne	to stop her	my attraction to her, her cunning, her beauty, intelligence	D.V. at NYC

ACT I, SCENE 1

SEQUENCE 3

SEQUENCE 3 TAG: INTERROGATING SUSANNE

OBJECTIVE	ACTION	OBSTACLE	INNER IMAGE
26. to put her on defensive	to change subject	She's elusive. It's Lucille's house.	Nocci's in N.O.
27. to put her on defensive	to attack	She's elusive. It's Lucille's house.	Defiance Church
28. to rattle her hope	to shut her up	her persistence, my attraction, her beauty, Lucille's clumsiness, glamour of L.A.	N.O. So. Rep.
29. to rush her out	to close subject	longer she is here more attracted I get, our being alone	
30. to deny, only desire for artist's life	to crack a joke	L.A., one-room apartment	UCLA— no car.
31. to get her to leave	to close a subject	her beauty, her soul that shines through	my empty account at Chase

ACT I, SCENE 1

SEQUENCE 4

SEQUENCE 4 TAG: HELPING LUCILLE

32. to get Lucille's sympathy	to reject	insufficient postage, my mailings	8 × 10 glossy photos
33. to help Lucille	to duck away	Lucille's absent-mindedness about all but art	cost of photos $925
34. to relieve Lucille	to do chores	her stubbornness in doing all herself just back from honeymoon	Fontainebleau— feeble help Ms. Gremillion cancer/bed

ACT I, SCENE 1

SEQUENCE 5

SEQUENCE 5 TAG: SUBDUING SUSANNE

35. to find a way to distance her	to watch	Lucille and help, all watching, lateness of hour uneasiness of being alone	Expos Blvd. lamps in oak trees
36. to find way to distance her	to mock	Susanne's beautiful voice and sweetness	beauty of Audubon Park at sundown
37. to halt conversation	to plea time	Beautiful night, Lucille's business	RPO
38. to alert Susanne to eavesdroppers	to question	people visiting, maids, nurse	garage in back

OBJECTIVE	ACTION	OBSTACLE	INNER IMAGE
39. to bring her out	call out Lucille	indoor/outdoor house	Bob outside window
40. to terminate Susanne	insist on time line my change	darkness, being alone with her	bomb in pocket "The Superior Man"
41. to gain her sympathy	to demonstrate my change	Susanne needs therapy	"Authentic Happiness" "The Superior Man"
42. to impress her with how rational I am	to keep rational	Susanne doesn't know me	consultant books Choice theory
43. to convince her I'm rational	to prove my determination	sex is driven	Rules I, Rules II
44. to discourage collaboration	to deny	isolation with Susanne	four friends in church in Defiance
45. to convince of isolation	describe weakness		JBO café
46. to throw her out my world	to reject pose	our past when she drew me	David Craig

ACT I, SCENE 1

SEQUENCE 6

SEQUENCE 6 TAG: KEEPING LUCILLE HERE

47. to keep Lucille out here	to guard	Uncle's health; just back from honeymoon full house of chores	Bob—D. V. alone

48. to get her to take care of me	to beg	her business, lateness, chores since wedding, Uncle's needs, Susanne's attentiveness	Mrs. G upstairs with cancer
49. to get her in bed	to seduce	Susanne's presence, Lucille's manners	yellowed cover, blue patchwork quilt

ACT I, SCENE 1

SEQUENCE 7

SEQUENCE 7 TAG: HIDING FROM SUSANNE

50. to hide my failure from her	to give her a clue	her knowledge of me, the art world, my shame	C.U. x. phone cell
51. to close subject	to pinpoint	her persistence	
52. to distract her with poetry	to toss off	solitude, her beauty	sweet Bud
53. to cancel subject	to stop up	her persistence, her knowledge of	"Agave"
54. to get her sympathy	to excuse	her beauty, money, success	Paris, vice
55. to distract her from my harsh reality	to wax poetic	her perception, my shame	Jung at UCLA
56. to get her sympathy	to defend	pain of failure, difficult to rehash	foyer at Cornell, waiting on sofa

OBJECTIVE	ACTION	OBSTACLE	INNER IMAGE
57. to get her to laugh	to joke	my shame at situation, my perfectionism	C.U. applications, meeting
58. to get her off my case	to confirm	her persistence, her knowledge of me	R.P—dog with rag in mouth
59. to can the subject	to shirk off	her persistence, her knowledge of me	C. U—B. L.
60. to can the subject	to insult	her knowledge of Hollywood Nurses and Maids	Keys to S.P.
61. to shut her up	to nail	shame—Lucille overhearing nurses and maids about Uncle's cancer	So. Rep—15 years.
62. to pry open her contents	to interrogate	her vagueness, her power as a star, her leaking info	
63. to humiliate her	to reject	my desire for drugs pot in my suitcase now, Lucille's ignorance	
64. to shame her for disbelief	to out her off	Lucille in next room	B—was a dider
65. to let her feel my desperation	to cave in	her success, her jealousy, difficulty in reaching her	R.O. at wedding

66. to get her off my back	to defend	outdoor life	
67. to get her off my back	to describe	her interest in athletics, outdoor life	Loyola gym
68. to get her off my back	to pinpoint		Nike tennis shoes
69. to hide shame	to quell nerves	her fortune, fame. Lucille and servants' big ear	Marlboro lover
70. to make her back off	to defy	her stare, intrusiveness, Lucille and servants' big ear	6 cigarettes a day
71. to shut her up	to concede	her stare, intrusiveness, Lucille and servants' big ear	
72. to punish her	to curse	my shame, Lucille's presence nearby	computer, TV—D. V
73. to get her compassion	to soften	her hardness, unsure of her mental state; is she still on drugs?	tobacco stains in R's purse
74. to keep her light	to mock	producer's death	funeral—dad caskets

OBJECTIVE	ACTION	OBSTACLE	INNER IMAGE
75. to keep her light	to joke	Lucille's proximity	Bu Hilton hotel
76. to get her off the topic	to deny involvement	Susanne's worldly ways	
77. to get her off the topic	to dismiss my involvement	her love of drama	T. McClain RP.
78. to hide my involvement	to reveal my stock	my nerves, Uncle's illness	
79. to hide my involvement	to admit	all the people to and fro for now	grey suit, plaid, hand-made
80. to hide my involvement	to defend		
81. to hide my involvement	to reveal	Lucille's ignorance of my California past	breast— Hollywood
82. to hide my involvement	to concede		
83. to deny my complicity	to expose his arousal		9″ thing
84. to get her sympathy	to defy	my experience with perverts, Lucille's proximity	
85. to get off the subject	to expose	her hardness, her listening, Lucille's proximity	car to Paris
86. to get her compassion	to defy humiliation		zipper
87. to get his compassion	to reveal my humiliation		B—O.S.

88. to get her under-standing	to deny	her attentiveness, others eavesdropping	No stuffing— Degas house
89. to prove my innocence	to defend	can't remember details, too painful, my police record	chase to Degas house
90. to prove my innocence	to defy		
91. to prove my innocence	to blame		ice bucket, pick
92. to prove they framed me	to denounce	upset stomach, lateness of the hour now	No mercy— blood floor
93. to reveal his twisted intentions	to repulse		no mercy cop
94. to get a reprieve	to cover my shame	resistance wearing down	C.U. gig.
95. grab on to Lucille	to cry for help	Lucille's prissiness and blindness. Lucille has worried because—	Bob clearing
96. to hide my failure	to insult	Susanne knows me, Lucille has worried because of her uncle's dislike	M.P.
97. to scare her away	to affirm	her celebrity status	

OBJECTIVE	ACTION	OBSTACLE	INNER IMAGE
98. to intimidate her	to appreciate for a second	she may want to help, lateness of hour	Tyler C
99. to admit vulnerability	to hold her close for a second	my need, Lucille's closeness, lateness of hour	NYC so far

ACT I, SCENE 1

SEQUENCE 8

SEQUENCE 8 TAG: REPRIMANDING LUCILLE

100. to punish her	to applaud	my caring for her, her ignorance of my love for Susanne	D.V. at N.O.
101. to repay her for abandoning me	to make light of	her prudishness	Larry—gin
102. to make her feel guilty	to attack	her attachment to Uncle, illness	M & B folders on drawer
103. to make her feel guilty	to defend	her vulnerability to Uncle, his illness	SCH rear room
104. to wrench her from Uncle's clutches	to order	I've no money, no job	S.H envelope
105. to get her to bond with me	to remind	she loves him, she needs his money, she loves this house	S.H. temple

106.	to get her to bond with me	to defend	she loves him, she needs his money, she loves this house	Favre with strings
107.	to wrench out her support	to justify	Lucille's hardheadedness	R & O will, sticker Fontainebleau
108.	to question her loyalty	to reject	my dislike for Uncle, his past sins	R.H. will tranquility
109.	to question her loyalty	to disbelieve	she's attracted to Uncle, both are devout Catholics, her treachery	Newcomb chapel attic Fontainebleau
110.	to demand her alliance	to hold accountable	her brainwashed state	B.H. in N.O.
111.	to reprimand her forgetfulness	to denounce	Lucille's blindness to Uncle's flaws, his presence upstairs	M.A.G., B. H. in N.O.
112.	to punish her shallowness	to curse	Lucille's blindness to Uncle's flaws	M.A. & B. H. in N.O.
113.	to hurt her	to decry	her naiveté, sweet nature	Fontainebleau
114.	to hurt her for supporting him	to dismiss	her double bend	d.r. table
115.	to criticize her family	to put down false rich	I need their money, support	M.S.—Paris trip
116.	to criticize her family	to insult their smallness	nurses, maids about	G.G. at L.U.

OBJECTIVE	ACTION	OBSTACLE	INNER IMAGE
117. to criticize her school	to denounce bureaucracy	I need her support	Loyola and So. Rep
118. to insult city of N.O.	to put down dilettantes	I'm in New Orleans, surrounded	
119. to dishonor her	to denounce	I like to please and placate	R. Dinner Theater
120. to expose her hypocrisy	to crack joke	pain of the joke	Degas in Paris, M.S.
121. to deride her	to laugh	painful jokes	Miriam S—turncoat
122. to get her on track	to refute	people eavesdropping	RPO Museum— turncoat
123. to get her on track	to deny	He's upstairs, he paid for food, all theater projects	SCH—T. V.
124. to expose the truth	to question	time running out. Need money for theater projects	dr. in white at Touro— unsure
125. to punish her for not telling her sooner	to curse	my insecurity fear of being stuck, broke in N.O.	Mame— feeding stops, hospice floor
125A. to hold honor tall	to shake her off	guilt for hating her uncle	J .S. Sargent

ACT I, SCENE 2.

SEQUENCE 1

SCENE TAG: SUPPRESSING DESIRE FOR SUSANNE

SEQUENCE 1 TAG: KEEPING SUSANNE AT ARM'S LENGTH

126. to wear self out	to work out	keep thinking of Susanne, I've been drinking	St. Char Ave. bed
127. to get her to leave	to set the boundary	time running out. Nurse and maids about	Marge in kitchen
128. to get her to art show	to unnerve	she's nonplused	
129. to denounce her I'm preoccupied	to freshen self	nerves, time	
130. to get her outside	to distance myself	her closeness, tense night air	ibuprofen wife's snoring
131. to encouraging her exit	to surround self with memories	heat, her closeness, time running out	Audubon Park, skip Marae
132. to keep her outside	to point out pals	her closeness lack of boundaries beauty	
133. to keep her outside	to point out gossip	lushness of outdoors	Autumn and other 30-year-olds
134. to keep her outside	to change topic	her beauty, time running out	
135. to keep her outside	to show my change support base	my horniness when with her	Ms. Garon

OBJECTIVE	ACTION	OBSTACLE	INNER IMAGE
136. to keep her outside	to stress my support base	It's a lie. I've no friends here.	J. Benry
137. to convince her, time's up	to absorb self dance	her beauty tense night air	ballet class—Loyola
138. to scare off	to stop touch	time's running out around us	B's hand on my head houses/people all about V.P.
139. to scare off	to warn with joke	my desire for her, caretakers around us	romance of R.V., wealthy houses/people all about V.P.
140. to keep her hands clean	to warn	Lucille's arrival, time running out	tires on gravel
141. to keep her hands clean	to release her	her beauty, softness	touch of B's hand
142. to keep her hands clean	to freeze her off	her closeness, soft breasts, soft skin	memory of S. L. with her
143. to keep her hands clean	to reprimand	she's gutless, a whore	R.C. is a nympho-maniac
144. to keep her hands clean	to order her off	her persistence, her lack of morals, the pleasure	M. with B.
145. to break free	to defy	people watching, Lucille returning, my body's excitement	O. S.
146. to break free	to silence her	Lucille's arrival, eavesdroppers Susanne's truth	D rubber boots

147. to convince her I'm happy	to defend my departure	my misery, my guilt	stuffing D. house
148. to convince her I'm happy	to reject wild sex	miss good sex, she's attractive, Lucille's not	O. S. with R. C.
149. to convince her I'm happy	to reject with drugs	yearning for a drink now	champagne NAC
150. to convince her I'm happy	to stop her fantasies	I'm flattered she still loves me	"with men you can count on"
151. to convince her I'm happy	to correct	can't forget her, her excitement glamour in this dull house	Susanne's yellow boots
152. to convince her I'm happy	to weaken	my fear on wedding day	R's face
153. to freeze her off	to scare her	time running out, crickets Lucille's approach	
154. to freeze her off	to quiet her guilty	her smell, closeness excitement of her presence	Red perfume
155. to freeze her off	to make her feel guilty	her shame-lessness, the excitement of her presence	opening at S.R.

ACT I, SCENE 2.

SEQUENCE 2

SEQUENCE 2 TAG: PUNISHING LUCILLE

156. to hide my feelings for Susanne	to justify	heat, time running out, strange aloneness discovered with Susanne	P.V. at S. R.

OBJECTIVE	ACTION	OBSTACLE	INNER IMAGE
157. to hide my feelings for Susanne	to explain her visit	awkwardness, Lucille's suspicions	
158. to hide my feelings for Susanne	to console	Lucille's suspicions, lateness of hour	
159. to stop Lucille's blathering about Uncle	to calm her	Uncle is dying, she's tired, lateness of hour	NOA
159A. to stop Lucille's blathering about Uncle	to calm her	Uncle is dying, she's tired, lateness of hour	NOA
160. to stop Lucille's blathering about Uncle	to condemn slave driver	it's his house, he raised her	SCH—Ella
161. to stop Lucille's blathering about Uncle	to condemn slave driver	I live here free	B.H.—Loyola
162. to wake her to danger	to confront danger reasons	her naiveté, I'm outside	envelope at hospital
163. to wake her to danger	to expose his reasons	his cancer, lawyers, papers about	Will in Waveland
164. to wake her to danger	to console	her angry attitude	book across room
165. to garner her support	to terrify her	time running out	potty on Fontainebleau

166.	to garner her support	to refuse	overhead of house	
167.	to garner her support	to act honorably	no employment here	Claudia pawned for stones
168.	to get her to back my acting	to reassure	30 days at pawn shop	gold bracelet, blue earrings, pawned for stones
169.	to get her to back my acting	to applaud	her disinterest	Montane Rep
170.	to avoid killing her	to free topic	her selfish attachment to New Orleans	Ohio "the pond"

NOTE: NEXT SECTION TO THE END OF ACT I IS FOR YOU TO SCORE.

ACT II, SCENE 1

SEQUENCE 1

SCENE TAG: CONFRONTING SUSANNE

SEQUENCE 1 TAG: SHUTTING TED UP

171.	to calm her nerves	to soothe Susanne	Ted's presence, Uncle dying upstairs, Lucille's in next room, I'm tired, disheveled	D. wisdom teeth
172.	clam up Ted	to mock	secret truth, Susanne's craziness	J.O. Tulo
173.	clam up Ted	to refute	attraction to Susanne tense house career	

OBJECTIVE	ACTION	OBSTACLE	INNER IMAGE
174. to blow him off	to set him straight	he's wealthy and he's made her career	R. Birk
175. to blow him off	to concede		

ACT II, SCENE 1

SEQUENCE 2

SEQUENCE 2 TAG: SCARING OFF SUSANNE

OBJECTIVE	ACTION	OBSTACLE	INNER IMAGE
176. to wake her into caring for herself	to confront	drugs, her disappointment, Ted and Lucille	Solitaire after review
177. to wake her into caring for herself	to terrorize	her numbness, distraction	bloody rag
178. to wake her into caring for herself	to joke	her distraction, detachment doped state	authentic happiness R. Dodds
179. to wake her into caring for herself	to attack	her disappointment, cough, illness	Fay critic Mafia

ACT II, SCENE 1

SEQUENCE 3

SEQUENCE 3 TAG: SHORING UP SUSANNE

OBJECTIVE	ACTION	OBSTACLE	INNER IMAGE
180. to console	to minimize	her disbelief	Solitaire review
181. to console	to show outrage	her glamorous state	review of my new work
182. to console	to expose me	ignorance of her recent past	Szanto RPO

183. to console	to mock	humor of put down	T.P. meeting
184. to console	to show under cut	despicable insult	R. Dodds
185. to protect	to warn	difficulty of her not listening	D.P. & T.P. critic
186. to protect	to expose jealousy	her need for love	Joe W.—Janet's
187. to protect	to decry art	her need for my love jealousy	Chinese show at NAC cast
188. to protect	to overrule	my inability to hold her, Lucille's jealousy	roses from Tomye to cast
189. to empower	to commiserate and arrows	her anguish, Lucille's nearby	C. U. phone
190. to empower	to explain slings and arrows	can't hold her, love her	B. H., N. H., M. H., JBO
191. to empower	to encourage	my bad marriage, my trap here	Carrollton by Fontainebleau hold out
192. to empower	to shore up bravery		R. Dodds
193. to empower	to encourage bravery	she's not listening	Cezanne at Louvre
194. to make her claim her genius	to link her pain with Monet	her depression, ignorance of Giverny	Giverny, water lilies in Paris
195. to make her claim her genius	to remind her of Faberge	she's not listening, she's self destructive	eggs at N.O.M.A

OBJECTIVE	ACTION	OBSTACLE	INNER IMAGE
196. to make her claim her genius	to dismiss	Lucille and Ted will be here	painful honey moon (JBO)
197. to get her to go it alone	to reject	my passion for her	Bob, Ohio pond
198. to get her to go it alone	to excuse	my weakness for Susanne	
199. to get her to go it alone	to dig	her seductiveness	D. V 20 seconds, Chicago-Lyn
200. to convince her of my strength	to overrule	my lack of confidence	third floor prod
201. to convince her of my strength	to identify	her disbelief	books on career
202. to convince her of my strength	to proclaim	her mockery	Swine Theater
203. to convince her of my strength	to find my bearings	her stone face	
204. to convince her of my strength	to give myself rope	fear of caving into her	"Can't out-passive passivity."
205. to convince her of my strength	to take lots of rope	fear of failure, fear of exposure	
206. to convince her of my strength	to concede	her disbelief	T. S. Playwright
207. to stall her	to encourage her taking time	her need for me	her limousine, and clothes

208. to stall her	to applaud her path	her desire for sex attraction, horny	O.U. in Louisville NYC
209. to stall her	to congratulate	my longing for work, magnetic attraction, horny	T.S. Playwright, back steps NYC
210. to stall her	to repeat	my marriage responsibilities	
211. to stall her	to insist	this neighbor, loud community	she's Madame
212. relieve her worry	to excuse	Susanne's sexuality	O.S. with B.C.
213. relieve her worry	to define	Susanne won't understand	D. Degas house
214. to inspire her greater purpose	to change topic	her terror	junk before PE B
215. to inspire her greater purpose	to overrule	she can't fix them	wrinkle of time, water marks
216. to inspire her greater purpose	to encourage work	she's lost her drive	R's passion for photographs
217. to inspire her greater purpose	to insist	is she hooked on drugs	her classes
218. to inspire finer new work	to soothe	her hyperactivity, Lucille's expected	little boy with bowl— Romania
219. to inspire finer new work	to stall	her fury	photos at Fordham

OBJECTIVE	ACTION	OBSTACLE	INNER IMAGE
220. to inspire finer new work	to admit	her crazed state	each placed on water
220A. to rescue paintings	to curse	people overhearing	
221. to rescue paintings	to forbid	her determination	Barret and his script
222. to rescue paintings	to warn to silence	all people in house	Fontainebleau staff
223. to rescue paintings	to silence	my love for her wife's fury	Rory's photo
224. to help her destroy paintings	to give in	my love for all she's touched, my wife's fury	exhibit at Fordham
225. to help her destroy paintings	to boost self up	love even her inferior work	Vodka in flask
226. to help her destroy paintings	to break up paintings	her manic state	R's disappoint-ment at her show's failure
227. to help her destroy paintings	to gloat	dislike destroying her art	paintings at Fordham
228. to help her destroy paintings	to kill dead babies	neighbors, danger of fire, fear	burning up art studio
229. to help her destroy paintings	to pin together	her beautiful painting, her crazed state	bathroom photos—Rory
230. to ease her loss	to search	her sadness, hatred for Uncle	pallet—red light Fontainebleau

231. to prepare her	to identify ambulance	her sadness, hatred for Uncle	pallet—red light Fontainebleau

ACT II, SCENE 2

SEQUENCE 1

SCENE TAG: TAKING CARE OF LUCILLE

SEQUENCE 1 TAG: PATCHING UP

232. to make up with Lucille	to find strength in book	too philosophical for my vulnerable state	Road less traveled
233. to make up with Lucille	to hug	she's frigid, mad	Mary after death
234. to make up with Lucille	to confirm	her emotions, anger	Buzz phone call
235. to make up with Lucille	to reassure	big hospital Touro	
236. to make up with Lucille	to correct	her aloofness, her brainwashed state	Road less traveled
237. to make up with Lucille	to insult		
238. to postpone her plan	to tread lightly	hate for legal documents Lucille's coldness	SCH envelope
239. to postpone her plan	to capitulate	difficulty in reading legal document	pages of Mama's will

OBJECTIVE	ACTION	OBSTACLE	INNER IMAGE
240. to postpone her plan	to beat about	pain in seeing her mistreated	Waveland— Will
241. to bolster her	to denounce coldness	she loves Uncle, he's dead	Will in Waveland
242. to bolster her	to justify my coldness	Lucille has stone feelings	markings on furniture
243. to bolster her up	to further justify my isolation	her love for Uncle, her disbelief	Waveland house will
244. to relax her nerves	to wave cover	her anger	B's dizzy spell outside
245. to relax her nerves	to grab about for a cover	hyperventilation, being trapped	pregnant now, pregnancy test
246. to destroy her suspicions	to shock	my passion for Susanne	memory of S. W. B.
247. to destroy her suspicions	to deny	my fear she sees through me	
248. to destroy her suspicions	to blame her	eavesdropping help	Nora in kitchen
249. to make her feel guilty	to shut her up	her attachment to Uncle	U. talk "nigger" at table
250. to make her feel guilty	to shut her up	nowhere to go, broke	walk around park
251. to make her feel guilty	to subdue her anger		Marlboros
252. to win her sympathy	to project rage		

253. to punish her greed	to joke	guilty in my action	Renoir
254. to punish her greed	to defy	Lucille's worship of painting	Lady with water pitcher
255. to punish her greed	to exult like Lucille	Lucille's hardheadedness	
256. to punish her greed	to denounce, rejects like Lucille	Lucille's rage	little girls at piano
257. to torture her for betrayal	to evade	Lucille's frenzied state	NC good news
258. to torture her for betrayal	to brag	Lucille's detachment	Aldon/NAC
259. to torture her for betrayal	to thrill in job offer	Lucille's disinterest	Theater on T. Square
260. to torture her for betrayal	to endorse	Lucille hates outdoor theater	Hamlet in *Hamlet*
261. to torture her for betrayal	to thrill in money	Lucille won't think it's much	$800 a week
262. to torture her for betrayal	to thrill in quick exit	Lucille's passivity	Need plane tix
263. to torture her for betrayal	to exult in call	desire to keep talking	Aldon on phone
264. to seduce her along	to amaze	pay is low, she hates city in summer	T. S. Play- wright

OBJECTIVE	ACTION	OBSTACLE	INNER IMAGE
265. to seduce her along	to delight	she hates NYC	T. S. traffic
266. to seduce her along	to encourage	her love of land	"the pond"
267. to seduce her along	to beg	her not listening	
268. to seduce her along	to tease	her piety	O.S.
269. to sweep her into my life	to toss off	her stubbornness	$$ Newcomb chapel
270. to sweep her into my life	to break free	her need to clean up all	Diehl gone—
271. to sweep her into my life	to concede	she loves owning	close door. Land
272. to sweep her into my life	to announce my exit	she's my anchor	
273. to sweep her into my life	reaffirm	she loves N.O.	window beauty— Ohio
274. to renew her loyalty	to remind of vows	her stubbornness	wedding license
275. to renew her loyalty	to refute	she's spoilt	tractor
276. to renew her loyalty	to castigate	used to having her way	"pond"
277. to renew her loyalty	to exaggerate	my vulnerability	Jason $400
278. to renew her loyalty	to reject	I'm broke	my prenuptial

279. to renew her loyalty	to correct	will be poor in NYC	write wills—
280. to renew her loyalty	to applaud	her sentiment	attic P & B Ohio view
281. to get her out now	to stress my identity	her disbelief	Ohio, pond
282. to get her out now	to name my path	her grief over Uncle	Carollton Ave.
283. to get her out now	to resolve	her attachment to the house	Favre ST.
284. to get her out now	to urge	her attachment to the house	B at NAC
285. to force her to come	to strike out	inner fear	garret
286. to force her to come	to reassure determination	my age future	at P & B
287. to force her to come	to reveal determination	youth driven profession, unsure of future	prof. with film contract
288. to get her to go	to convince of my strength	her disbelief, my recent failures my age	*Doubt* got the Pulitzer
289. to get her to go	to admit uncertainty	she thinks the worst, time running out	bomb in pocket
290. to get her to go	to praise my focus clear-sightedness	her wanting her best interest	P & B, NYC
291. to get her to go	to applaud my clear-sightedness	she wants me weak	"the land"

OBJECTIVE	ACTION	OBSTACLE	INNER IMAGE
292. to get her to go	to identify bravery	her manipulating me	RPO Carrollton owe—I want all you've got
293. to get her to go	to denounce her disloyalty	her depression. She's set in her ways	R.G. Picture on wall
294. to get her to go	to proclaim independence	her stubbornness, refused to listen	

ACT II, SCENE 2

SEQUENCE 2

SEQUENCE 2 TAG: SPARING LUCILLE

295. to get out without a scene	to collect my things	noise, Lucille nearby, servants about	back door, run at Carrollton
296. to get out without a scene	to evade subjects	humiliation before Susanne	at S.R.
297. to get out without a scene	to declare exit	beauty of house, ease of life security	bedroom at Carrollton Ave
298. to get out without a scene	to celebrate	pain of leaving	"the land" don't look back
299. to get out without a scene	to stay vogue	her prying, not wanting her to follow	TSP in NYC Third Ave producers
300. to get oput without a scene	to cut off her hopes	her beauty, my longing, don't want to do this alone	$$ carefree

301. to get out without a scene	to specify poverty	she has money, she has beauty	D.V. at N.O.
302. to get out without a scene	to praise loners	her persistence, knowledge	JBO Montana
303. to get out without a scene	to demand payment	she's rich, hard	V. Bogneris
304. to get out without a scene	to insist on solitude	her sexuality, her beauty	Paris—tree
305. to get out without a scene	to put down middle class values	she's no desire for domesticity	all divorced Ron & Ray
306. to get out without a scene	to remind of B.	she's been in rehab—too hard to shock	B on 6 cigs
307. to get on without a scene	to decry B Summer	my desire for her, our aloneness	Dale's friends by river with gun
308. to get on without a scene	to insist we're unconventional	her not listening, looking at me with love, running out of excuses	Michelle G.
309. to get with Susanne without a scene	to give in finally acquiesce	time running out	O.S. big hands—Bob

APPENDIX B

■ IMPROVISATIONS, GAMES, EXERCISES

APPENDIX C

■ KEY TERMS

APPENDIX D

■ GLOSSARY

Active verbs (use of): wording your objective or action so it inspires pursuit

Animal traits (use of): studying expressive movements of animals to communicate character

Atmosphere: the emotional sphere enveloping the space

Background: the character's experiences, responded to intuitively, that affect feelings about each situation

Beat: a slice of a scene with the same ingredients; the smallest unit of conflict

Becoming the character: developing the physical and psychological traits of the role

Build of a scene: momentum of a scene

Character analysis: evaluation of the play for background, the sum of your character's experiences, training or education and relationships

Difficult obstacle: barriers that are harder to overcome, thus committing the character to action

Emotional memory: technique for reliving a detail of a past event to evoke a feeling, such as sadness

Endow: to deal with a false object as if it possesses real qualities

Endowing objects: capturing physical adjustments to stimulate unconscious thoughts and feelings

Era: time period influencing your character's clothing and physical behavior

Feeling the part: ripening yourself to key words and events to experience your character's thoughts

Floor plan: the well-laid-out space for a scene

Fourth wall: the wall behind the audience that your character focuses on when looking out

Future circumstances: the real (what actually will occur) and the expected (what the character imagines)

Handicap: a permanent disability, physical or professional, with which some characters operate

History: a written record of events and feelings in a character's life

Imaginary garment (use of): performing tasks as if restricted by clothing, then using it as an imaginary influence on behavior

Improvisation: composing a sequence without previous preparation, spontaneously reacting to fellow actors

Inner images: mental pictures that feed you, pictures flashing before your mind's eye

Inner monologue: a silent conversation with yourself as the character

Inner problem: a secret trouble worrying your character so that you operate from dissatisfaction onstage

Intention: what your character wants, your reason for doing something

Journal: notebook used to stimulate your imagination and record observations to broaden the sources for expanding a role

Life script: a character's history that reflects expectations at a certain age at a particular time

Line-by-line actions: tiny doings that your character plays on or does between different lines

Line-by-line objectives: series of immediate needs that emotionally charges action

Living the role: providing yourself with a direct experience of your character's circumstances

Machine traits (use of): using the rhythmic sounds or movements of a machine to influence your character's actions

Magic If (use of): using the "what if" phrase to hurl yourself into your character's circumstances

Main action: the major thing your character does in a scene

Major objective: your character's overall need in a scene

Major obstacle: what blocks your character's main action

Observation: the acting technique of watching yourself and others offstage

Observation exercise: an exercise in which an actor notices and records another's behavior and restages it

Obstacle: something that stands in the way of your character's action

Open scene (use of): performing a physical task, focusing on an objective and allowing for a great range of interpretation

Opposing objectives: needs that totally conflict

Personalizing relationships: relating the character's relationship to someone in your own life

Physical endowment (use of): using stage props as if they have the sensual characteristics of real objects

Physical obstacle: a natural barrier that blocks action externally

Physical task: an activity that helps engage focus and express your character's thoughts to the audience

Physical traits: external traits: sex, age, size, color, health, fitness, vocal quality, physical quality

Physicalizating relationship: character's body language when adjusting to a relationship

Physicalize: to find outward physical expression of the internal, psychological action

Place: the specific location of the action

Playing games: using exercises to loosen up and relax you, to get your character in touch with impulses, and make contact with others

Present circumstances: conditions hitting your character as you enter the stage

Previous circumstances: anything that happened recently to your character that affects you right now onstage

Primary fourth wall (use of): dealing directly with something on the wall behind the audience

Privacy (use of): acting as if no one is watching you

Professional traits: career and work habits that either restrain or free a character

Prompt book: notebook or journal used for scoring a script and holding notes in scenes

Psychological endowment (use of): revealing the way certain objects are manipulated because of their sentiment or value

Psychological obstacle: a deliberate disjunction of impressions working against what your character hears, feels, or thinks

Psychological relationship: mental bond that influences connections between characters

Psychological traits: distinguishing qualities of your character

Psychophysical action: what you do with your body and what you think. All action is psychophysical.

Relationship: invisible link between characters

Relaxation: vocal, physical warm-ups and controlled breathing exercises that ready your mind and body for suggestion

Responsiveness: electricity between characters

Scene breakdown (use of): evaluating the play scene by scene—diagram includes a scene tag, setting, and characters

Score: written account you keep scene by scene of how to play a role

Secondary fourth wall (use of): dealing indirectly with the wall behind the audience, using it as a backdrop

Sending inner images: provoking another character to experience your thoughts

Sense memory: technique for reliving physical sensations by using certain inner images to trigger them

Setting: time and place of a scene

Stage time: special period in which your character's action occurs

Stamina: endurance to sustain a range of actions and behave imaginatively in whatever role played

Structured improvisations: progressive exercises that are rehearsed and have a framework of conflict supporting them

Substitutions: images from your life that replace each thought of the character

Subtext: hidden information you use below the line to strengthen meaning

Super objective: an overall aim of the character or play

Through line or spine: the track your character pursues to reach his destination or super objective

Time running out (use of): using a "clock winding down" to increase urgency in a scene

Urgency (use of): heightening what's at stake for your character in a scene to increase interest in it

Vulnerability: ability to be wounded easily

APPENDIX E

■ SCENE SELECTIONS

Man-Woman Scenes

All My Sons—Arthur Miller

The American Plan—
Richard Greenberg

Angels in America: A Gay Fantasia on National Themes—Tony Kushner

Another Antigone—A. R. Gurney Jr.

Another Part of the Forest—
Lillian Hellman

The Autumn Garden—Lillian Hellman

Barefoot in the Park—Neil Simon

Beau Jest—James Sherman

Betrayal—Harold Pinter

Beyond Therapy—Christopher Durang

Blithe Spirit—Noel Coward

Blue Window—Craig Lucas

Burn This—Lanford Wilson

Butterflies Are Free—Leonard Gershe

Cat on a Hot Tin Roof—
Tennessee Williams

The Chase—Horton Foote

Children of a Lesser God—
Mark Medoff

Cloud Nine—Caryl Churchill

Come Blow Your Horn—Neil Simon

A Coupla White Chicks Sitting Around Talking—John Ford Noonan

Crimes of the Heart—Beth Henley

Crossing Delancey—Susan Sandler

The Crucible—Arthur Miller

The Day They Shot John Lennon—James McLure

Driving Miss Daisy—Alfred Uhry

Epitaph for George Dillon—
John Osborne and Anthony Creighton

Fences—August Wilson

Fool for Love—Sam Shepard

Forty Carats—Pierre Barillet and Jean Pierre Gredy

The Fourposter—Jan de Hartog

Frankie and Johnny in the Clair de Lune—Terrence McNally

The Glass Menagerie—
Tennessee Williams

Golden Boy—Clifford Odets

The Graduate—Calder Willingham

The Heidi Chronicles—Wendy Wasserstein

Here We Are—Dorothy Parker
I Am a Camera—John Van Druten
The Immigrant—Mark Harelik
In the Boom Boom Room—David Rabe
Joe Egg—Peter Nichols
Landscape of the Body—John Guare
La Ronde—Arthur Schnitzler
Last of the Red-Hot Lovers—Neil Simon
Les Liaisons Dangereuses—Christopher Hampton
A Lie of the Mind—Sam Shepard
Loose Ends—Michael Weller
Lovers and Other Strangers—Renee Taylor and Joseph Bologna
Luv—Murray Schisgal
Mary, Mary—Jean Kerr
Monday After the Miracle—William Gibson
The Norman Conquests: Table Manners—Alan Ayckbourn
Oleanna—David Mamet
Our Town—Thornton Wilder
Period of Adjustment—Tennessee Williams
The Piano Lesson—August Wilson
Picnic—William Inge
Plaza Suite—Neil Simon
Prelude to a Kiss—Craig Lucas
The Prime of Miss Jean Brodie—Jay Presson Allen

The Prisoner of Second Avenue—Neil Simon
A Raisin in the Sun—Lorraine Hansberry
Ring Round the Moon—Jean Anouilh
The Rose Tattoo—Tennessee Williams
Speed-the-Plow—David Mamet
A Streetcar Named Desire—Tennessee Williams
The Substance of Fire—Jon Robin Baitz
Suddenly Last Summer—Tennessee Williams
Summer and Smoke—Tennessee Williams
Summertree—Ron Cowen
Sweet Bird of Youth—Tennessee Williams
This Property Is Condemned—Tennessee Williams
The Three Sisters—Anton Chekhov
The Tiger—Murray Schisgal
The Time of Your Life—William Saroyan
To Gillian on Her 37th Birthday—Michael Brady
Tomorrow—Horton Foote
The Traveling Lady—Horton Foote
Two for the Seesaw—William Gibson
The Typists—Murray Schisgal
Uncle Vanya—Anton Chekhov
A View from the Bridge—Arthur Miller

When You Comin' Back, Red Ryder?—Mark Medoff
Who's Afraid of Virginia Woolf?—Edward Albee

Woman-Woman Scenes

Absent Friends—Alan Ayckbourn
Agnes of God—John Pielmeier
All My Sons—Arthur Miller
Amphitryon 38—Jean Giraudoux
And a Nightingale Sang—C. P. Taylor
And Miss Reardon Drinks a Little—Paul Zindel
Any Wednesday—Muriel Resnik
Bell, Book and Candle—John Van Druten
Blithe Spirit—Noel Coward
Butterflies Are Free—Leonard Gershe
Cactus Flower—Abe Burrows
The Chalk Garden—Enid Bagnold
The Children's Hour—Lillian Hellman
Cloud Nine—Caryl Churchill
A Coupla White Chicks Sitting Around Talking—John Ford Noonan
Crimes of the Heart—Beth Henley
The Dining Room—A. R. Gurney Jr.
The Effect of Gamma Rays . . .—Paul Zindel
The Gingerbread Lady—Neil Simon

The Glass Menagerie—Tennessee Williams
The Immigrant—Mark Harelik
In the Boom Boom Room—David Rabe
Isn't It Romantic?—Wendy Wasserstein
Joe Egg—Peter Nichols
Keely and Du—Jane Martin
Key Exchange—Kevin Wade
Laundry and Bourbon—James McLure
A Lie of the Mind—Sam Shepard
Light Up the Sky—Moss Hart
Look Back in Anger—John Osborne
Middle of the Night—Paddy Chayevsky
The Miracle Worker—William Gibson
The Miss Firecracker Contest—Beth Henley
My Sister Eileen—Joseph Fields and Jerome Chodorov
Night of the Iguana—Tennessee Williams
Other People's Money—Jerry Sterner
Picnic—William Inge
The Prime of Miss Jean Brodie—Jay Presson Allen
Separate Tables—Terence Rattigan
The Skin of Our Teeth—Thornton Wilder
Steel Magnolias—Robert Harling

A Streetcar Named Desire—
Tennessee Williams
Toys in the Attic—Lillian
Hellman
Vanities—Jack Heifner
A View from the Bridge—
Arthur Miller
What I Did Last Summer—
A. R. Gurney Jr.
A Young Lady of Property—
Horton Foote

Man-Man Scenes

Ah, Wilderness!—Eugene
O'Neill
All the Way Home—Tad Mosel
All My Sons—Arthur Miller
American Buffalo—David
Mamet
The American Plan—
Richard Greenberg
*Angels in America: A Gay Fan-
tasia on National Themes*—
Tony Kushner
Another Part of the Forest—
Lillian Hellman
The Bald Soprano—Eugene
Ionesco
Betrayal—Harold Pinter
Biloxi Blues—Neil Simon
Brighton Beach Memoirs—Neil
Simon
Buried Child—Sam
Shepard
The Chase—Horton Foote
Come Blow Your Horn—Neil
Simon
Death of a Salesman—Arthur
Miller

The Dining Room—
A. R. Gurney Jr.
Driving Miss Daisy—Alfred
Uhry
Equus—Peter Shaffer
Father's Day—Oliver Hailey
Feiffer's People—Jules
Feiffer
Fences—August Wilson
Fifth of July—Lanford
Wilson
Fool for Love—Sam Shepard
The Glass Menagerie—
Tennessee Williams
Glengarry Glen Ross—David
Mamet
A Hatful of Rain—Michael
Gazzo
Hurlyburly—David Rabe
The Immigrant—Mark
Harelik
Key Exchange—Kevin Wade
A Lie of the Mind—Sam
Shepard
Lone Star—James McLure
*Long Day's Journey into
Night*—Eugene O'Neill
Look Homeward, Angel—Ketti
Frings
*The Man with the Flower
in His Mouth*—Luigi
Pirandello
The Master Builder—Henrik
Ibsen
M. Butterfly—David Henry
Hwang
The Nerd—Larry Shue
The Odd Couple—Neil Simon
Period of Adjustment—
Tennessee Williams

Precious Sons—George Furth

Private Wars—James McLure

Relatively Speaking—Alan Ayckbourn

Sexual Perversity in Chicago—David Mamet

A Soldier's Play—Charles Fuller

Speed-the-Plow—David Mamet

Streamers—David Rabe

That Championship Season—Jason Miller

True West—Sam Shepard

A View from the Bridge—Arthur Miller

Waiting for Godot—Samuel Beckett

We Bombed in New Haven—Joseph Heller

Who's Afraid of Virginia Woolf?—Edward Albee

The Widow Claire—Horton Foote

The Zoo Story—Edward Albee

APPENDIX F

■ MONOLOGUE SELECTIONS

Women

Absent Friends—Alan Ayckbourn

Agnes of God—John Pielmeier

Blue Window—Craig Lucas

Burn This—Lanford Wilson

Butterflies Are Free—Leonard Gershe

Chapter Two—Neil Simon

A Chorus Line—Michael Bennett

The Colored Museum—George C. Wolfe

The Country Girl—Clifford Odets

Crossing Delancey—Susan Sandler

A Delicate Balance—Edward Albee

The Diary of Anne Frank—Frances Goodrich and Albert Hackett

Dream Girl—Elmer Rice

The Effect of Gamma Rays . . .—Paul Zindel

Fences—August Wilson

Fool for Love—Sam Shepard

For Colored Girls Who Have Considered Suicide When the Rainbow Is Enough—Ntozake Shange

Frankie and Johnny in the Clair de Lune—Terrence McNally

The Gingerbread Lady—Neil Simon

The Heidi Chronicles—Wendy Wasserstein

House of Blue Leaves—John Guare

Hurlyburly—David Rabe

In the Boom Boom Room—David Rabe

Isn't It Romantic?—Wendy Wasserstein

Joe Turner's Come and Gone—August Wilson

Keely and Du—Jane Martin

Kennedy's Children—Robert Patrick

The Lady of Larkspur Lotion—Tennessee Williams

Laundry and Bourbon—James McLure

Les Belles Soeurs—Michel Tremblay

Lips Together, Teeth Apart—Terrence McNally

Ludlow Fair—Lanford Wilson

Luv—Murray Schisgal

Ma Rainey's Black Bottom—August Wilson

The Matchmaker—Thornton Wilder

Miss Margarida's Way—Roberto Athayde

'Night, Mother—Marsha Norman

Oleanna—David Mamet

Orpheus Descending—Tennessee Williams

Otherwise Engaged—Simon Gray

Our Town—Thornton Wilder

The Philadelphia Story—Philip Barry

Plaza Suite—Neil Simon

Shirley Valentine—Willy Russell

The Sign in Sidney Brustein's Window—Lorraine Hansberry

Sister Mary Ignatius Explains It All for You—Christopher Durang

Six Degrees of Separation—John Guare

The Skin of Our Teeth—Thornton Wilder

Spring Dance—Horton Foote

The Star-Spangled Girl—Neil Simon

Steel Magnolias—Robert Harling

A Streetcar Named Desire—Tennessee Williams

Suddenly Last Summer—Tennessee Williams

Summertree—Ron Cowen

Talking With . . .—Jane Martin

To Be Young, Gifted, and Black—Lorraine Hansberry

Two for the Seesaw—William Gibson

Vanities—Jack Heifner

Zooman and the Sign—Charles Fuller

Men

The Actor's Nightmare—Christopher Durang

Ah, Wilderness!—Eugene O'Neill

All My Sons—Arthur Miller

Amadeus—Peter Shaffer

The American Plan—Richard Greenberg

The Baltimore Waltz—Paula Vogel

The Boor—Anton Chekhov

Burn This—Lanford Wilson

Butterflies Are Free—Leonard Gershe

Children of a Lesser God—Mark Medoff

A Chorus Line—Michael Bennett

Come Blow Your Horn—Neil Simon

Crossing Delancey—Susan Sandler

Dream Girl—Elmer Rice

The Dresser—Ronald Harwood

Epitaph for George Dillon—John Osborne and Anthony Creighton

Equus—Peter Shaffer

Fences—August Wilson

Fool for Love—Sam Shepard

Frankie and Johnny in the Clair de Lune—Terrence McNally

The Gingerbread Lady—Neil Simon

The Glass Menagerie—Tennessee Williams

Glengarry Glen Ross—David Mamet

House of Blue Leaves—John Guare

House Party—Ed Bullins

Hurlyburly—David Rabe

I Am a Camera—John Van Druten

In the Boom Boom Room—David Rabe

Joe Egg—Peter Nichols

Joe Turner's Come and Gone—August Wilson

Long Day's Journey into Night—Eugene O'Neill

Look Homeward, Angel—Ketti Frings

Luv—Murray Schisgal

Ma Rainey's Black Bottom—August Wilson

Mass Appeal—Bill C. Davis

Master Harold and the Boys—Athol Fugard

Moon for the Misbegotten—Eugene O'Neill

Oleanna—David Mamet

The Piano Lesson—August Wilson

The Prisoner of Second Avenue—Neil Simon

The Proposal—Anton Chekhov

A Raisin in the Sun—Lorraine Hansberry

The Rimers of Eldritch—Lanford Wilson

The River Niger—Joseph A. Walker

The Seven-Year Itch—George Axelrod

Six Degrees of Separation—John Guare

Talley's Folly—Lanford Wilson

That Championship Season—Jason Miller

A Thousand Clowns—Herb Gardner

Tobacco Road—Erskine Caldwell

Two for the Seesaw—William Gibson

Uncle Vanya—Anton Chekhov

The Zoo Story—Edward Albee

Zooman and the Sign—Charles Fuller

READING LIST

This brief list is offered as a starting point for those seeking further reading on the theater and acting.

Consult your library for additional suggestions.

■ ACTORS AND ACTING

Barton, Margaret. *Garrick.* 1949. Reprint 1978. An account of the life of one of the greatest actors, responsible for a radical change in the style of English acting in the eighteenth century.

Bernhardt, Sarah. *The Art of the Theatre.* 1924. Reprint 1969. The French personality actress sums up her career and her technique.

Chaliapin, Feodor. *Man and Mask: Forty Years in the Life of a Singer.* 1932. *Chaliapin, an Autobiography,* as told to Maxim Gorky. 1969. Autobiographies of the great Russian bass (1873–1938), known for his excellent acting as much as for his magnificent singing.

Courtney, Marguerite. *Laurette.* 1955. Reprint 1968. Biography of Laurette Taylor, who first appeared on the stage as a child, took the world by storm in *Peg O' My Heart* in 1912, and returned in 1945 to triumph again in *The Glass Menagerie;* by her daughter.

French, Yvonne. *Mrs. Siddons: Tragic Actress.* 1936. Reprint 1981. Main events in the life of this great English tragic actress (1755–1831), stressing her illustrious career and her brilliant technique.

Hillebrand, Harold Newcomb. *Edmund Kean.* 1933. Reprint 1967. A judicious life story of the great English tragedian (1787–1833): gives details of Kean's roles from contemporary criticism and commentary.

Macready, W. C. *The Journal of William Charles Macready, 1832–1851.* Abridged and edited by J. C. Trewin. 1967. The editor's notes give background to the great tragedian's diary entries.

Richardson, Joanna. *Rachel.* 1956. Portrait of one of the greatest actresses that France, or perhaps the world, has ever known, seen in her nineteenth-century setting.

Salvini, Tommaso. *Leaves from the Autobiography of Tommaso Salvini.* 1893. Reprint 1971. Memoirs of the great Italian tragedian whose performance as Othello inspired Stanislavski to search for a universal law of creativity.

Stanislavski, Constantin. *An Actor's Handbook.* Edited and translated by Elizabeth Reynolds Hapgood. 1963. Describes the key principles of the Stanislavski system in alphabetical order.

———. *An Actor Prepares.* Translated by Elizabeth Reynolds Hapgood. 1936. Sets down the concepts of sensory recall, emotion, memory, relaxation, concentration units and objectives, super objectives, communion, adaptation, and through line of action.

———. *My Life in Art.* Translated by J. J. Robbins. 1924. Reprinted 1956. Tells of his career in the theater and how he came to develop his system.

Weaver, William. *Duse: A Biography.* 1984. The life of Eleonora Duse (1859–1924), Italian acting genius, who rose from a poor itinerant acting family to be a great international actress. Notes, bibliography, and index add much to the usefulness of the book.

Young, Stark. *Theatre Practice.* 1926. Mostly on acting, with final chapter on Duse.

■ CRITICISM

Clurman, Harold. *Lies Like Truth: Theatre Reviews and Essays.* 1958. *The Naked Image: Observations on the Modern Theatre.* 1966. *The Divine Pastime: Theatre Essays.* 1974. Wise and discerning essays by the late director and critic.

Craig, Gordon. *On the Art of the Theatre.* 1911. Reprint 1925, 1958. Dissatisfied with the acting of his time, this designer-director wrote, "Today they impersonate and interpret; tomorrow they must represent and interpret; and the third day they must create." *Towards a New Theatre: Forty Designs for Stage Scenes, with Critical Notes by the Inventor.* 1913. Reprint 1968.

Hazlitt, William. *The Characters of Shakespeare's Plays.* 1817. Reprint 1962. *Hazlitt on Theatre.* 1895, as Volume 2 of *Dramatic Essays.* Reprint 1957. Selections from *A View of the English Stage* and other essays on the theater and actors.

Jones, Robert Edmond. *The Dramatic Imagination: Reflections and Speculations on the Art of the Theatre.* 1941. The great designer presents an aesthetics of theater.

Lewes, George Henry. *On Actors and the Art of Acting.* 1875. Reprint 1957. This nineteenth-century English critic understood acting as few other critics of that or any other period have.

Shaw, George Bernard. *Play and Players: Essays on the Theatre.* 1952. *Dramatic Criticism: A Selection.* 1959. Shaw was drama critic for the *Saturday Review* from January 1895 to May 1898. His weekly writings in that capacity were collected in three volumes as *Our Theatres in the Nineties* (1932). Prior to the publication of this set, which is available and highly recommended, a selection had been edited by Huneker under the title *Dramatic Opinions and Essays.*

Young, Stark. *The Theatre.* 1927. Reprint 1958, 1980. *Immortal Shadows: A Book of Dramatic Criticism.* 1948. *The Flower in Drama, and Glamour: Theatre Essays and Criticism.* 1955. Stark Young, great American critic and practical man of the theater, has written about acting with more perception than almost any other.

■ DANCE

Cohen, Selma Jeanne, comp. *Dance as a Theatre Art; Source Readings in Dance History from 1581 to the Present.* 1974. An overall view of the history of theatrical dance in Europe and America. Theoretical essays, librettos, and excerpts from technical manuals combine with Cohen's introductions and headnotes to give the first adequate coverage of the subject.

De Mille, Agnes. *Dance to the Piper.* 1952. Autobiographical volume by the American dancer and choreographer whose dances for *Oklahoma!* revolutionized musical theater.

Graham, Martha. "God's Athlete," in Karl Leabo, ed. *Martha Graham.* 1961. Also in *This I Believe*, edited by Edward R. Murrow (1954).

Horst, Louis. *Pre-Classic Dance Forms.* 1937. Reprint 1987. Descriptions of court dances of the early sixteenth century, prior to ballet.

Leatherman, Le Roy. *Martha Graham: Portrait of the Lady as an Artist.* Photographs by Martha Swope. 1967. Text covers her entire career up to 1965; photographs, only her late work.

Morgan, Barbara. *Martha Graham: Sixteen Dances in Photographs.* 1941. Reprint 1980.

■ THEATER HISTORY

General

Brockett, Oscar Gross. *History of the Theatre.* 1968. 4th ed., 1981. A freshly written and illustrated story of the theater from the Egyptian passion play to "happenings" and other recent developments. Controversial new theories as well as long-accepted facts are presented.

Southern, Richard. *The Seven Ages of the Theatre.* 1961. World theater is presented by phases instead of time periods or countries. Theater history in different periods or countries shows a surprising similarity in phases.

Special Place, Time, or Perspective

Clurman, Harold. *The Fervent Years: The Story of the Group Theatre and the Thirties.* 1945. Reprint 1957. New ed. 1975. An account of one of the most vital theater organizations of the period.

Crowley, Alice Lewisohn. *The Neighborhood Playhouse: Leaves from a Theatre Scrapbook.* 1959. The story of one producing theater (1915–1927) that, growing out of the dramatic program of a settlement house, helped to bring the American theater to its maturity.

O'Neill, Rosary H. *The Director As Artist: Play Direction Today.* 1987. Challenges in twentieth-century directing.

CREDITS

■ **CHAPTER 1**

From *Beyond the Horizon*, in *The Plays of Eugene O'Neill*, by Eugene O'Neill. Published by Random House, Inc.

From *The Importance of Being Earnest*, by Oscar Wilde, 1899.

From Ketti Frings's dramatization of Thomas Wolfe's *Look Homeward, Angel*. Copyright © 1958 by Edward C. Aswell as administrator C.T.A. of the estate of Thomas Wolfe and/or Fred W. Wolfe and Ketti Frings; renewed 1986 by Howard B. Olson, executor of Ketti Frings and by Peter Frings and Kathie Mixon.

From *A View from the Bridge*, by Arthur Miller. Copyright © 1955, 1957, renewed 1983, 1985 by Arthur Miller. Used by permission of Viking Penguin, a division of Penguin Putnam, Inc.

■ **CHAPTER 2**

From *My Life in Art*, by Constantin Stanislavski. Translated by J. J. Robbins. Copyright 1924 by Little, Brown, and Company. Copyright 1948 Elizabeth Reynolds Hapgood; copyright renewed 1952. Published since 1948 by Routledge/Theatre Arts Books, New York.

From *Death of a Salesman*, by Arthur Miller. Copyright © 1949, renewed 1977 by Arthur Miller. Used by permission of Viking Penguin, a division of Penguin Putnam, Inc.

From *Buried Child*, in *Sam Shepard: Seven Plays*, by Sam Shepard. Copyright © 1981 by Sam Shepard. Used by permission of Bantam Books, a division of Bantam Doubleday Dell Publishing Group, Inc.

From *'Night Mother*, by Marsha Norman. Copyright © 1983 by Marsha Norman. Published by Hill and Wang, a division of Farrar, Straus & Giroux, Inc.

From *Serenading Louie*, by Lanford Wilson. Copyright © 1985 by Lanford Wilson. Published by Hill and Wang, a division of Farrar, Straus & Giroux, Inc.

From *The Ghost Sonata*, by August Strindberg. Published by Penguin Books (USA), Inc.

From *Ludlow Fair*, in *Balm in Gilead and Other Plays*, by Lanford Wilson. Copyright © 1965 by Lanford Wilson. Published by Hill and Wang, a division of Farrar, Straus & Giroux, Inc.

■ **CHAPTER 3**

From *My Life in Art*, by Constantin Stanislavski. Translated by J. J. Robbins. Copyright 1924 by Little, Brown, and Company. Copyright 1948 Elizabeth Reynolds Hapgood;

■ CHAPTER 4

■ CHAPTER 5

■ CHAPTER 6

■ CHAPTER 7

From *Laundry and Bourbon*, by James McLure. Copyright © 1982 James McLure. Professionals and amateurs are hereby warned that *Laundry and Bourbon* is subject to a royalty. It is fully protected under the copyright laws of the United States of America, and of all countries covered by the International Copyright Union (including the Dominion of Canada and the rest of the British Commonwealth), and of all countries covered by the Pan-American Copyright Convention and the Universal Copyright Convention, and all countries with which the United States has reciprocal copyright relations. All rights, including professional, amateur, motion picture, recitation, lecturing, public reading, radio broadcasting, television, video or sound taping, all other forms of mechanical or electronic reproductions such as information storage and retrieval systems and photocopying and the rights of translation into foreign languages, are strictly reserved. All inquiries should be addressed to Mary Harden at Harden-Curtis Associates, 850 Seventh Avenue, Suite 405, New York, NY 10019.

From *The Glass Menagerie*, by Tennessee Williams. Published by Random House, Inc.

From Ketti Frings's dramatization of Thomas Wolfe's *Look Homeward, Angel*. Copyright © 1958 by Edward C. Aswell as administrator C.T.A. of the estate of Thomas Wolfe and/or Fred W. Wolfe and Ketti Frings; renewed 1986 by Howard B. Olson, executor of Ketti Frings and by Peter Frings and Kathie Mixon.

From *Hedda Gabler*, by Henrik Ibsen, 1890. Translated from the original Norwegian by Edmund Gosse and William Archer, 1891.

■ CHAPTER 8

From *An Actor's Handbook*, by Constantin Stanislavski. Copyright © 1963. Reproduced by permission of Routledge, Inc., a part of Taylor & Francis Group.

Plot summary of *The Glass Menagerie* from *Plot Outlines of 100 Famous Plays* by Van Cartmell. Copyright © 1945 by Doubleday.

From *A Streetcar Named Desire*, by Tennessee Williams. Copyright © 1947 by Tennessee Williams. Published by New Directions Publishing Corporation.

From *The Importance of Being Earnest*, by Oscar Wilde, 1899.

From *Ah, Wilderness!*, in *The Plays of Eugene O'Neill*, by Eugene O'Neill. Copyright 1933, renewed 1960 by Carlotta Monterey O'Neill, the widow of the author. Used by permission of Random House, Inc.

From *Man and His Symbols*, edited by Carl Jung (Aldus Books, 1964). Permission granted by the J. G. Ferguson Publishing Company.

■ CHAPTER 9

From *Respect for Acting*, by Uta Hagen. Copyright © 1973 by Uta Hagen. Published by Macmillan Publishing Co., Inc., New York.

■ APPENDIX A